REBOUND

ALSO BY STEPHEN J. ROSE

Social Stratification in the United States, 5th Edition

WHY AMERICA WILL EMERGE STRONGER FROM THE FINANCIAL CRISIS

STEPHEN J. ROSE

St. Martin's Press ★ New York

www.stmartins.com

Design by Patrice Sheridan

Library of Congress Cataloging-in-Publication Data

Rose, Stephen J., (Stephen Jay), 1947–
    Rebound : why America will emerge stronger from the financial crisis / Stephen J. Rose.
      p. cm.
    ISBN 978-0-312-57542-7
    1. Economic forecasting—United States.   2. United States—Economic conditions—2009–
3. Financial crises—United States.   I. Title.
    HC106.84.R67 2010
    330.973—dc22

    2009040248

First Edition: April 2010

10 9 8 7 6 5 4 3 2 1

To Christina and Marija

CONTENTS

ACKNOWLEDGMENTS

THIS WORK is the product of thirty years of research on the state of the middle class. I've mostly eschewed academia and directed my work to the public policy community and the general public. Like most long-time researchers, my intellectual debts are many and I have developed my ideas in many interactions with friends and critics.

I have given presentations at or gotten support from a number of institutions in Washington, D.C.: Joint Economic Committee, National Commission for Employment Policy, Economic Policy Institute, Institute for Women's Policy Research, Washington Office of the Education Testing Service, Third Way, Center for Economic and Policy Research, Pew Economic Mobility Project, and Information Technology and Innovation Foundation.

Individually, my strongest debts are due to my coauthors: Barry Bluestone, Anthony Carnevale, William Dickens, David Fasenfest, Heidi Hartmann, Anne Kim, Jim Kessler, and Scott Winship. Ruy Teixeira posted my original critique of doom and gloom thinking, setting off a series of online debates. Participants in these debates included: Larry Mishel, Jacob Hacker, Matthew Ygelsias, Jeff Madrick, Tamara Draut, Elizabeth Warren, Jason Furman, John Schmitt, Heather Boushey, and Dean Baker (see http://www.prospect.org/cs/articles?article=debating_the_middle). In addition, I have had personal and e-mail exchanges with Jim Klumpner, Peter Gosselin, Emanuel Saez, Art Wilmarth, Rob Atkinson, Robert Lerman, Frank Levy, Jared Bernstein,

Paul Taylor, and Steve Quick. In writing the manuscript, I talked many times with Bill Dickens about my evolving ideas about the financial crisis, Paul Taylor suggested how I might reorganize the two financial chapters, and David Fasenfest and Christina Cerna read and commented on the entire manuscript.

Finally, many people helped me move from an idea for a book to its completion. Peter Bernstein was my agent and a wonderful advocate for my ideas. Phil Revzin at St. Martin's helped transform the book to accommodate the massive changes in the economy due to the financial crisis; in fact, it was he who suggested the current title. Others at St. Martin's, especially Kylah McNeill, made the transition from my original manuscript to final production smooth and stress free.

INTRODUCTION

IN APRIL 2008, the American and world economies started spiraling down. The U.S. unemployment rate, which was at 5.0 percent in April, increased to 10.2 percent by October 2009. Because of population growth, the number of jobs usually increases by 2.3 million over a 17-month period. Hence, the 6.9 million decline in the number of employed from April 2008 to October 2009 represents a 9.5 million shortfall in job creation.

There is a split between those who have confidence that America will bounce back in the future and those who think that the decline is much more serious and long-lasting. Paralleling this division, there is a dispute about the causes of the financial meltdown that first began in 2007 and exploded in full force in September 2008. Those, like me, who think that the economy is going to rebound feel that the crisis was due to unusual events that did not have to happen and that can be reversed; witness the relatively steady economic growth from 1945 to 2007, based on an effective mix of private entrepreneurship and government regulation. By contrast, the "negativists" see an American economy that has not been serving the interests of the majority of the country for decades; consequently they see the current problems as structural and requiring more fundamental changes to get the economy back on track.

In this book, I will show why the economy will rebound and how many critics were wrong in their analysis of the past thirty years. Chapters 1 and 2 address the financial crisis—how it happened and what we can do to avoid it happening again. Chapters 3 through 7 look at the incomes and jobs of middle-class Americans. I'll refute a number of myths about the declining middle class and offer a more bittersweet (some bad, but mostly good) view of the economy. Once we realize that the economy was stronger in the years before the 2008 crash than is generally thought, it's easier to see how the economy can rebound strongly once the financial mess has been cleared.

The first two chapters trace the good, the bad, and the ugly of modern finance. Starting with the September 2008 testimony of Hank Paulson, George W. Bush's treasury secretary and Federal Reserve Chairman Ben Bernanke, many public figures have talked about needing to bail out Wall Street in order to save Main Street. Although Presidents Bush and Obama, and other major public figures, have often repeated this mantra, the public has not been totally convinced. Part of the reason for this skepticism is that these are complex issues and vast sums of money are involved. Further, people are angry at financiers who commanded huge salaries and caused the collapse of the world financial system with their recklessness. For many, it is hard to comprehend why these corporations need to be "made whole" with massive infusions of public money.

The first chapter describes the financial practices that caused the crisis under the rubric of "brilliant idiocy."[1] Each of the decisions and new financial instruments made a lot of sense as long as home prices were rising and the economy was strong. When interest rates were low from 2001 through 2004, a wave of refinancing and an expansion of subprime lending led to great profits for firms involved in creating and selling mortgage-backed securities. When interest rates rose in 2005, this market dried up. Faced with losing a wonderful cash cow, financial firms and mortgage lenders changed the qualifying rules (permitting borrowers to have lower credit scores, giving high loan-to-value-of-home loans, requiring no documentation of income and assets, and permitting a ratio of higher debt payments to income) to allow less financially capable borrowers to obtain a mortgage.

All of the major actors—home buyers, investors, financial firms, credit rating agencies, home appraisers, mortgage brokers, and govern-

---

[1] Paradoxically, Warren Buffett, ever leery about unnecessary complexity, once proposed that all financial managers be given IQ tests for the ironic purpose of weeding out anyone who scored over 115 (that is, people that were "too smart" for their own and everyone else's good!).

ment regulators—were caught in the euphoria of the moment and turned a blind eye to any risk. Further, the enthusiasm for the new debt instruments spread to commercial real estate, credit card and student debt, corporate loans, and funding for leveraged buyouts. For a while, the money poured in as fees, profits, and compensation in large financial institutions skyrocketed.

The poster child of this crisis was Merrill Lynch. In late 2002, Stan O'Neal became its new chief executive officer (CEO) and decided that the company was missing a profit opportunity in mortgage-backed securities. By 2008, the company had gigantic losses and only avoided bankruptcy by a government-brokered bailout by Bank of America (and then its losses almost brought down Bank of America). Merrill Lynch did not have to go down this road, and one can argue the financial system as a whole did not have to suspend critical judgment and build a financial edifice based on subprime and other loans and instruments that could have high default rates.

Chapter 2 begins with the counterintuitive claims that finance promotes mobility and opportunity and that borrowing is often a sign of economic strength. The reason that so many people have a visceral dislike for financiers is because they view lending through the eyes of a borrower with all of the accompanying worries about meeting payment deadlines and fears about the consequences if these deadlines are not met. The perspective of the lenders, however, is very different; they are concerned with finding responsible borrowers who will pay their loans in full and on time. Finance brings lenders and borrowers together, permitting borrowers to build businesses and make purchases that would be difficult to do without the outside resources.

Because finance is a bridge over time (money is lent to be repaid later), it is possible that the business may not perform as expected or that the valuation of various assets can change. Further, as an intermediary between those with resources and those with capital needs, financial institutions are mostly dealing with other people's money. This can be a dangerous mix because people can easily overstep in their pursuit of profits, especially when all of the incentives push them to make ever larger and riskier investments.

Consequently, "financial crises, panics, and crashes" (also the title of a 1974 book on the history of financial blowups) have occurred with great regularity. The calmest period was the one between the end of World War II and the inflation of the 1970s, and was characterized by severe restrictions on financial institutions. On the other hand, the period from 1980 to 2006 had many crises that seemed to be large when they first appeared but then turned out to have little long-lasting effect. These experiences led many to think that financial crises were a thing of the past, given the ability of the government to come in with lots of resources to clean up any messes.

The financial actors who developed ever more complex financial instruments with many of the assets "off the books" and outside any regulatory purview made three common errors. First, they followed the "herd"—if other companies were making lots of profits by making risky loans, they had to do the same. Not only would they miss out on profits, they could potentially lose their relative standing in the industry. Second, they trusted the experts who used complex mathematical models that showed that the chances of large losses were remote. Of course, the experts were paid handsomely if they came up with an answer that supported the sale of the assets. Third, financial leaders were optimists and severely underestimated the downside risk. This was easier to do because they felt that they had a "back stop"—if the worst did arise, the government would have to bail them out because "they were too big to fail."

Chapters 3 through 7 examine the period from 1979 to 2007. Many analysts have argued that rising income inequality meant that the economic growth of these years did not benefit most Americans. The following statements highlight these sentiments:

> A war is raging in America . . . and that war is nothing less than an all-out assault on the middle class.
>
> Each night, I have the gut-sick feeling that we have chronicled another twenty-four hours in the decline of our great democratic republic and the bankrupting of our free enterprise economy.
>
> —Lou Dobbs
> Host, *Lou Dobbs Tonight*
> Quotes from *War on the Middle Class*

> With most people, the intensity, the insecurity, and the arduousness of their economic struggles are woven into the fabric of their lives—and are central to their identity.
>
> —Larry Mishel
> President, Economic Policy Institute
> Quote from *Talking Past Each Other*

The middle class is vanishing.
—ELIZABETH WARREN
Author
Quote from *Huffington Post blog*

Thomas Frank in *What's the Matter with Kansas?* Juxtaposes economic decline with the voting for President Bush in 2004 by low- and moderate-income people as follows:

The country seems more like a panorama of madness and delusion . . . of sturdy blue-collar patriots reciting the Pledge while they strangle their own life chances; of small farmers proudly voting themselves off the land; of devoted family men carefully seeing to it that their children will never be able to afford college or proper health care; of working-class guys in Midwestern cities cheering as they deliver up a landslide for a candidate whose policies will end their way of life.

Although this level of doom and gloom is a minority position in the country, it gets a lot of play in mass media and in the progressive wing of the Democratic Party. For the media, good news is boring and there is always more emphasis placed on what is wrong than on what is right. Further, the negative story generates controversy and interest, while tales of people who played "by the rules" don't elicit pathos and sympathy. As for the progressives, it is an occupational hazard of those with big hearts to overestimate the share of the population living in economic distress. They are sensitive to problems and see them everywhere (behavioral psychologists call this "confirmation bias"). In a large country, even a small share of the population experiencing economic distress translates into a large number of people. But it makes a big difference whether the share of the population just scraping by is 20 percent, or if it is 50 percent or more.

Chapters 3 through 7 debunk various "myths" that have been successfully propagated about our economic performance. If these claims were correct, the kind of society that would emerge from the financial crisis would inadequately serve most Americans. It is important to emphasize that inequality has indeed risen since 1979, but the issues are "how much?" and "to what effect?" Some argue that the standards of living of the broad middle class have stagnated at best and perhaps even moved backward. I show that this is a large overstatement by presenting new ways of looking at the data.

Contrary to the popular conceit that economics is a science, it is important to understand that socioeconomic analysis requires making decisions on the proper ways to organize the data and to interpret the results. This book is meant to break through the clutter of faulty analysis and to explain why the economy is going to rebound.

Also, I will try to make economics as easy to understand as possible by focusing on two fundamental questions. First, the size of the economy—measured by real (readjusted for inflation) Gross Domestic Product per person (GDP)—is mainly determined by our level of productivity, skills, number of workers, and ability to wisely use all of our resources (e.g., low unemployment). Second, there is the distribution of incomes and consumption among the population. In the workplace, the distribution of the revenues is accomplished by the varying pay of different types of workers, retirement and health insurance benefits, the profits for the owners, and the interest for those who lent money to the company. Society as a whole supports a number of nonworkers: children, the elderly, the infirm, people taking care of families, the unemployed, and the poor. In the past, these functions were usually provided within families, but over the last century, government has played a bigger role in arranging transfers from working people to many classes of nonworkers, with the biggest programs being Social Security and Medicare for the elderly.

Many of the arguments in these chapters may appear "rose-colored." The reason for this is that the negative economic stories have great resonance because they have been repeated so often. In fact, the story of decline does not pass the smell test. The proliferation of suburbs, McMansions, cell phones, iPods, HDTVs, camcorders, game consoles, luxury cars, other high-end baubles, and crowded malls belie the negative story. Further, when millions of copies of *Grand Theft Auto* and iPhones are sold within days of their release, and $59 billion is spent fighting fat, it is clear that many people have money to spend.

The data presented in chapters 3 through 7 will track the experiences of people from 1979 through 2007; these are the years when inequality rose, manufacturing employment declined, and our trade deficit rose. Both 1979 and 2007 were business cycle peaks, and most economic researchers think it best to avoid distortions by comparing years at similar points in the business cycle.

An obvious question is "What about the effects of the recession that started in December 2007?" As of June 2009, the decline in total output per person adjusted for inflation (real GDP per capital) was 5 percent (this is the latest data available in December 2009). There is a greater lag in reporting detailed data on personal incomes, so the latest information applies to 2008. During that year, median income adjusted for inflation declined by 3.6 percent. Given the decline in real median income, it is probable that the median income will fall another 2 percent in 2009. Relative to the decline in incomes of other recent recessions, this is a quite large decline but not that large when compared with the recession of 1982 or the Great Depression of the 1930s.

Chapter 3 addresses "the barbell" myth—the claim that the rich have captured all of the income gains of recent years and the rest of society has experienced a decline. If this were true, then over 75 percent of all income would be controlled by the richest 20 percent of the population. This describes conditions in a Third World country, not one with the mass market that we have. In fact, when calculated correctly, real middle-class incomes have risen 32 percent, or $18,000, since 1979. Yes, the incomes of rich Americans have risen more, but, the rich have not captured all of the gains.

Appendix 3 refutes three studies showing that the standard of living of middle-class Americans has declined. These widely cited studies have been used by many commentators as proof that the middle class is in dire shape today. I show that each of these studies is seriously flawed.

Chapter 4 confronts "the declining middle class" myth. Yes, fewer people now live in "middle class" households with incomes between $35,000 and $105,000 (inflation-adjusted 2008 dollars) than they did in 1979, but the reason for this is that more people live in households with incomes above $105,000. The share of adults in households with incomes over $105,000 grew from 11 percent in 1979 to 24 percent in 2007, while the share of households with incomes below $35,000 was slightly smaller. Rather than being a cause for alarm, the disappearing middle class is a good sign for America because more people have higher incomes and provide the demand to keep our economy moving forward.

Chapter 5 refutes the claim that the number of good jobs has declined because of the decline in manufacturing; by contrast, "the McJobs" myth holds that most new jobs are low-skill, dead-end service jobs. If true, this finding would be very odd because so many more people today have two- and four-year college degrees or have attended several years of post-secondary education. At the same time, the share of the workforce without a high school diploma or GED (passing the high school equivalency test) has declined from 50 percent in 1960 to 11 percent in 2007.

In reality, a more educated workforce has better jobs because many service jobs are not dead-end jobs but managerial and professional jobs. A new functional approach is used to quantify the shift from manual jobs in manufacturing to jobs in front offices, business services, and high-skill services such as health care, education, and communication. Further, occupations are divided into three tiers: elite managerial and professional jobs; good jobs that require either job-specific skills or a moderate level of education; and less-skilled jobs. Using this division, I show that the share of elite jobs grew (staffed by the growing numbers of college-educated workers) while the share of less-skilled jobs declined. In other words, job quality has improved, not declined, and the legions of high-end workers provide the economic strength that supports economic growth.

Globalization is on everyone's mind, and there is a sense that China and India will undermine local employment because they can produce most things more cheaply than we can. Alan Blinder, a Princeton University economics professor and former vice-chair of the Federal Reserve Board, has estimated that 40 million new jobs are at risk of being outsourced. The specter of a large segment of the workforce being unemployable looms.

Chapter 6 addresses the "exporting our jobs" myth and shows that foreign trade has not lead to rising overall unemployment in any period in U.S. history. In a dynamic economy, plants close and people lose their jobs while new jobs open up. Except when the economy is contracting, the number of hires is greater than the number of job losers. For example, in the fourteen years after the passage of the 1993 North American Free Trade Agreement—which supposedly devastated the U.S. job market— employment grew by over 26 million. This 21 percent growth was spread across all states; even in the Midwest states that lost many manufacturing jobs, employment grew by 15 to 20 percent.

The employment declines after April 2008 are due to the contraction of the economy, not trade. While many worry that we won't be able to compete in the future, the World Economic Forum rated the United States as the world's most competitive country, a rating that it has held for most of the last fifteen years. Due to the negative effects of our depression, the United States fell to the second most competitive economy in the world in 2009 after Switzerland.

The impact of trade on wages has been mixed: Women's wages have increased dramatically across the board as have the earnings of men in the top third of the labor force. Male workers in the middle third have seen their wages stagnate while male workers in the bottom third have lost ground.

Overall, trade is like productivity—there are individual losers but the economy as a whole is larger. Some estimates put the positive effects of trade at $1 trillion a year. People mistakenly think that having lower costs (i.e., cheap labor) is the way to economic success. The race to the bottom argument has never held up to close scrutiny, and economies grow primarily because of the high skills of their people. America is blessed with a huge market, the world's commercial language, the best universities in the world, an established legal system, the largest venture capital pool in the world, and an openness that results in the most entrepreneurial country in the world.

Chapter 7 addresses the claim that the "social contract" is unraveling as companies cut back on health and retirement benefits. Once again, this claim is not supported by the facts: While the share that companies pay into retirement programs for their workers has remained constant, the costs of health insurance have skyrocketed as health care spending went from 5 percent of GDP (when company health insurance payments were 1 percent of payrolls) in 1960 to over 17 percent in 2009 (when company payments rose to over 8 percent of payrolls). The rise of copayments and higher insurance premiums paid by workers is simply the sharing of this rising expense.

This chapter has a wider discussion of issues relating to health care, wealth, debts, and preparation for retirement. There is more pressure on the former social contract because it has grown in size and expense. Further, it is not large companies that are abandoning their commitments to their workers but smaller ones that can't keep up with the rising costs. The Social Security system already provides a basic floor for the retired, and new initiatives by the Obama administration are doing the same for health care for the population as a whole.

The concluding chapter summarizes the strengths of the American economy and why we will emerge from the recent financial crisis stronger than ever. As noted in chapter 5, America was recently rated the most or second-most competitive economy in the world, a rating that it has held for most of the previous twenty years. The focus on declining employment in manufacturing creates an unduly negative impression and misses our strengths in innovation, research, entertainment, sales, and finance. The combination of the size of our market, our international leadership, and our ability to adapt has placed America at the head of the leading economic powers. While other industrialized countries are not far behind, they have chosen a different path that is in many ways more generous to the least well-off in their societies.

The framework developed in chapter 5 is based on the importance of office work and high-skilled services in education, health care, and communications. The old manufacturing-based economy often had inventory swings that caused frequent recessions. By contrast, up until the finance-induced recession of 2007, the office economy had long periods of economic growth and short shallow recessions. The current recession has not destroyed any physical, organizational, or intellectual capital, and this economic structure combined with judicious government regulation and intervention will provide the foundation for future economic growth.

Further, our future economy will be stronger because the stupendous growth of the financial sector distorted the distribution of rewards in our economy: From 1979 to 1986, the share of income of the top 1 percent of taxpayers varied within a narrow range of 8 to 9 percent of all income; from 1988 to 1995, the share going to the top 1 percent varied between 12 and 13 percent; but in the years from 1996 to 2006, the share of top-income holders grew steadily to 18 percent.

In essence, we shifted our economy to one that used more financial services, and this sector more than any other had a large number of people whose earnings and bonuses were very high. We now know that some of this money was ill-deserved because the assets that were bought and sold were mispriced. After the crisis, we will have a smaller financial sector and we will shift our consumption back to goods and services that are not so top-heavy with big earners.

Unfortunately, this was a crisis that was waiting to happen. As we progressively decreased our regulation of financial transactions, we were forgetting the lessons of history. The minicrises that occurred from 1980 to 2005 did not develop into full-blown crises because we had developed mechanisms to combat financial disruptions. But with each successful avoidance of a crisis, financial institutions developed new ways to make riskier and riskier bets.

The financial meltdown that started in 2007 has led to large losses and rising unemployment. But now that we have had this crisis, we will not soon make the same mistakes about financial deregulation again. People in and out of the financial industry have been rudely made aware of what can happen without proper oversight. It seems crazy that we need a crisis to cleanse the system of its excesses; one would have thought that we could have managed this in some other, less disruptive way. But this is not the case, and our best days are still ahead of us, and we will recover quicker than many people think.

While this is good news on the macroeconomic front, we still face many challenges in the years ahead: creating a new financial architecture to avoid crises like the one we just experienced; finding a way to increase access to health care while reining in costs; providing for comfortable retirement; making investments in infrastructure and new energy-saving innovations; developing new policies that allow parents to combine work and home responsibilities; education reform, particularly among the young, and increasing access to postsecondary education; changes in how we finance government; and better policies to help low-income people.

In the end, to say that the glass is three-quarters full rather than three-quarters empty means that one-quarter of the population has some sort of trouble keeping up. Especially in the deep recession of 2008 to 2009, a large number of people faced economic tough times. An agenda for change will be outlined in the final pages of the conclusion. A strong economy has two advantages in dealing with these challenges: The problem is smaller, and there are more resources available. The issue thus becomes one of political balance versus one of economic necessity.

Evolution of the Project

Like many of my generation, I was "radicalized" by the antiwar and civil rights movements of the 1960s. In a bold step, I quit medical school to make "social change." Being intellectually inclined, I gravitated to graduate school in economics so that I could teach. In the 1970s, I had a rather dim view of the fate of the American economy and was sure that we were in a long-term crisis. The stagflation of that decade seemed to be the forerunner of tougher times to come.

In 1972, I moved to Baltimore to do community organizing (a profession with a much higher profile since Obama came on the scene) and teaching. After not meeting with as much success as I had expected, I started studying the status of the middle class and prepared the *Social*

Stratification in the United States poster and factbook in 1978—what some have called "Sociology 101 on a Poster" (the fifth edition was released in 2007). Consisting of 1,000 colored icons, the purpose was to visually present data of income, wealth, gender, household status, race/ethnicity, and occupation. At the time, I wanted people to be able to easily identify the constituencies that they were organizing.

In 1983, when the *Social Stratification* poster was first updated, I reported information about a shrinking middle class and rising inequality. This conclusion was based on information from the deep recession of 1982 and was a confirmation of the inequities of modern America. However, in 1987, I produced the *American Economy* poster and factbook and found a lot of data showing the strength of the American economy. At a summer conference of the Union for Radical Political Economics, I said that "after sixteen years of making apocalyptic statements, I am hesitant to make any more" and my days of thinking that the American economy was about to collapse were over. Ironically, this quote was picked up by *The New York Times, Newsweek,* and *Fortune* and presented as a radical recanting his old beliefs.

Over the next eighteen years, I produced a few dozen papers and monographs on the state of the middle class arguing the results were "bittersweet"—not as bad as some thought and not as good as what we could do. I argued privately with friends who still felt that the economy was a basket case and that most Americans shared none of the prosperity of the Reagan, Bush, and Clinton years. In 1992, I moved to Washington, D.C., to become a staff economist at the Joint Economic Committee. When Bill Clinton won the election, I was appointed chief economist at the National Commission for Employment Policy before becoming a senior adviser to Secretary of Labor Robert Reich.

After Reich left in the second term, I worked at several think tanks and consulting firms continuing my research on middle-class living conditions and the state of the American economy. John Kerry's loss in the 2004 presidential election led to many arguments within the Democratic Party on how to proceed. The Left wanted Democrats to run as progressives and not closet Republicans, while the moderates thought that Americans were not looking for a return to classic liberal policies.

Into this mix, Thomas Frank wrote *What's the Matter with Kansas?* which argued that Americans were voting against their self-interest as evidenced by the last sentences of his introduction (quoted above on p. 5). Since the Left has always proclaimed to represent the masses, they are consistently disappointed when the masses don't follow them. To explain this anomaly, they have often argued that people have been "duped" and have "false consciousness."

After nearly twenty years of quiet critique of the persistent doom and gloomers, I published a lengthy rebuttal of Frank, showing that the glass was not three-quarters empty but three-quarters full (see www.emerg-ingdemocratweblog.com/rose/rose.html). Given my background in the progressive movement, my critiques could not be easily dismissed as coming from a right-wing crazy. So, a number of debates and online forums were organized around my analysis of the middle class. Even though I was called a few names, I stood my ground and never felt that my critics rebutted my arguments.

With the onset of the financial crisis, the negativists appeared vindicated in their analysis about the failings of modern American capitalism. This book is meant to show that they are wrong and that we will soon be on the rebound.

It is ironic that I, as an economist active in the Democratic Party, am criticizing claims of economic distress usually associated with the liberal wing of the Democratic Party. I am doing this because I think that the facts don't support the claims and that they are trying to "scare" people into supporting their agenda. Ultimately, their intellectual strategy is to demonstrate that the middle class is in the same economic state as the poor in the United States. Therefore, they write as if the vast majority of Americans have a stake in electing liberal Democrats (e.g., the stance of Thomas Frank). If they are wrong, this is not a good strategy because people will not see their policy prescriptions as helping them.

CHAPTER 1

The Financial Crisis:
What Just Happened?

"MONEY MAKES THE WORLD GO 'ROUND" is a catchy tune from *Cabaret,* and few people doubt the relevance of this statement. Yet, we have a very ambivalent attitude toward money and those that handle it. We like what money buys but feel that paying too much attention to material rewards is a bad way to live. We glorify the entrepreneur but not the financier; moneylenders are considered unsavory and "Wall Street" connotes feelings of people living well—off of other people's money. While we don't quite know what they do, we know they make enormous salaries.

And now, finance has imploded and brought the rest of the world economy down with it. In pursuit of superprofits and big bonuses, financiers' bets turned out to be wrong, leading to massive losses. The financial crisis, in turn, has undermined the real economy, leading to huge declines in wealth, income, and jobs. Yet, the only way out of the mess seems to be to bail out the banks by covering their losses. There is a palpable sense of public outrage even though our business and political leaders say there is no better alternative.

This chapter carefully traces the events leading up to the financial collapse of 2008. I call the process one of "brilliant idiocy." It was brilliant because it seemed to transfer risk to those who wanted to hold it, and because it provided capital to those who could put it to work. The share of homeowners, especially among low-income people, rose, and many firms (including nonprofits) got access to cheaper loans, freeing up resources for more activities and higher profits. It seemed like a classic win–win situation.

It was idiocy because many mortgages were given to people who had little chance to pay them off and no chance to pay them off if housing prices stopped climbing at 10 percent per year. It was idiocy because the system was very fragile: So many investors maximized yield by using lots of debt (leverage), which made losses pile up very fast. It was also idiocy because so many instruments were bought by investors that were unable to evaluate the quality of the instruments and who trusted the sales pitch (and ratings) that these instruments were very safe. Finally, it was idiocy because there were so many interlocking contracts that it was impossible to disentangle them when the system was stressed. Once confidence disappeared, the price of a variety of assets plummeted (no one knew what they were worth), many financial firms failed, credit collapsed, and the real economy spiraled downward.

Some have presented the crisis as a reflection of long-term problems that were not sustainable. By contrast, I will argue that finance is certainly prone to excesses, but that the crisis was caused by a series of bad decisions, and that a new set of financial rules can—and will—be drawn up to prevent similar crises in the future.

The perfect exemplar of this crisis is the experience of Merrill Lynch. In late 2002, Stan O'Neal became the CEO, and immediately began acquiring other companies to increase the company's presence in mortgage-backed securities. In 2005 and 2006, the company generated record profits, in large part due to subprime mortgage securitization. In 2007, the profits turned to losses, and in September 2008, the company was on the edge of bankruptcy and was bought by Bank of America with a partial government guarantee against future losses.

Even as late as January 2007, Merrill was convinced that the subprime market was where the profits were, and paid $1.3 billion for First Franklin Bank, a major subprime originator. This purchase was the beginning of Mr. O'Neal's demise; he was relieved of his position in September 2007.[2] But much as Merrill Lynch did not have to pursue this business strategy, the financial industry as a whole could have avoided the actions that caused the financial meltdown of 2008.

---

[2] The timing was propitious for O'Neal, if not for the company, as he walked away with a $161 million "golden parachute."

To understand why Stan O'Neal and the rest of the financiers did what they did requires tracing the history of the evolution of the mortgage market through the use of securitization and the expansion of subprime lending. When private subprime mortgage securitization expanded in 2002, it seemed to be on sound footing. When interest rates rose in 2005, subprime mortgage lending and securitization changed and loans were made that were certain to have default rates greater than the financial instruments that were created could sustain. This was especially true because the additional loans provided some of the fuel that drove housing prices up at a record pace.

In 2008, three processes interacted to create a powerful negative economic spiral. First, the popping of the housing bubble coupled with the negative effects of lending to low-creditworthy purchasers led to a huge rise in the number of foreclosures. Second, the decline in housing prices led to a sharp decline in the home construction industry. Third, the problems of the financial firms created great uncertainties and losses, which led to the drying up of bank lending. From September 2008 onward, layoffs led to more layoffs as companies were forced to cut back because demand was falling and financing tightened up.

While subprime lending has gotten the most attention, financial institutions were active in expanding and securitizing other lines of lending—e.g., commercial real estate, normal business loans, leverage buyout loans, credit card debt, and student loans. None of these loans was as susceptible to default as subprime mortgages, but the downturn in the economy markedly increased delinquencies and defaults of these loans as well. The rest of this chapter will focus on the ups and downs of subprime mortgages but similar events were happening in these other markets as well.

Even though a few people predicted an upcoming disaster as early as 2005, most of the financial community dismissed these statements as alarmist because the banks were well capitalized. Further, the expansion of crazy subprime lending was only a small part of the market. There was only a little more than $1 trillion in outstanding subprime loans, whereas the value of all outstanding debt instruments around the world amounted to tens of trillions. So it seemed reasonable to think that even if the worst happened in the subprime market, it would be an isolated and easily reparable problem.

This confidence in the resiliency of the financial system, however, turned out to be misplaced. The losses in subprime mortgages totaled about $250 billion at the end of 2008, and are projected to reach a maximum of $500 billion by 2012. By comparison, worldwide global losses of financial institutions are projected by the International Monetary Fund (IMF) to surpass $4 trillion. Global output in 2009 through 2011 is expected to be about $8 trillion less than initially projected, and values on worldwide global stock markets were down $26 trillion at the end of 2008. What the optimists failed to appreciate was how a small spark could lead to such a conflagration.

How this happened is a complex story based on thirty years of financial consolidation and innovation. There were minicrises from 1982 to 2003. While each started with damaging revelations of large losses that portended a serious downturn, the macroeconomic effects (e.g., the rise in unemployment and the decline in GDP) turned out to be small. This created a false sense of confidence that major crises were a thing of the past. Since this was particularly evident in the mortgage market, this chapter will focus on the changes in this area and the eleven actors that made poor decisions. The other crises of the 1980s and the lessons learned from thirty years of financial expansion will be discussed in the next chapter.

The Changing Mortgage Market

The era of long (typically thirty-year), subsidized mortgages for residential homes became the norm in the 1950s. In the 1920s, only 40 percent of Americans owned their homes. Required down payments were often for 50 percent of the value of the home, and mortgages were typically for three to five years with the payments only going to pay off the interest on the loan. With the onset of the Depression, many banks did not renew these loans even for financially viable customers. This was a key factor in the tidal wave of foreclosures in 1930 to 1932.

In response to this problem, the Roosevelt administration created the Home Owners Loan Corporation in 1933 to issue mortgages with repayment periods of up to fifteen years. The Federal Housing Administration went further by offering insurance to lenders for mortgages that could last up to twenty years and could cover up to 80 percent of the value of the home. This program was expanded with the creation of the Federal National Mortgage Association ("Fannie Mae") in 1938. In addition to guaranteeing loans, the government created a special niche for

Savings and Loans ("S&Ls") banks to provide mortgages to local residents (they were forbidden from making loans for properties that were more than fifty miles from their offices).

After the war was over, this system was expanded to amortizing loans running for thirty years. As a result, the face of America changed with suburbs mushrooming around each large city. S&Ls were the primary source of home financing and the economy flourished with new road construction and a self-reinforcing consumption cycle of housing, auto, and consumer durables to fill the new homes. As a result, home ownership leapt to 60 percent of all households by 1959 from 40 percent in 1945. Home ownership climbed to 64 percent by the mid-1960s and remained at that level through 1995.

The dominant image of bankers during this period was one of individuals who were very conservative in their lending, with loans only going to those who passed the 4C test: capacity, collateral, credit, and character. In the 1950s, some people described this banking model as being based on the numbers 3-6-3. This stood for paying your depositors 3 percent, charging your borrowers 6 percent, and bank managers being on the golf course by 3:00 P.M. In most cases, the S&Ls serviced the loan and kept the loan on their books. For the more enterprising institutions, they could sell the loan to Fannie Mae. Although they would still service the loan, the sale of the mortgage provided them with added capital to make additional loans.

In order to keep Fannie Mae's debt off the federal government accounts (a worry for the increasingly stressed Johnson administration), Fannie Mae was privatized in 1968. At the same time, the Government National Mortgage Association ("Ginnie Mae") was split off to guarantee federal government loans to low-income borrowers. In 1970, another private corporation, the Federal Home Loan Mortgage Corporation ("Freddie Mac"), was created to provide a competitive check on Fannie.

Although private companies, Fannie and Freddie had the implicit guarantee of the federal government (they were called Government-Sponsored Enterprises—GSEs). This allowed them to borrow more cheaply, and the saving was passed on to people taking out mortgages in the form of lower interest rates. In return for this guarantee, the GSEs agreed to pursue "public purposes" from guidelines set every four years by the U.S. Department of Housing and Urban Development (HUD).

The qualifications for a "conforming" or "prime" loan (eligible for a GSE guarantee) were high and newly set each year by HUD. The size of their loans was limited (to avoid serving the wealthy) and only financially strong borrowers who made substantial down payments were eligible. The indicators of a strong loan were: loan amount to value (lower was better), debt payments as a share of income (lower is better), zero or few bad credit problems (e.g., no bankruptcy, previous delinquencies on debt payments, etc.), and presence of other assets. Detailed loan applications with appropriate documentation (e.g., tax forms and bank records) were required, as professional "underwriters" determined whether a prospective borrower was eligible for a prime loan.

There were three types of borrowers that were not eligible for mortgages backed by Fannie, Freddie, or Ginnie. First, there were large loans for very expensive homes. These "jumbo loans" carried only a slightly higher interest rate than the conforming loans as long as the borrowers had the income to show that they could make their payments.

Second, some people's incomes were hard to verify—those with high amounts of investment income and the self-employed who did not have a W-2 form. Since the required documentation for a conforming loan was high, a new class of loans, "Alt-A," was created for borrowers with "stated incomes." Except for their income sources, they would have qualified for a conforming loan, but this exception cost them and they had to pay higher interest rates for their mortgages.

Third, some people did not qualify for a conforming loan either because their income was too low (and did not qualify for a Ginnie Mae loan) or because they had a negative credit event that made them a high risk. Starting in the 1970s, a few nonbank loan companies created an alternative ("subprime" loans) for these borrowers. The Money Store, for example, flooded the New York region with catchy commercials from Phil Rizzuto (a former baseball player and announcer) offering financing to those with damaged credit. To make this a profitable endeavor, these lenders would only provide money to home owners who had significant equity in their homes (up to 50 percent of the appraised value).[3]

The inflation of 1970s put pressure on the 3-6-3 banking model because banks could not attract deposits paying only 3 percent when

---

[3] But even this strategy did not work: After the Money Store was bought by Wachovia for over $2 billion in 1998, many of the loans turned out to be losers and Wachovia had to absorb the losses.

inflation was running at a considerably higher rate. While they could charge higher interest rates on their new mortgages, they were stuck with lots of loans with low interest rates from their previous lending. In effect, these loans represented a bad investment and resulted in big hits to the banks' balance sheets if their values were determined by current interest rates.

When the S&Ls imploded at the end of the 1980s (discussed in the next chapter), the mortgage market changed in five important ways.

First, securitization (i.e., getting money from investors rather than depositors) would play a bigger role in providing capital to this market. Instead of just guaranteeing the mortgages for a small fee, Fannie and Freddie would buy the mortgages from approved institutions. The loans were packaged together and sold as bonds that paid a fixed rate of return. These bonds, in turn, were bought by large investors who saw them as close substitutes for Treasury bonds with a slightly higher yield.

Second, instead of S&Ls initiating and holding loans with GSE guarantees (the "originate to hold" model), a new structure developed (the "originate to distribute" model) that was based on mortgage brokers, small mortgage lenders, and large financial organizations. The brokers worked with real estate agents or went directly to home owners to push refinancing as well as mortgages for first-time buyers. Their business was based strictly on commissions—they offered the buyer a chance to deal with multiple lenders and the lender a preliminary screening of what loan the client would most likely qualify for. The new small lenders got their funds through lines of credit with large banks or other financial institutions. After initiating the loan, the lenders sold the loans to their financial backer. For banks that remained in the home mortgage business, securitization meant that they were provided with new capital to make additional loans.

Third, more loans had adjustable interest rates. The fixed-rate mortgage with the option to refinance can be a very good deal for the borrower: If interest rates rise, you have a mortgage with a much lower interest rate than you could get; if interest rates fall, you refinance and get the lower rate. To protect lenders, the fixed rate has a risk premium for possible future interest rate increases to provide some security for the financing institution.

It should be noted that the mortgages in many other countries—e.g., England, Canada, and Ireland—are predominantly adjustable rate; they are quite popular in Australia and New Zealand, as well. The advantage is that there is a lower initial interest rate. Of course, the lender then is at the mercy of the market and can end up paying more when interest rates rise.

Fourth, World Savings Bank of California developed a variation of ARM mortgages known as the "pay option" or "pick a payment" loan. This gives the lender four options of what to pay each month; one of the options does not even cover the interest payment and hence *increases* the amount of the loan ("negative amortization"). In 1980s and 1990s, this alternative was rarely used except by a few self-employed professionals who had large swings in income. Used carefully, this was very effective for these borrowers. As we will see below, this option can lead to quick defaults for borrowers who choose low payments without offsetting them by higher payments in other months.

Fifth, mortgages had a privileged place in people's financial decisions because of a 1986 law that maintained the mortgage interest deduction on federal income tax returns, but prohibited deductions of interest payments on credit cards, auto loans, and all types of personal loans. As a consequence, individuals tended to keep large mortgages (or to take out home equity loans) in order to keep the balances on the other debts low.

As the 1990s progressed, this complex system of loans functioned well because inflation and interest rates were relatively low. The size of the mortgage market kept growing and would eventually surpass $10 trillion by 2006. This was much bigger than the size of the corporate bond market, and enterprising financial companies seized the opportunity to earn fees from securitizing mortgages by the 1980s.

However, there were inherent weaknesses in the new system. Formerly, if a person defaulted on a loan, all the costs of foreclosure and resale would fall on the institution that made the loan. This created a strong incentive to make good loans. By contrast, many of the participants in the new mortgage market did not "have skin in the game" because they did not hold the mortgage, but instead sold it to someone else. When that someone else became more removed from the original loan (and by implication, the properties backing them), there was less scrutiny about the quality of the mortgages.[4] As the mortgages of high-risk borrowers be-

[4] Art Wilmarth cites five studies that show that loans that were destined for securitization were of poorer quality than other loans ("The Dark Side of Universal Banking: Financial Conglomerates and the Origins of the Subprime Financial Crisis," *Connecticut Law Review,* May 2009, p. 963–1050, footnote 310).

came easy to sell, the brokers and small mortgage companies were happy to collect their fees and not have to think about the consequences of any defaults.

A Perfect Storm that Changed the System Even More

Between 2001 and 2003, several things happened that changed the face of the housing market. The trends to be more aggressive with subprime lending were in place, so perhaps things would have moved this way under all circumstances. But there was a burst of activity and innovation that reached a crescendo in 2005 that lasted through the beginning of 2007 when everything started falling apart.

Six trends came together in 2003:

1. *Interest rates were low:* Following the dot-com bust that started in March 2000, the economy went into a recession. This was quickly followed by the unexpected attacks of September 11, 2001, which led the Federal Reserve to reduce the federal fund interest rate (that which is charged on bank overnight lending) to 1 percent in 2002, and to keep interest rates low for eighteen months.
2. *The decline in the stock market* made investors look for other investment outlets.
3. *The U.S. current account deficit grew* to very high levels and stayed there. This issue will be discussed more fully in chapter 6, but the relevance here is that the United States was awash with foreign capital. This pushed interest rates lower than they would have been without this capital flow, and as Charles Kindleberger notes in his discussion of financial crises, excess liquidity almost always ends in excess credit expansion that is often located in the housing market.
4. *Fannie Mae and Freddie Mac accounting difficulties:* In 2003, there was an accounting scandal at Fannie Mae over the timing of profits. While this did not affect the housing market directly, it did cause Fannie and Freddie to reduce their securitization business that year. Given this opening, there was a huge rise in the share of "private label" mortgage-backed securities, more of which contained subprime mortgages.

5. *More large financial actors:* Following the 1999 repeal of the Depression-era rules separating investment and commercial banks into separate entities, commercial banks were now able to compete with investment banks in creating bonds.[5]

6. *Subprime promotion:* Official government policy from Clinton through Bush was to encourage home ownership for low-income people. HUD operationalized these policies by setting targets for Fannie and Freddie that included purchasing subprime mortgage securities. It is important to emphasize that subprime mortgages can be an effective way to expand homeownership among low-income households. For example, the Community Action Program, a partnership between the Ford Foundation, Fannie Mae, and Self-Help (a community development lender in North Carolina) has initiated 50,000 loans to low-income families since 1998 with low default rates.[6] Further, writing in *The New Yorker* magazine, Connie Bruck shows how Angelo Mozilla (one of the supposed bad actors who started the financial crisis) initiated programs in the mid-1990s to expand home ownership in low-income areas.[7]

In the low-interest rate environment of 2003 and 2004, there were $6.4 trillion in new mortgages and refinancing. Anyone who didn't refinance during these years was probably missing an opportunity to reduce their payments, and some people refinanced in both years or flipped houses that they had bought for speculation.

Also during these years, many of the mortgages were issued to nonprime borrowers. In 1994, subprime mortgages were just 5.6 percent of mortgage issuance and that Alt-A issuance was just 0.2 percent. Even in 2001, these two types of mortgages together only accounted for 8.7 percent of all mortgages issued. By 2004, this share had risen to 28 percent and over $1.1 trillion additional subprime and Alt-A mortgages were created in 2003 and 2004.

---

[5] The consolidation movement in the financial industry had been ongoing for many years (with special regulatory exemptions granted) and the 1999 law was just the formalization of this reality: between 1990 and 2005, there were 5,400 financial mergers involving $5 trillion in assets.

[6] See Lei Ding, Roberto G. Quercia, Janneke Ratcliff, and Wei Li, "Risky Borrowers or Risky Mortgages," Center for Community Capital, University of North Carolina, September 13, 2008 (under review) PDF and October 18, 2008 PDF.

[7] "Angelo's Ashes" June 29, 2009.

The low-interest rates could not last forever and the Fed orchestrated a steady rise in interest rates from 2004 through 2006. As the attractiveness of refinancing disappeared for prime borrowers, the mortgage industry became more aggressive at the bottom end of the market; by 2006, subprime and Alt-A mortgages were responsible for 39.2 percent of the issuance. Related to this shift was a decline in the share of conforming mortgages from 61.4 percent in 2001 to 39.6 percent in 2006.

Caution Is Thrown to the Wind and Responsibility Is Abdicated

With higher interest rates, fixed-rate subprime mortgages were no longer affordable for most subprime borrowers: Fixed rate mortgages that in 2003 had interest rates of 8 to 10 percent went up to 12 percent and higher by the middle of 2005. Consequently, the vast majority of subprime mortgages during these years were adjustable-rate mortgages (92 percent in 2006). Often times, these ARMs had "teaser rates"—lower than normal interest rates for the first six months or year. Once the teaser rates ended, the interest rates on ARMs would rise by several percentage points, making the monthly payments no longer sustainable for many borrowers.

To avoid defaulting on their loan, many borrowers expected to refinance their loan with either another ARM or a fixed-rate mortgage if interest rates declined or if their financial situation changed and they could qualify for a conforming loan. This is a very risky strategy because refinancing may not be available, forcing these borrowers to face the terrible choice of crushing mortgage costs or foreclosure.

The lenders knew that ARMs were a short-term fix that would not work for many borrowers. However, they had a false sense of security because housing prices kept rising by over 10 percent each year. Therefore, if they had to foreclose, the costs of foreclosure would be modest and the abandoned homes could be sold for a higher price than their original sales price.

Given the euphoria of rising prices (between 2001 and 2006, home prices increased on average by 50 percent) and the newfound enthusiasm of Fannie and Freddie in purchasing subprime securities, there seemed no limit. This was a period in which new types of mortgages appeared: "Liar loans" earned their name because people with low-paying jobs went unchallenged when they stated that their incomes were much higher than they actually were; "NINJA" loans were the comedic name for "no income, no job, and no assets" (obviously you could only get a NINJA loan because you lied).

Finally, payment-option loans, which originally had only been given to professionals with varying salaries, were made more widely available. Perhaps these loans could work for housing speculators who intended to sell the properties quickly. But for the rest of the people who got these loans, the temptation to pay small amounts was great; of course, this led to unaffordable balloon payments later. Once the option of refinancing disappeared, the majority of these loans went into default.

The proliferation of all these loans was based on feeding the money-making machine of subprime securitization. Borrowers who would not have qualified for a mortgage in the past were now cleared for loans, even if the loans were for 100 percent of the value of the home (the share of homes purchased with 100 percent financing went from 3 percent in 2003, to 33 percent in 2006). The tenor of the times was characterized by the slogan of the successful 2006 ad campaign of Washington Mutual—GETTING TO YES.

Overall, the subprime and Alt-A mortgages of 2005 through 2007 were of worse quality than those of 2003 and 2004; and they were of much worse quality than the subprime mortgages of the 1980s and 1990s. By a variety of measures (e.g., housing value to GDP, rate of increase in prices), home prices were too high across the board and way too high in selective submarkets. The combination of weak borrowers and a housing bubble was a time bomb waiting to explode.

At the same time that quality of the underlying mortgages was changing, the specific form of securitization was also changing to a much more opaque system based on something called "structured finance." The specific details of the alphabet soup of CDOs, CDSs, MBSs, ABSs, and SIVs are explained in Appendix 1. Suffice it to say that many of the CEOs of large financial firms reluctantly admitted that they did not understand all of the details of each of these "innovations." What they did understand was that at each step along the way, high fees were charged that fed directly to the firm's bottom line: It is estimated that fee share of earnings at the largest U.S. banks went from 40 percent in 1995 to 70 percent in 2007.

The new financial architecture relied on three new practices that hid what was happening.

First, the key to these innovations was the increased use of mathematical modeling to "effectively" estimate the price and risk of these instruments. The "quants" and their computers developed new approaches to price options (the Black–Sholes equation), structured finance (Gaussian cupola), and risk (VAR—value at risk). Great confidence was put in these computations even though they had never stood the test of time. However, as Nassim Nicholas Taleb shows in his book *The Black Swan,* unusual events occur much more frequently than are accounted for in these models. Because all financial institutions were operating with minimal capital (to maximize their rate of return), a Black Swan event without adequate insurance immediately undermined the stability of many companies.

Second, the new system was often conducted "over the counter." These were private contracts between consenting firms that were not regulated by any government body.[8] In addition, there weren't even formal markets of any sort as contracts were determined over the phone with direct negotiation. Without a market or even a market-maker (a single firm that guarantees that all trades will be consummated), no one knew the size of the exposure of any firm or even the total size of the market.

Third, in order to avoid having to raise additional capital, many financial firms set up "special purpose entities," which were technically not part of the company. These trusts and companies were often registered in poorly regulated places like the Cayman Islands. This "shadow banking system" could take the largest risks while having the least regulation and protection. Nonetheless, the confidence in this system (that totaled nearly $10 trillion) was high because the quants had worked it out.[9]

---

[8] There was a famous 1999 meeting between Brooksley Born, chair of the obscure Commodities Futures Trading Commission and Treasury Secretary Robert Rubin, Federal Reserve Chair Alan Greenspan, and Securities and Exchange Chair Arthur Levitt. Ms. Born's attempt to have her commission regulate these over-the-counter derivatives was successfully opposed by this powerful threesome. After four congressional hearings, Born's commission was forbidden from regulating derivatives, and she resigned.

[9] Some media report the "notional value" of the CDSs was $50 trillion. This number, however, is an exaggeration because of multiple hedges on the same loan and the real value of these instruments was about one-tenth of that amount.

The System Implodes in 2008

The Case-Shiller Home Price Index of the twenty largest metropolitan areas reached its high in August 2006. Since the stability of the system was based on rising prices, the day of reckoning could not be far away. The first signs that a crisis was beginning occurred in February 2007, when the interest rate spreads rose (meaning that the market was increasing the probability of their risk of default) for the lowest rated bonds of mortgage-backed securities. Nonetheless the balance sheet of banks looked good—they had substantial liquidity and their capitalization was above the legal minimum.

By August 2007, two Bear Stearns hedge funds that invested heavily in subprime-heavy securities went bankrupt. At this point, subprime lending stopped and the market for reselling all of the mortgage-backed securities almost disappeared: Sales were only completed if the buyer accepted 10 to 25 percent of the face value of bonds. On a different front, housing prices were down 5 percent from their peak and appeared to be on a downward path. Since the run-up in housing prices had stimulated a massive building spree, the imbalance between a large supply and few buyers added to downward pressure on price. All of a sudden, the flippers who were buying to resell and those with ARMs who anticipated refinancing when their interest rates were reset were left with mortgages that they were unable to sustain.

But trouble in housing spreads slowly because it takes a lot of time to move from delinquency (payments 30 to 90 days late) to foreclosure proceedings, to eviction, to resale at bargain basement prices. When the market froze, the originate-to-distribute model stopped working and lots of firms were stuck holding mortgages that were in the securitization pipeline. So, instead of passing on the mortgages, they remained on the books of commercial banks that specialized in subprime lending and investment banks that had not yet created and sold the bonds that included these mortgages.[10]

At the beginning of 2008, home prices were down 10 percent from their peak, mortgage delinquencies were increasing at a fast rate, unemployment was rising, and there was no market for the exotic bonds.

---

[10] George Washington University law professor Art Wilmarth perceptively calls this backlog in the system "originate *not* to distribute" because firms had exposure to subprime foreclosures when they thought that they didn't.

In January, the rating agencies announced a downgrading of 6,000 bonds connected to the various mortgage-backed bonds. The financial institutions that held these bonds faced the dilemma of what value to use for their official balance sheet. The new "mark-to-market" rules meant that they were supposed to value these bonds at what they could be sold at—but there was no effective market price.

There was a lot of improvising going on as the size of the problem kept changing. Banks started announcing "write-downs" for anticipated losses—e.g., the world's largest bank, HSBC of Hong Kong, announced a $10 billion write-down on its subprime holdings. In March, a thunderbolt hit when Bear Stearns, the fifth largest investment bank in America with assets of nearly $400 billion, collapsed and was bought by J. P. Morgan with a $29 billion Federal Reserve guarantee against bond losses. At its peak in the middle of 2007, shares in Bear sold for $170 a share; JPMorgan Chase eventually paid $10 a share (after the initial deal was announced at $2 a share) even though the stock sold for $60 a share one week before the collapse in March 2008.

While President Bush, Secretary of the Treasury Henry Paulson, and new Federal Reserve Chairman Ben Bernanke were making soothing comments about the strength of the economy and of the financial sector, bad news kept coming. Each month, banks were revising upward the size of their expected losses, and oil and other commodity prices shot up. Although not officially called until the end of 2008, the Business Cycle Dating Committee of the National Bureau for Economic Research, a private body of economists that officially calls the starts and ends of business cycles, stated the recession started in December 2007.

The mortgage industry was in crisis as hundreds of small and large lenders went out of business. Countrywide, the largest mortgage lender in the United States, went from being a huge profit generator to having to be bought in January 2008 by Bank of America at a distressed price. A number of other major mortgage lenders closed their doors, and in July, IndyMac, another subprime lender, became the fourth largest bank failure in U.S. history.

The situation worsened in September of that same year when Fannie Mae and Freddie Mac were put into receivership, Merrill Lynch was taken over by Bank of America, Lehman Brothers was allowed to go bankrupt, the huge insurer AIG was given emergency funding by the Federal Reserve in return for an 80 percent ownership stake, and Washington Mutual Bank was seized by the Office of Thrift Supervision. So much was happening that it made the mind spin as Paulson and Bernanke warned that they needed a $700 billion injection of funds immediately to avoid a complete financial meltdown.[11]

Basically, we witnessed the fragility of financial institutions that are always subject to the loss of confidence by their depositors or investors. As discussed in the following chapter, financial institutions use very little of their own capital to conduct their normal business of lending and trading. National and international regulators have tried to set guidelines on capital requirements depending on the business that a specific financial institution conducts.

For example, Fannie and Freddie had very low capital requirements because they were thought to guarantee loans with the implicit support of the U.S. Treasury. As they switched to issuing and holding mortgage-backed securities, however, their required capital base should have been increased. When the value of these instruments plummeted, they had nothing to fall back on and quickly needed the government to bail them out.

Investment banks also had small capital bases because they were thought to be involved mainly in trading and providing financial advice and services for mergers, acquisitions, and initial public offerings. The collapse of Bear Stearns over one week in March 2008 revealed how dependent the company was on market confidence. Their financial strategy was based on two cheap sources of liquidity to conduct their daily business. On the one hand, they made one-day loans by using repurchase or "repo" agreements (Bear got cash in exchange for securities that would be repurchased by Bear at a fixed price the next day); over $50 billion of repo loans were made each day for years at a time. On the other hand, Bear was the prime broker for many hedge funds. As active traders, the hedge fund accounts often had billions of dollars in uncommitted funds on any given day. Bear could legally use these billions for its use in trading activities.

Even though this strategy had been used successfully for a long time, market players were getting progressively worried about the financial health of Bear given its large exposure to subprime mortgage securities. Over the course of a few days, other financial institutions stopped mak-

---

[11] For a detailed description of the daily crises faced by Hank Paulson and Bernanke see David Wessel's *In Fed We Trust,* Andrew Ross Sorkin's *Too Big to Fail,* and James Stewart's "Eight Days" (*The New Yorker,* September 21, 2009).

ing new repo agreements with Bear and hedge funds started withdrawing their funds. Not quite a typical bank run, but the effect was the same as Bear had to close its doors and agree to be bought out by a stronger institution (with a government guarantee).[12]

The history of AIG (American International Group, Inc.) provides another example of how losses in one division could undermine an entire company. Formed in China by American C.V. Starr in 1919, AIG grew to be the ninth-largest company (by stock value) in America.[13] Over the previous fifty years, the company had earned a high reputation for prudent insurance and investment activities. In 2004, the financial products division began offering credit default swaps (CDSs) for mortgage-related securities. These were basically insurance guarantees that limited the buyer's loss. At first, profits soared and this division expanded greatly. The fees on the CDSs were treated as free money as the company put no money aside as a reserve against losses. In their core insurance businesses, they never would have thought of acting (or been permitted to act) in this way.

They used the wrong models in determining their risks and were totally unprepared when the mortgage-backed bond markets collapsed at the beginning of 2008. The terms of the CDSs required that AIG put more "collateral" in the accounts of the CDS buyers as added protection for the CDS holder. They were bleeding money, and as more money was being put aside for collateral, the rating agencies downgraded the creditworthiness of AIG bonds from the AAA status. This, in turn, triggered the need for more collateral. So, AIG's balance sheet was progressively undermined by direct losses on having to pay CDS claims and by money that had to be given to its "counterparties" (the term used for those on the other side of a financial contract) for potential future CDS losses.

Since so many firms were losing money on mortgage-based assets, their capital position deteriorated below the legal limits. This forced them to sell other assets to improve their cash position. Of course, when lots of sellers come to market, prices are bid down resulting in less money for the sellers. Further, because of the mark-to-market rules (assets had to

---

[12] A detailed history of Bear's collapse is presented in Lawrence McDonald's *A Colossal Failure of Common Sense*.

[13] For a history of the company see Ron Shelp, *Fallen Giant* (Hoboken, N.J.: John Wiley & Sons, 2009).

be evaluated on your balance sheet to the value that they could fetch in today's market rather than their face value), all financial institutions had to reduce the value of similar assets that were on their books. Consequently, the solvency of many institutions was threatened as the prices of virtually all financial assets were depressed.

A quadruple-whammy developed: first, the financial crisis; second, declining employment; third, falling stock prices; and fourth, falling housing prices. There developed an "adverse feedback loop" across the economy as each of these factors interacted to make everything worse. As individuals' personal wealth took a big hit because of declining stock and housing prices, they cut back on their consumption in order to increase savings (economists call this the "wealth effect" and estimate that people spend between 3 to 5 cents less for each dollar of their declining wealth).

Declining consumer expenditures, in turn, led producers to cut back production. Of course, this is a self-reinforcing process—as one company laid workers off, demand fell, which led to other companies laying workers off, which led to demand falling further and making the first company think that they might not have laid off enough workers. It takes a while for this vicious cycle to end, and the unemployment rate rose rapidly from September 2008 through September 2009.

On the financial front, the problems of the real economy made its problems worse. First, deterioration in the quality of other credit instruments, such as commercial mortgages and bonds based on auto and credit card debt, led to further losses and write-downs. Second, the freezing up of the credit system made it even more difficult for businesses to manage cash flow and for consumers to get access to loans for large purchases. Third, the fear of uncovering more problems in the future made investors wary of buying stocks and bonds, even when prices were low.

Causes of Crisis—Eleven Actors

Could/should this have been foreseen? The answer is yes, but no one wanted to. Also no one listened to the few people who knew enough to see that there was a great systemic risk of a meltdown and who were courageous enough to speak out. Everyone was part of the great money-making machine, and people who were supposed to say "stop," either didn't or were told to shut up. As Kenneth Lewis, CEO of Bank of America, said in May 2007, "We are close to a time when we'll look back and say we did some stupid things. . . . We need a little more sanity in a period in which everyone feels invincible."[14]

It is useful to list all the players and review their roles in one of the largest financial boondoggles in history (and that is saying a lot considering the history of past abuses):

1. Home buyers

If you only refinanced your mortgage in 2001 to 2003, you did fine. If you refinanced (or took out a home equity loan) and took money out of your home, you did what many others did. At the time, it seemed like a reasonable strategy to treat your home as a "personal ATM." Many people did a quick mental calculation and decided that they had reached (or were close to) their savings target for retirement. From this perspective, it made sense to take money out of your accumulated home equity and enjoy it today. An estimated $2 trillion was taken out of homes from 2002 to 2007; many wish they had that money today.

An indication of the evolving attitudes of consumers to mortgages is evident in the share of home values that was supported by debt: This figure went from 14 percent in 1945, to 32 percent in 1985, to 45 percent in 2001, to 55 percent in the second quarter of 2008.

A lot of people made bad decisions. Some were bamboozled by smooth-talking brokers to take mortgages that they would later default on. Others knowingly lied to get big mortgages.[15] There are stories galore of maids working at the big Las Vegas hotels who got mortgages for $500,000 houses in the suburbs. On the up side, they got to live in these homes for a couple of years. But their day of reckoning has either come or is about to come as they are now unable to make their mortgage payments.

Another active group of home buyers were speculators who tried to "flip" homes—own them for a short period of time (sometimes as little

---

[14] *Bloomberg News*, "Bank of America's Lewis Calls for Lending 'Sanity,'" by Warren Giles and Mark Pittman, May 9, 2007.

[15] Often, we think that people who lied on their loan forms were low-income people, trying to pull a fast one. Edmund Andrews is a *New York Times* economics writer who had covered the excesses of the housing market. Yet when he got remarried, he ended up with a no-doc liar loan because he would not have qualified without the deception (he had high child support payments and his wife had just moved to the area and did not have a job yet). "My Personal Credit Crisis," *New York Times Magazine,* May 17, 2009, p. 47.

as a few days) and then resell them at a higher price. For those who timed the market right, this was a winning strategy. For those who continued to pursue this strategy after September 2006, the housing bust left them with many properties that they were unprepared to pay for.[16]

Finally, there were the people who remodeled their homes with money from refinancing. These people reasoned that their homes were "worth" much more and they might as well outfit them with the latest amenities—new kitchens and baths and added rooms. Even though they may still be financially sound, they are "underwater" or "upside down" in their homes—what they owe on the mortgage is more than they could sell it for.

A few of these people have had to move, and just gave the bank the keys to the house and walked away. Consider the couple who had a $450,000 mortgage on a house that was once worth $480,000. If that home can only sell for $300,000 today, then they would have to come up with $150,000 at closing to fully pay off the loan. Alternatively, if they abandoned the property, they would not have to pay the $150,000, but their credit ratings would suffer and it would be very difficult for them to buy another home.

2. The home appraisers

These people played a small but significant role in the mortgage fiasco. By making a high appraisal (one estimate identified 21 percent of appraisals as being too high), the loan-to-value ratio would be lower and the buyer would have an easier time obtaining a mortgage, especially for those with low income and low-credit scores. Since getting more business was often based on connections with real estate agents and brokers, appraisers were clearly pressured to come up with high valuations. Of course, the appraisers could justify this by saying that it was hard to know where the market was going given how much it was appreciating each year.

3. The mortgage brokers

These people had the least skin in the game. When the market was superhot, they had no problems finding willing lenders so they pro-

---

[16] In many cases, "straw buyers" were used to hide the true owner (they already had too much mortgage exposure) or to serve as the front person with enough creditworthiness to get the loan.

ceeded to create as much business as possible and did not care whether the mortgages were viable for the buyer or lender.[17] The quality of mortgage brokers varied from very good to totally crooked. One key dimension defining their role in all this was the fact that most were paid a fee for initiating the mortgage and were not financially invested in the performance of the mortgage.

4. The small mortgage lenders

These institutions initiated the original mortgage with funds borrowed from larger financial institutions. Richard Bitner tells a remarkable tale in his *Confessions of a Subprime Lender: An Insider's Tale of Greed, Fraud, and Ignorance*. He recounts his experiences in Dallas from the time that he opened a small mortgage company in 2000 to the time that it went bankrupt in 2007. In the introduction, he laments that, "Even those with the best of intentions . . . found it difficult to effectively manage risk [because one had] to stay competitive in the marketplace." Because financial institutions preferred the high interest rate on subprime mortgages, they paid the lenders three to four times more for these mortgages versus prime mortgages.

Over time, however, the lending standards were loosened and he traces the specific institutions that offered new terms to attract more borrowers. Further, as the number of competitors rose, the pressure to accept applications from mortgage brokers increased tremendously: The logic was that, if not you, then someone else was ready to provide the funding. These firms were thinly capitalized and quickly fell into bankruptcy once the mortgage mill slowed down; the decline of more than 374 such institutions is chronicled on an "implode-o-meter" (at ml-implode.com).

5. Account executives at financial institutions

The larger commercial and investment banks bought many mortgages from smaller institutions to create mortgage-backed securities.

---

[17] There were many abuses in which smooth-talking mortgage brokers convinced home owners who had no mortgage to refinance that they could have money for needed repairs or to pay off credit card balances. Many of these buyers were old or unsophisticated about financial matters and did not understand what they were agreeing to. Most of the actions described in this section describe mistakes; by contrast, many mortgage brokers were con men engaged in fraud and misrepresentation.

The person responsible for making this purchase was the account executive. At the height of the boom, these people, relatively low on the institutional totem pole, were making up to $1 million a year once their bonus was included. This is the best indication of how generous the money-making machine of the subprime securitization process was to its participants. It is not hard to imagine that people were giddy with enthusiasm to package more and more mortgages. Further, if some academic or outsider told them how much risk they were creating for their company, it is quite easy to see how they would have discounted this unwanted opinion. (Behavioral psychologists call this inability to make clear value judgments when you have a strong personal stake "confirmation bias.")

6. The credit officers at financial institutions

In order to identify growing risks early, large financial institutions have compliance departments staffed with credit officers to review approved loans to assure that they are creditworthy. Other people in compliance departments review the overall exposure of the company to losses from a large number of defaults and file regular reports on the strength of the company's loan portfolio.

As the number of subprime mortgages grew, the compliance departments had to approve the new mix of mortgages. In some cases, they evaluated the loans and went along with the prevailing wisdom that subprime mortgages added no additional risk. In other cases, however, they reviewed the files and thought that the company was taking on excessive risk. In several prominent cases, their concerns were rejected by senior managers who were intoxicated with the added profits that resulted from these loans. For many companies, the prevailing culture was to move product. Even though compliance offices were established to warn top executives when risks were rising, they were ignored and on occasion were threatened with termination if they persisted.

Consider the experiences described by Sherri Zaback, a mortgage screener at Washington Mutual. When she refused to approve loans, she said that "[the account executives] would be furious. They would put it on you that they weren't going to get paid if you stood in the way." She further relates how, when she called a loan officer to verify a balance she was often yelled at. A colleague of hers, Keysha Cooper, eventually lost her job because she would not approve various loans. Of course, this did not stop the loans from being approved because her supervisor overrode her decision.[18]

Looking back in 2008, Betsy Bayer, a compliance officer for Countrywide Financial Corporation (originator of 20 percent of all mortgages in 2006) summarized the rise of subprime mortgages as "to get volume, you lose quality."

7. The re-underwriters

When making a mortgage-backed bond, there is a legal requirement that each of the loans to be scrutinized has to be rated on a scale from 1 to 3 (where 3 means unacceptable). Just a few companies (Clayton Holding, Bohan, or Opus) specialize in this task and they hire temporary employees to do the review, giving them one hour for each loan. This is a pretty minor review with a very low rejection rate. But, during the height of the subprime boom, supervisors pressured re-underwriters to change their scoring whenever a single mortgage application was rated as a three.[19] Apparently, not a single opportunity was passed up in creating MBSs.

8. The credit rating agencies

The three major firms responsible for rating bonds (Standard and Poor's, Moody's, and Fitch) have been discredited by their actions in this financial mess. The conflict of interest was straightforward—they got very lucrative business if they came up with AAA ratings and they lost business if they did not.[20] Since structured finance was much more complicated, the fees for rating these bonds were several times higher than rating corporate or municipal bonds; by 2006, fully 40 percent of Moody's revenues were from structured finance.

It should be emphasized that determining how mortgage-backed and related securities would perform was not an easy task. It was further complicated by a lack of cooperation from the big financial firms. In

[18] Reported in "Saying Yes, WaMu Built Empire on Shaky Loans," Peter S. Goodman and Gretchen Morgenson, *New York Times,* December 27, 2008, A1. Also in "Was There a Loan It Didn't Like," Gretchen Morgenson, *New York Times,* November 1, 2008.
[19] See Paul Muolo and Mathew Padilla, *Chain of Blame: How Wall Street Caused the Mortgage and Credit Crisis.* (Hoboken, NJ: John Wiley and Sons, 2008): 183.
[20] The practice of not paying the rating agency until they produced a preliminary rating has since been discontinued.

most cases, the rating agencies were not given the full documentation on the loans that made up the pooled securities. An honorable approach might have been to refuse to rate bonds without full information; the firms did not pursue this strategy.

Even without the specifics, the agencies were told that they were being paid handsomely to come up with default estimates. They used the history of the previous ten to twenty years to project what future default rates might be. But as has been emphasized, the subprime mortgages created after 2005 were very different from the subprime mortgages of prior years, and housing prices were more out of line in 2006 than ever before. To put it perhaps uncharitably, the rating agencies were using the weather history of Miami over the previous twenty years to project temperatures in Boston in February.

In computer vernacular, this is called GIGO—"garbage in, garbage out," only in this case, they got paid up to $1 million to give their imprimatur. In the end, the courts will have to determine whether the rating agencies were merely incompetent, criminally liable, or just "journalists" writing a story (apparently this is their major line of defense).

9. Federal agencies

The deregulation creed has been a central part of Republican thinking and a disputed part of Democratic thinking over the last thirty-five years. President George W. Bush's first chair of the Securities and Exchange Commission (SEC), Harvey Pitt, promised a "kinder, gentler" agency. After the second chair was let go for being too zealous, Chris Cox, the third and last Bush appointment for this post, began his tenure by saying that he wanted to take a chainsaw to the more than 9,000 pages of banking regulations.[21]

Even after the crisis erupted, the Bush administration stuck to their deregulatory guns. When a number of states passed laws about predatory lending, the administration used an obscure 1863 law to claim federal jurisdiction. Despite the fact that all fifty state attorneys general protested, the administration prevailed.

---

[21] The story of how Cox and some of his colleagues impeded enforcement actions is told by Zachary Goldfarb, "The Cox Year at the SEC, Policies Undercut Action," *Washington Post,* June 1, 2009, A1.

The SEC enforcement division was so lacking in enforcement follow-through that they ignored many detailed warnings that Bernie Madoff was running an illegal Ponzi scheme. In 2006, they finally opened an investigation. Despite the fact that financial analyst Harry Markopolos had given them a 22-point explanation of why Madoff could not be a real investor, the division found no problems and cleared Madoff of wrongdoing just months before he confessed to his misdeeds.[22]

Finally, Robert Shiller, a leading financial economist at Yale University, describes giving a talk in 2005 to several senior employees at the Office of Thrift Supervision and the FDIC during which he warned of upcoming difficulties in the housing market. Even though the people in attendance had no financial stake in this issue, his arguments were dismissed. Apparently, the prevailing wisdom about the strength of the housing market pervaded the government bureaucracy as well as the financial professionals.

10. Bond purchasers

What were investors thinking? They were being offered AAA bonds that paid up to 2.5 percentage points more than AAA corporate bonds. Hadn't they ever heard the warning about things being "too good to be true"? Common sense was thrown out the window as they were blinded by the high returns and the evaluations of the rating agencies.

We now know that many investors did not understand what they were buying. Unbelievably, four Norwegian towns from north of the Arctic Circle (Rana, Hemnes, Hattjelldal, and Narvik) lost most of their $120 million investment in bonds backed by American subprime mortgages. Or take, for instance, the case of the retirement accounts of the school districts of Whitefish Bay, Wisconsin, and four surrounding communities. After two days of training, David Noack, their investment adviser, told them that they could get an extra 0.8 of a percentage point of returns by investing their $35 million in a mortgage-backed bond and borrowing $165 million. He assured them that the chances of default were remote even though he did not correctly describe the contents of the specific bond he was selling them. The investors dutifully initialed

---

[22] Even though Madoff's funds were continuing to report monthly gains throughout 2008, his investors needed to sell some of their holdings to pay for other losses. The lack of new investment and the need to meet these redemptions exposed the scam for what it was. Ironically, without the crisis, the scheme might still be functioning.

each page of the forty-page contract attesting to the fact that they knew what they were doing.

When the investment went sour, they quickly lost all of their money and had to inform the Irish bank that held their loan that they would not be repaying it. This tragic comedy of errors is now in court. Do investors give up personal responsibility when they follow the advice of their longtime broker? How would you decide?

Another case pushes the limits of professed ignorance even further. Buffalo's M&T Bank is now suing Deutsche Bank for an $80 million loss. They claimed that they had been told that this investment was "a layup" and "fully rock solid." Yet, at the same time (early 2007), Greg Lippmann, who headed Deutsche's bond trading department, advised hedge funds to bet against mortgage investments. Despite signing the 390-page offering document, M&T is claiming that it was misled and should not be held responsible for its decision.

When banks are arguing that they are unsophisticated investors we know that the instruments have become too complicated. Most investors were playing the odds in search of a little extra return, and now that their gamble has failed, they are looking to hold others responsible.[23]

11. The leaders of the financial industry

Since enough negative things have been said about these people, let's make a bit of an effort to understand why they did what they did. Even as the crisis was becoming eminently clear, Citigroup CEO Chuck Prince said in June 2007: "When the music stops, in terms of liquidity, things will be complicated . . . but as long as the music is playing, you've got to get up and dance."[24]

Put another way, if you were the CEO of a big financial institution in 2006, do you think that you could have justified to the business press and your stockholders that you were not pursuing the profitable mortgage-backed security business because of concerns about its future

---

[23] Even nonprofit organizations utilized financial innovation by using auction-late securities, interest-rate arbitrage, and complex swaps that backfired on them (see Stephanie Strom, "Non-Profits Paying Price for Gambles on Finance." *New York Times,* September 23, 2009).

[24] "Counting the Reasons Not to Be Cheerful" Investment Adviser, *FT Business,* July 23, 2007.

viability? It would have been very difficult to heed the warnings of the analysts who were (correctly) predicting an imminent crash because their own employees would have been outraged by not being able to earn the bonuses that their counterparts at other firms were making by selling these securities. Clearly, they would have been tempted to change jobs if they saw that these opportunities were not as available in their current firm.

Another issue to consider is that, by the time one becomes a CEO of a major financial firm, your wealth is already in the stratosphere. At a personal level, you are working very hard to build a legacy of accomplishment. Even though Stan O'Neal walked away with a huge amount of money, it is hard to believe that he intentionally put Merrill Lynch at risk simply for a couple of years of extraordinary profits.

Or, consider the case of Jimmy Cayne, CEO of Bear Stearns. He was so confident in the strength of his company that he kept a substantial portion of his fortune in company stock. At the end of 2007, his total holdings reached $1.2 billion; when the firm was sold to JP Morgan Chase, he received $61 million. Even though this is a large amount of money, he undoubtedly would have preferred to avoid losing over $1.1 billion.

Let's not go too far and give them a free pass, however. They were the ones who created a bonus system that rewarded short-term thinking at the expense of long-term stability. *Washington Post* columnist Steven Pearlstein describes Wall Street firms as having a "scummy culture [that has] contempt for customers, and that glorifies risk-taking, games-playing, and corner-cutting."[25] They were caught up in a wave of profit-making that was built on a foundation of poor quality subprime loans. They devised strategies to maximize every dollar of profit they could make, not realizing how vulnerable this made their companies to a series of losses. And they did all this without fully understanding the financial instruments they were using.

Conclusion

Many commentators have described the current crisis as being caused by "risky financial practices" that have to be curtailed in the future.

---

[25] Steven Pearlstein, "Obama's SEC Pick Is No Joe Kennedy," *Washington Post,* January 7, 2009, D1.

This is the wrong way to describe what happened, and tends to throw the baby out with the bath water.

Risk is at the heart of capitalism. Without a penchant for risk, Bill Gates would be a Harvard graduate and corporate lawyer in Seattle, and Warren Buffett would be a financial analyst rather than the lead investor of Berkshire Hathaway. Unless people were willing to throw caution to the wind, there wouldn't be a couple of million people who start new businesses each year. All successful entrepreneurs have taken risks and lost; the key to their success is taking enough prudent risks that the successes outnumber the failures.

Many people think that financiers are different because they were not risking their own money. In fact, some claim that financiers were getting huge salaries by selling bonds that they knew were going to fail. This is a bold statement that is supported by a few random comments cited in some e-mails. If they were so sure that these instruments would fail, why did Jimmy Cayne and so many other executives have so much money invested in their own companies? Furthermore, the big bonuses that many financial executives received were in the form of stock options that could not be exercised for many years.

Unfortunately, there is no good data on how much money financial executives lost in the crash. Clearly those that quit while they were ahead and diversified their investments were left with big nest eggs, but a much higher percentage seems to have kept their own money on the table. The most successful business executives were still left with large fortunes (Jimmy Cayne is still worth several hundreds of millions of dollars) but their actions at the end of the crisis show how badly they felt about the downfall of their companies and the loss of the jobs of many of their employees.

By comparison, how many people knew when to quit when the NASDAQ was rising to unbelievable levels? Human nature seems to doom us to be unable to walk away from big winnings and stop taking more gambles. *New York Times* reporters Louise Story and Landon Thomas Jr. tried to track down several Lehman employees to determine what they were doing one year after the company went bankrupt.[26] They found a person who quit early and lived in comfort, a person who was running a corner gas station, and a person who lost $6.6 million and was unemployed.

[26] "Tales From Lehman's Crypt," *New York Times,* September 13, 2009, B1.

One shouldn't feel sorry for the losers: They took risks and paid the consequences. One certainly can be angry, though, at the executives that were bailed out and are taking big bonuses today—while they may have lost a lot of money in the crash, they seem well on their way to rebuilding their large fortunes. Oddly there is very little that the government can do to stop these practices because there are no laws that permit the government to dictate what companies pay their workers. Apparently public disgrace and the pressures of the market are not enough to rein in high business salaries: When Goldman Sachs announced high profits for the third quarter of 2009, the simultaneous announcement of high bonuses presented a "public relations problem" for the company.[27]

The key lesson is that individual actors and companies can't see the systemic risk embodied in a series of similar bad decisions. Taking risks works when each actor pays the consequences for his or her failure and when the risks are reasonably small in relation to the whole economy. In the run-up to the crisis, there was a housing bubble, a lack of supervision over mortgages (because of the move to securitization and the originate-to-distribute model), a failure of rating agencies to properly quantify the possibilities of defaults, an explosion of private equity purchases financed with cheap credit, the creation of opaque financial instruments, a failure to regulate, and a lack of investor awareness of what they were purchasing.

With the benefit of hindsight, this does not look like risk but folly. No one was in a position to see how all of the pieces were dependent on one another. The financiers are at the center of the economy (capital is its life blood), and they mainly use other people's money. When the weakest link started to fail (the subprime mortgages), it was hard to contain the problems and present them from affecting other financial instruments, which led the banks to insolvency and the economy to the edge of collapse. The government had no alternative but to step in and stop the economy from spiraling downward.

A long time ago all advanced countries learned that unregulated industries can result in deadly actions.[28] After Upton Sinclair exposed in

---

[27] See Graham Bowley, "Bonuses Put Goldman in Public Relations Bind," *New York Times,* October 15, 2009, B1.]
[28] Less-developed countries have not had this luxury and paid the price in several different ways. In 2008, a number of Chinese babies died because producers cut costs by adding melamine to their milk. When an earthquake struck, lots of public schools

The Jungle the poor sanitary conditions in the Chicago stockyards at the beginning of the twentieth century, many firms in the industry joined the public in establishing food safety standards enforced by new government bodies. This is just one example of many in which minimum standards for product safety, air quality, and working conditions (including minimum wages) have been established. These countries have also "interfered" in the free operation of the market in terms of creating unemployment insurance, welfare for the needy, and Social Security for the elderly.

As a result, all advanced economies have become "mixed economies," balancing social needs with an open market. Yet, as I noted in a *Wall Street Journal* op-ed, "we are not French" and have more open markets, smaller government spending, lower taxes, and fewer regulations.[29] Our recent experiences with the gradual loosening of the restrictions on finance have had unexpectedly negative consequences.

The actions that led to the financial crisis of 2008 were the result of overconfidence. Many thought the "market" would be self-regulating because business leaders would not pursue strategies that could threaten the very existence of the company, but, as the next chapter will show, there have been many "manias, panics, and crashes" (the title of Charles Kindleberger's book on the prevalence of financial crises through the last three centuries). We've recovered from the past crises and built a stronger set of rules and regulations; we will recover from this crisis as well.

The bottom line is that one still can't "make a silk purse from a sow's ear." The centrality of subprime mortgages in the current financial collapse is due to the relatively high interest rates subprime borrowers paid. This high rate was used to support multiple transformations in which a generous fee was deducted at each step. In order for the final product to be competitive, one needed the "spread" (the difference in the interest rate from those of treasury bonds) to support all these deductions. The originate-to-distribute model and the development of new financial instruments allowed the financial titans and purchasers of mortgage-backed bonds to "trust" that the quality of the underlying assets was strong. How could it not be, given that the rating agencies gave the bonds the coveted AAA rating?

---

collapsed because of shoddy construction. Plus, a series of product recalls were required because of safety hazards (e.g., use of lead paint in toys).
[29] "Democrats and the Economy," March 25, 2008.

Of course, the high interest rates for subprime mortgages were due to the higher probability of default. Therefore, this cushion was not as large as it appeared because the effective payments were always going to be less due to higher default rates. The subprime model worked only for the few years while housing prices were increasing at an unusual and unsustainable rate. Increasing prices permitted people to refinance properties, which were now deemed to be "worth" more. After several iterations of this process, housing values were increasingly out of line with their long-term historic trajectory. This only made the inevitable crash that much larger.

In the end, the notion that rich people could make lots of money by lending to poor people and others with poor credit histories was preposterous. A company like Walmart is successful selling to the lower and middle classes by having very thin profit margins and very high volume (recall that just 12 percent of all income is held by the bottom 40 percent of the population). Most other successful companies either serve businesses or cater to the upper-middle and upper-income classes.

CHAPTER 2

The Financial Crisis:
What Will Happen Next?

"CAN'T LIVE WITH HIM, can't live without him" is a phrase an exasperated wife might say after her husband has repeated a behavior that annoys her. In much the same way, President Barack Obama explains to the public that bailing out Wall Street is necessary for the health of Main Street, even though many would rather punish the leaders of our financial institutions. Obama is saying that "we can't live without them" and that we have to come to their assistance while making sure that they never have the opportunity to create such a mess again.

Obama's strategy is based on the premise that the financial system can be restored close to the form that existed before. There certainly will be new regulations and requirements put on the surviving financial institutions, but the fundamental structure of private firms raising and allocating money will be maintained. Even though the government is lending many institutions enough money to buy up all of their shares, the administration has rebuffed demands that the government "nationalize" the ailing banks because of its strong commitment to private ownership of banks.

To understand why a Democratic president has chosen to rebuild the private financial sector, one must understand the role that finance plays in the economy. Consequently, this chapter starts with the counterintuitive claim that debt can promote mobility and add to overall profitability. Since capital is relatively expensive and hard to raise, access to borrowing permits firms to manage their finances much more easily.

At the same time, we need to understand the limitations of these institutions, especially since they seem to lurch into crisis every five years or so. I'll discuss in some detail each of the seven major financial crises from 1982 to 2001 to show where regulators and investors went wrong.

Finally, the last part of the chapter will present an analysis of the lessons learned from the seven small crises and the one large one that was analyzed in Chapter 1. These lessons, in turn, will be used to develop common-sense regulatory changes that can be implemented once the economic downturn has ended.

The Role of Finance in a Free-Market Economy

Most people don't understand finance because they see the world through the eyes of a borrower. While Shakespeare intoned that one should be neither a borrower nor a lender, most people do not have lots of extra cash to invest, but do require loans to buy a house or car or perhaps to send a son or daughter to college. They also use credit cards (called "revolving debt") and frequently don't pay their full monthly balances, and therefore pay interest and other charges. The borrower's anxieties, e.g., repayments, terms, pressure not to be late, potential default-foreclosure-repossession, bring a strong sense of foreboding to the act of borrowing money. So whenever people hear that personal, corporate, government, or international debt is rising, they interpret this as a sign of economic distress.

The perspective of the borrower was very influential in having two of the world's great religions—Christianity and Islam—prohibit the charging of interest during the Middle Ages (and operating under Islamic law in some countries results in provisions that make charging interest difficult).[30] Saint Thomas Aquinas, writing in the thirteenth century, gives the best explanation for the logic behind this position. He looked at the act of lending and asked why someone would need to go into debt. He concluded that people would only incur debt if some calamity had befallen them. Since this was not a very entrepreneurial

---

[30] To the degree that loans share in the profits of the enterprise as a way to avoid the appearance of charging interest, this is closer to being a partner rather than a lender.

age, the notion that debt could be used as part of the investment process to expand business activity did not enter into his thoughts. Therefore, it would be unethical to "traffic in the misery of others" to require that the borrower repay more than the amount of the loan.

The negative view of finance is also evident in Margaret Atwood's 2008 book *Payback: Debt and the Shadow Side of Wealth*. Ms. Atwood is an acclaimed writer of fiction, poetry, and nonfiction, and investigates the idea of debt from the ancients onward in literature and culture. She shows how debt has often been equated with sin and how the Faustian bargain is one in which a promise today leads to a life of eternal damnation. Since economic activity is portrayed as either taking or trading, there is once again no room for debt to be used beneficially. For her, neither the borrower nor the lender is acting responsibly and we would all be better off if borrowing were still banned.

The view of debt from the point of view of the lender, however, is very different. The person with money is trying to decide how to safely get the highest return possible. The lender has various options and weighs the potential rewards and risks. There is no sense of urgency because these are the lender's surplus funds that can easily find a safe haven. Before making the loan, the intelligent lender will investigate the creditworthiness and collateral of the borrower and only lend money once the appropriate conditions are met. From this prospective, debt is not menacing, just profitable.

Putting the perspectives of the borrower and lender together, one can make the counter-intuitive proposition that the widespread use of debt is a sign of economic strength because lenders are confident that their money is safe even if it is committed for a long period of time. Conversely, excessively high interest rates and reluctance to lend are clear signals that potential lenders have worries and concerns about future economic instability.

In the same vein, one can argue that debt promotes mobility. Although borrowers worry about repayments, debt provides them with access to resources, be it a new house, furthering their education, or starting a new business. As Glenn Yago puts it: "In the absence of inherited wealth or the granting of seigniorial rights to property, debt has been a central tool for acquiring productive assets."[31] Without debt, many people would

---

[31] In *Junk Bonds: How High Yield Securities Restructured Corporate America*. (New York: Oxford University Press, 1991): 109.

have had to do without; debt makes the money of the wealthy (and the combined smaller resources of the near wealthy) more widely available to those who are not wealthy.

Think for a moment about the poorest countries in the world, and think about what their banking systems are like. Three researchers have found that countries lacking a developed banking system tend to have greater income inequality.[32] In fact, some of the most interesting ideas about helping poor countries move forward involve better systems to clarify land ownership and microfinancing so individuals can start new businesses. Furthermore, even in the United States, another group of researchers found that banking deregulation over the last twenty-five years helped reduce inequality.[33]

To fully understand the positive role of debt, we can begin with the basic capitalist act of starting a business to make a profit. This process starts with a leap of faith that putting up money today will lead to more money in the future. Even established companies are constantly expanding and changing product lines to respond to the signals from the market.

Since today's activities are initiated in anticipation of a future sale, a crucial problem facing all businesses is managing time. If the owners knew their product would not sell at the appropriate price, they would not start the process. They would like to sell their product before they incurred the costs to produce it, but this is rarely possible. Consequently, the money to pay their workers and suppliers must come from either accumulated capital or loans.

Another component of the time problem involves long-lived inputs, such as machinery and buildings, which are used in multiple production cycles spanning several years. In these circumstances, an outlay today will not be fully repaid for many years. Therefore, to start production, owners need even more money and don't fully expect to recover their costs for many years. Since the payoff period is longer, there are more things that can go wrong and owners will need better incentives—i.e., high expected profits when sales meet expectations—to make the initial commitment to begin production.

[32] Thorsten Beck, Asli Demirgüç-Kunt, and Ross Levine, "Finance, Inequality and the Poor: Cross-Country Evidence," *Journal of Economic Growth,* 12:1 (2007): 27–49.
[33] Thorsten Beck, Ross Levine, and Alexey Levkov, "Big Bad Banks?: The Impact of U.S. Branch Deregulation on Income Distribution" (2008), http://www.econ.brown.edu/fac/Ross_Levine/Publication/Forthcoming/2007_big_bad_banks.pdf.

Even without fraud and swindling, the bridge over time may fail for various reasons: output may not sell at the expected price, customers may not pay their bills, or goods may not sell quickly enough. Each of these events cuts into profits, and if severe enough, leads to losses. If the losses build up, the owners may have to sell their enterprises, or in severe cases, they may be unable to pay their creditors and be forced into bankruptcy. But if their creditors are depending on this money to repay their own obligations, a negative snowball effect may help to spread bankruptcies from business to business.

Finance helps businesses manage time and conserve capital. Consider a hypothetical Ms. Smith who needs further capitalization to build a new office complex which she plans to sell to a developer.[34] Her cousin John has some money and thinks this is a good idea. He can either become a part-owner in the company, or he can lend her the money at a given interest rate over a certain period of time using his cousin's house as collateral.

In both situations, John's money is being used to finance the project. If he becomes a partner, his returns vary with the fate of the company: making a lot of money if the project is successful or potentially getting no return on his investment if sales don't meet projections. If he opts to make the loan instead, his return is fixed unless the company does very badly. Even then, he can get his principal back because he has first claim on the assets of his cousin's business.

So, the difference between ownership and loans has to do with dividing the spoils and allocating the risk. As long as a company performs reasonably well, the cash flow will support either profits or repayment of debts. The owner with an "equity" stake can share in the division of high profits while the lender has agreed to a fixed rate of return. Offsetting this ownership advantage is the downside risk of lower returns and potential losses if the company does not meet expectations.

The use of a bank rather than a personal loan only makes the chain longer. Instead of borrowing from a friend, you go to a bank holding the money of many individual depositors. The bank plays the role of financial intermediary between you and your creditors. Banks have several advantages over person to person contacts: expertise in evaluating proposals, staff to do the paperwork and oversee timely payments, and

---

[34] In the real world, development projects like this are almost always funded with loans from a bank or other financial institution.

spreading the risk by lending to many companies (a few failures to repay without the collateral covering the loss does not jeopardize the return on a large number of loans). Therefore, having a banking system is much more efficient than having borrowers locate their own lenders.

Should Ms. Smith have a preference for a loan or equity partnership? Consider the following two ways of funding a $100-million office complex that is expected to sell for $112 million one year later. If Ms. Smith puts up the entire amount, the profit rate is 12 percent. An alternative way of financing this project is to borrow $50 million and personally invest the other $50 million. If the interest rate of the loan is 10 percent, then $55 million must be paid back to the bank at the end of the year. After the sale and repayment to the bank, Ms. Smith is left with $57 million and a profit of $7 million on a $50 million investment. By using a loan, Ms. Smith has put up less money and increased her return on investment from 12 percent to 14 percent.

In financial parlance, the use of the loan permitted the investor to "leverage" her $50 million into $100 million much as the individual purchasing a home leverages the down payment on a home using the bank's money. The use of loans in this fashion results in wider variations of profits for the owners. If the office complex could only sell for $106 million rather than the planned $112 million, the profit rates on the two financing schemes change dramatically. In the first case where the investor put up the entire amount, the profit rate would be 6 percent. The leveraged investor on the other hand would still have to pay back $55 million, leaving only $1 million of profits, or a 2 percent rate of return. So, the use of debt financing magnifies both the risks and rewards of the equity owners.

This case is tame compared with the use of much greater amounts of leverage. Let's say Ms. Smith only put up $20 million, and borrowed $80 million to make the $100 million investment. In the example of the $112 million sale, she would have $24 million after paying back the $88 million in loans and interest, for a $4 million or 20 percent return on her investment. But if the economy soured and the property only sold for $70 million, she still owes her borrowers $88 million. Because the expected profits have not materialized, not only has the $20 million investment been lost, Ms. Smith has to come up with $18 million more to repay the lender. In a nutshell, this is the explosive downside risk of high leverage, and this is what happened in 2007 and 2008.

So, loans start out as a way to move capital from those who have it to those who want to use it to create or expand a business (see Appendix 2 for a listing of different kinds of financial institutions and how they raise and make money). The fact that loans can be used to increase the rate of return on owner's capital shows the incentive for owners to use debts to deal with short-term costs associated with changes in payrolls and other purchases. For them, their own capital is precious and they seek a high rate of return on their investment. Therefore, even if they are well capitalized, they will use loans regularly in financing their needs.

Of course, loans are made to consumers as well as businesses. By far, the largest component of consumer borrowing (75 percent of all personal debts) is for the financing of a mortgage on one's principal residence. Unlike pure consumption loans (e.g., credit card balances) mortgage loans have a real asset that can be sold as a form of collateral against the debt. This loan helps people buy an asset that they will use over many years. Without the opportunity to take on this debt and because most people do not have the savings needed to pay for a house, the home-ownership rate would be much lower than the 67 percent it is today. Other common reasons for consumer borrowing, such as purchasing an auto or sending a child to college, also involve items whose benefits are spread out over many years. The exact distribution of consumer borrowing and credit card use will be addressed in chapter 7.[35]

From Investing to Insurance
to Gambling

The previous discussion is the positive side of finance being used to support consumption and production. The interest rate on loans is based on two components: a minimum rate that is determined by the interest rate of the safest asset (usually a U.S. government bond) and a risk premium to cover the expected losses from loans associated with each class of borrower. The "interest spread" or risk premium varies widely depending on the quality of borrower and the state of the market.

---

[35] Public lending is yet a different case although most local and state lending is for infrastructure projects.

Because finance is so connected with time and uncertainty, every financial asset is constantly changing in price as people reassess what the future will hold. Anyone who follows the stock market closely knows that, even in good times, there is a substantial amount of daily, weekly, and monthly variation. And from time to time, there are massive movements up or down as perceptions of future conditions and current prices change dramatically.

In such a changing world, strategies have been developed to protect against unexpected price swings. Farmers' lives, for example, often revolved around a single crop. In addition to the obvious perils of bad weather—too much rain, too little rain, too much heat, extreme cold—and other calamities such as insect infestation, they faced price uncertainty for their crop. Because they have to make decisions on how much to plant at the beginning of the season they could be very disappointed and lose lots of money if, when they are ready to sell, the commodity price is lower than anticipated. The obvious solution is to lock in a price before you have planted your crop. If the price is higher when you were ready to sell, then you passed up on some profit. But if the price is lower when the harvest comes in, you would not have to face the possibility of losing your farm. So you have "hedged your bets" by minimizing your losses against falling prices. Farmers gain security by forgoing higher profits by capping losses.

If you could find a buyer who also wanted to lock in a price for your product, you were set. Bakers, for example, might want to agree on a future delivery of wheat with a known price. For their own reasons, these two parties can agree to a "futures contract" on the price and quantity of a commodity to be delivered when the harvest is ready.

It should be noted that this contract is not based on an existing asset but on something of expected value. In financial parlance, the value of future contracts is "derived" from something that is not immediately part of the contract. Thus, derivatives began as a risk avoidance strategy so people would not be "putting all their eggs in one basket." As early as 1862, the Chicago Board of Trade was opened to create a futures market for commodities (the first type of futures contracts date back to the fourteenth century and perhaps earlier). In the 1970s, its competitor (and now partner), the Chicago Mercantile Exchange began trading in financial and monetary instruments.

Today, there are very active futures markets in country currencies, the Dow Jones average and other broad market baskets, individual stocks, and other entities. Again, there are good reasons to make these trades as a way to avoid risk. For example, consider if I plan on selling wheat to Russia to be delivered in three months. We've agreed on a price so I don't need to buy a futures contract to avoid the dangers of the falling price of wheat. But I now have a currency exposure to the exchange rate of the dollar with the ruble: If the value of the ruble rises, I'll get fewer dollars back than I expect. So to avoid this risk, I can buy a futures contract that locks in the dollar-ruble exchange rate.

Basically, all investing is "betting on" the future. Under normal circumstances, this is a reasonably safe bet because profits are able to sustain stock prices and repay loans with interest, and there are strategies to limit downside risk. But the markets today are structured to let the betting juices flow freely. In many cases, the buying and selling of options and future contracts is not based on insurance but on a confidence that you know what the future is going to look like.[36] The currency markets, in particular, have daily trading volumes way out of proportion to what is needed to manage exchange rate risk.

Similarly, the original selling of stock is a means for companies to obtain capital. Once issued, however, the buying and selling of stock is based on the relative perceptions of the future company's. While companies can benefit from high share prices (it's easier to sell more stock and employee morale will be high), the capital position of the company is unchanged.

Most of the discussion of finance involves investing in stocks or businesses because you want to share in their profits. There are many books on how to accurately evaluate companies in order to pick winners. But what if you think that a company is overvalued? In today's market, you can "sell a company short" and make money if the stock price goes down.

Short selling is usually accomplished by borrowing a stock and agreeing to return it after a specified time period. When you originally borrow the stock, you immediately sell it at its current price of

---

[36] A way to protect yourself against stock price declines is to buy "put options": For a small fee someone agrees to buy the stock if the price falls by a specified amount over a certain time period. For example, if XYZ Biotech is selling for $50 a share and I want to protect myself from losing too much money on this investment, I can buy a put option with a "strike price" of $45. I am worried that their new drug trial will turn out badly and the stock price will fall dramatically. By buying a put option, I have limited my losses and still have the upside potential if the stock rises when the trial is successful.

$50. In three months, you sell back the stock at $50 a share after having paid a small fee for borrowing the stock. If you are correct and the price is $40 after three months, you will purchase the stock at the current price of $40, immediately resell it at $50, and pocket the difference as profits.

The negativists who sell short have a bad reputation because they are anticipating other people's decline. For example, financier George Soros made a famous bet that the British pound was going to be devalued within the week. He made several billion dollars when his prediction turned out to be true. Of course, the British Chancellor of the Exchequer gave a news conference bitterly complaining about the attack of financial barracudas (i.e., Soros's betting against the pound) that forced the country into a devaluation. And it certainly seems odd that someone can make this amount of money in such a socially nonproductive fashion.[37]

The Growing Role of Finance

Between 1982 and 2001, the S&P 500 stock index grew by 15 percent per year. This astonishing "bull run" changed how many people thought about wealth and investing. At the end of the 1980s (an era of leveraged buyouts with junk bonds), there was a double-dip recession and Clinton won the election on a platform to improve the economy. Fortunately, the economy was already rebounding and the 1990s were characterized by strong economic growth, rising employment, and an even bigger bull run. As 401(k) plans became more common, we were becoming an

---

[37] An alternative view of short sellers is presented by David Einhorn in his book, *Fooling Some of the People All of the Time*. He recounts his long battle with Allied Capital over their accounting practices. After responding to a public question for his current best investment tip, he responded by saying that he was shorting this stock. Thus began a five-year battle with the company that used a variety of contacts in the press and elective offices to attack Einhorn for starting a "short attack" from which he would gain. Ingenuously, he questioned how come many people could get air time every day listing the stocks that they thought were good investments and were not accused of artificially pumping up the stock from which they would gain. In the end, a wholly-owned subsidiary of the company was shown to have perpetrated fraud against the Small Business Administration. Yet, along the way, Einhorn had his phone records stolen, was investigated by the SEC and the N.Y. state attorney general, and was called "scum" by a *Washington Post* columnist.

"investor society" with half of all households holding equities directly or indirectly in their pension accounts.

As the 1990s progressed, the mania about investment grew year by year. On August 9, 1995, the Netscape IPO hit the market. Even though the company had been in existence just fifteen months and had never made a profit, the stock closed at $75 a share after having opened at $28 a share (the original offering price three weeks earlier had been estimated to be $14 a share). It seemed like any company with a hi-tech name could "go public" and see their stock prices zoom through the roof.

The signs of public mass "irrational exuberance" were everywhere. I remember going into a McDonald's restaurant one day in the late 1990s in the suburbs of Washington, D.C., and finding the one TV set tuned to the business channel, CNBC. On the Web, the Motley Fool became a center for analysis promoting the long-term investment prospects of hi-tech stocks. Finally, many stock analysts, TV commentators, and authors competed with each other over who could be the most enthusiastic about the future of the stock market.

As the clamor for investing advice grew, analysts competed to get attention by developing new metrics of company growth. For example, many people started to talk about the importance of "EBITDA" (earnings before interest, taxes, depreciation, and amortization). Lynn Turner, the chief accountant at the SEC, sarcastically called this approach "EBBS"—earnings before bad stuff. Alex Berenson in *The Number: How the Drive for Quarterly Earnings Corrupted Wall Street and Corporate America* chronicled how the focus on the quarterly earnings, stock options, and CEO pay led to a series of deceptive practices.[38]

All this was happening while finance's role in the economy was growing. In terms of corporate profits, the share controlled by financial corporations averaged 10 percent of all profits from 1960 through 1984 (Figure 2.1). After that year, finance's share of profits bounced around each year (rising higher during recessions reaching 40 percent in 2001 to 2003) but trended upward ending at about one-quarter of all profits from 2004 to 2005. However, when finance's share of corporate profits is over 20 percent, it is fair to think, as Benjamin Friedman does, that finance's ability to make money has gotten too big.[39]

---

[38] New York: Random House Publishing Group, 2004.

[39] In "The Failure of the Economy & the Economists," *New York Review of Books,* May 28, 2009. It should be noted that there is no easy computation to determine the

Figure 2.1: Financial Share of Corporate profits, 1948–2007

National Income and Product Accounts

Another sign of the growing importance of finance is its share of value added in the economy (Figure 2.2): financial companies grew from 3.3 percent of the economy in 1960, to 4.6 percent in 1980, to 8.2 percent in 2001 through 2007. As our society has become wealthier and as the economies of the world have become more integrated, the growing share of finance in terms of value added is to be expected and is part of the expansion of the office economy (see discussion in chapter 5). Consequently, the increase in this measure is more appropriate than the increase in finance's corporate profit share. However, with a decrease in

---

share of finance of corporate profits. The numbers cited here use a methodology suggested by Benjamin Friedman based on Table 6.17 of the National Income and Product Accounts. On the one hand there is a line for "management of companies," which includes bank and other holding companies. Although this entry is composed predominantly of bank-holding companies, the BEA does not make available what percent are nonbank holding companies. On the other hand, these data are reported at the enterprise level. Therefore, a lending company such as GMAC (which made mortgage as well as car loans) would not be considered a financial company.

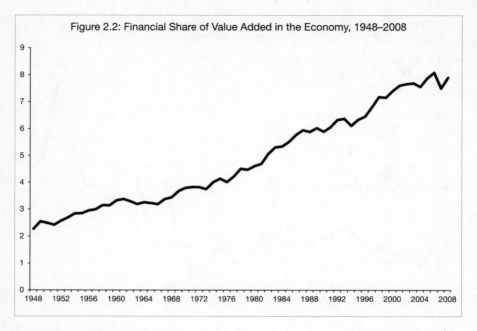

Figure 2.2: Financial Share of Value Added in the Economy, 1948–2008

National Income and Product Accounts

the high salaries of so many financial profits, this measure will probably edge downward in the years ahead.

The Rise of Bonuses and Executive Pay

Determining how to pay people for their work is much a more complex process than most people realize. The problem arises because of the disconnect between getting paid and doing the work. After the salary is paid, the workers have the opportunity to not work up to their potential or can "shirk" their responsibilities.

Making sure that workers work is one of the major tasks of management, which offer a series of "carrots and sticks." The highest form of punishment is to fire the worker. But this usually requires close monitoring and some sort of proof that the worker is not doing his or her job. Further, other downsides of dismissing workers are that it can undermine the remaining workers' morale and that it is expensive to recruit and retrain new workers.

An alternative to close supervision is "piece work"—to pay workers on the basis of their output. This is often not an option when the individual worker's output cannot be separately tallied.

Obviously, the best option for management is for workers to police themselves. The Japanese and Germans, for example, are known as hard workers because their sense of duty is very high. Virtually all workers, however, have pride in what they do, especially because of their desire to be respected by their co-workers.

Management can foster these feelings by creating a "team" atmosphere and demonstrating that they care about the workers' attitudes and feelings. In fact, some economists have postulated that in many cases companies pay slightly above the going rate to foster positive feelings among workers for the company. This "efficiency wage," as it is called, relies on workers avoiding shirking responsibilities because they want to reward the company that is rewarding them.

Bonuses are a form of piece work aimed at highly paid workers. They are based on the premise that workers need to be highly incentivized to work their hardest. Cash is used as the carrot in place of professional ethics and the normal work ethic.

It wasn't always this way as executive bonuses were very small before 1980. In 1978, the company Toys 'R Us broke with the tradition of offering their executives a few stock options as a token of appreciation of a job well done. Instead, a large number of options were offered, and the earnings of their CEO Charles Lazarus in 1980 were twice that of any other executive because of the value of the options he received. At that point, the average CEO made forty times the salary of the average worker, but the expanding use of stock options was going to change this dramatically. An odd accounting convention permitted options to not be treated as a cost in the year in which they were given. This permitted companies to grant options without immediately affecting their reported earnings. Since reported earnings were often the basis of movements of stock prices, the exclusion of costing out options artificially inflated stock prices, which in turn increased the value of the options.

When used wisely, options make a lot of sense. Start-up firms could attract talented workers on the basis of future gains and not have to pay high salaries immediately. For this reason, hi-tech firms were at the forefront of granting options widely and were the biggest defenders of continuing to keep options off of a company's yearly income statement.[40]

Then options became crazy, and by 1999, CEO pay had increased by twenty times, and the ratio of CEO pay to average-worker pay grew to 150. Plus, options and bonuses were not limited to CEOs and spread to most of the professional staff on Wall Street. In fact, the salaries of these workers were set relatively low based on yearly bonuses (comprised heavily of options) that could be up to one to four times one's salary.

Not surprisingly, bonus announcements became the central part of the year. Instead of using bonuses as a small incentive to have workers avoid shirking, their size meant that all actions during the course of the year revolved around maximizing one's bonus. This certainly made people work long hours and try to make lots of money for the company. On the other hand, incentives were so skewed to reward high profits that it led traders and managers to take big risks in order to receive high yearly bonuses. Many commentators have argued that the compensation practices that developed in the 1990s led to short-term thinking, which did not adequately serve the long-term interest of the company.

Financial Crises

There is something magical about money, and there is a strong tendency for there to be overenthusiasm and a herd mentality.[41] The problem comes when the herd turns and everyone runs to one of the few exit doors at the same time. At these moments of financial panic, markets collapse as everyone becomes a seller—credit dries up, liquidity disappears, and the best laid plans to respond to market turns become impossible to execute. Macroeconomist Hyman Minsky analyzed this movement of excessive optimism leading to sudden collapses and developed a typology to describe each stage of this repeating process. He talked about a "world

[40] Options did become a company expense in the year in which they were cashed in. But sometimes this was treated as an "unusual expense" and discounted when earnings were reported before unusual items.

[41] One school of investment focuses on "momentum" buying—this is where stock investors buy stocks that have been rising in price, which of course tends to lead to further price rises. Fed Chairman Alan Greenspan called this "irrational exuberance," and then did nothing to stop it.

in which businessmen and financial intermediaries who aggressively seek profit, innovators will always outpace regulators" and find a way to create "fringe banks" to fund these activities (in the current crisis, this would be the shadow banking system of SIVs, CDOs, CDSs, and related instruments).[42] He distinguished between three kinds of financing:

> *Hedge:* This is the normal financing in which the borrower is able to pay the interest while paying down the debt.
>
> *Speculative:* Riskier financing where the lender only has enough cash flow to cover the interest payments and profits are made because the lender expects a rise in price of the underlying investment.
>
> *Ponzi:* The riskiest financing where the lender does not even have the cash flow to pay the interest on the loan and expects to be able to refinance because the underlying asset will increase in value enough to support getting a larger loan in the future.

Others before Minsky had noted the tendency of finance to go through periodic crashes. In 1976, Charles Kindleberger published the first edition of *Manias, Panics, and Crashes: A History of Financial Crises* and identified forty separate cases from 1720 through 1975 in which a country's (and sometime many countries') economic health was thrown into distress because of a financial meltdown. The fifth edition of this classic was released in 2005 (Robert Aliber finished the manuscript after Kindleberger died in 2003), and there was plenty of new material on crises to be added.

Paul Samuelson, a Nobel laureate and one of the leading economists in the world over the last sixty years, made a prescient comment for the book jacket: "Sometime in the next five years you may kick yourself for not reading and rereading Kindleberger's [book]." Apparently, in the thirty years since the original publication of this book, financial leaders have not learned about the recurrence of financial crises. They have devised ever more creative strategies to make large amounts of money, not realizing the dangers of financial ruin for many (but not you!) a few years in the future.

---

[42] *Stabilizing an Unstable Economy.* (New York: McGraw Hill, 1986). Cited in Paul McCulley, "The Shadow Banking System and Hyman Minsky's Economic Journey," p. 11; available at: www.highlinewealth.com/upload_passprotected.asp? OrgID=2401&SPID=89778&up_lid=87179

From 1946 through 1973, the constraints of Glass-Steagall, the 1930 law that severely limited the growth of large financial institutions, and a remarkably strong worldwide economic recovery from the Depression and war led to a very stable financial system. The inflation and slow growth of the next nine years, however, convinced political leaders to let the competitive juices flow more freely in order to begin a deregulatory process that would result in great financial expansion. From 1982 to 2007, there were a number of financial minicollapses that did not have large macroeconomic impacts. At the onset of many of these events, there were some people who said that this or that crisis "was going to be the largest one since the Great Depression." The lack of impact of these events and the poor track record of predicting economic decline gave many a sense that we were in a new age in which major economic dislocations could no longer occur.

One of the reasons for this belief was that the Federal Reserve was quick to bail out troubled firms and maintain financial stability. Some people called these actions "Greenspan's Put" (a put is an option that limits your downside risk) because any time the stock market fell, the Fed opened the monetary spigots to keep the economy and stock market from declining. Others worried that these actions might have the unanticipated effect of encouraging riskier and riskier behavior. This is called "moral hazard" because if the costs of a negative event (e.g., a flood) are minimized (by subsidized insurance), then reckless behavior (building houses on flood plains) will become more common.

Let's look at seven major crises that occurred from 1982 through 2003:

1. Savings and Loan (S&L) Bankruptcies: The old 3-6-3 banking model relied on low and stable interest rates. Because S&Ls mainly made residential mortgages that they held on their books, they had a fixed revenue stream. This was not a problem because they were limited by law on how much they could pay their depositors (Regulation Q). As the inflation rate crept up in the 1970s, however, other institutions were able to attract deposits away from the S&Ls. Even after a 1980 law was passed that did away with the interest rate ceiling that S&Ls could pay their depositors, the S&Ls had already been weakened and many of them no longer had enough capital, and were subjected to being closed by the banking authorities.

Nevertheless, the regulators did not close all the weak banks and S&Ls, and instead provided them with the opportunity to earn their way back to solvency. This would turn out to be a moral hazard on steroids. The first response of these banks was to attract deposits by offering certificates of deposits (CDs) of up to $100,000 that paid very high interest rates. They had nothing more to lose, and buyers often went through brokers who looked for the very highest rates of return for their clients.

This created a difficult situation because the banks now had to make loans with interest rates high enough to pay off their CDs and still earn a substantial profit. The only loans that would carry such high interest rates were risky ventures that could not easily get conventional financing. The banks could make these loans with impunity because they had no capital left to lose, and because the loss would be covered by the government through deposit insurance.

Some investors saw owning an S&L as an opportunity to use the new cash flow to provide loans for development projects for which they were unable to obtain funding. In a number of cases, illegal "flipping" schemes were used to bilk the government. In one case, developer/bank owners bought a property for $3 million and sold it to a company that they owned the next day for $47 million using bank loans. The bank regulators weren't looking closely for conflicts of interest and, in fact, were being pressured by elected representatives to allow free enterprise to work its magic and to stop "harassing" S&L bank officials. The most famous cases of political pressure involved Arizona businessman Charles Keating and President George H. W. Bush's son Neil, (one of George W. Bush's brothers).

In the end, most risky loans did not come through. Partly, this was due to the regional decline in the oil and coal patch of Texas, Louisiana, and Colorado, but mainly it was due to poor business judgments that were backed by taxpayer dollars. By 1990, nearly 50 percent of the S&Ls that were in business in 1980 no longer existed. If these institutions had been closed or consolidated with other institutions at the beginning of the 1980s, the estimated cost to the government would have been $10 billion. Whereas by staying open for another five to seven years and by pursuing a go-for-broke strategy, the cost to the tax payers was

$124 billion (the eventual cost of bailing out Keating's Lincoln Savings was $2.6 billion alone). Of the S&Ls that closed, fraud was found to have occurred in half of them and 550 S&L managers and owners were convicted of crimes.

When the Resolution Trust Corporation (RTC) was set up to handle the failed assets of the S&Ls, some projections of the costs ran to $600 billion to $800 billion. In the end, the total cost was $153 billion ($124 billion by tax payers and $29 billion by the S&Ls). This is certainly a high number, especially when compared with the $10 billion that it would have cost to shut these banks in 1982. The confusion over the value of the "toxic loans" demonstrates the problems of evaluating financial assets. At the time of the crisis, prices were very low and costs would have been very high if all the properties had been immediately sold, but by waiting, the RTC was able to get a much higher price and reduce taxpayer exposure.

2. The Stock Market Collapse of 1987: Out of the blue, stock prices declined by over 20 percent without any real change in employment, inflation, or output. Most people attribute this decline to "portfolio insurance," which represented a new strategy of selling short whenever a large-scale market decline occurred. Although this was an old strategy, the new wrinkle was that the selling would be done by a computer model that would kick in automatically.

This is a classic case of what is "good for one" may not work when everyone is trying to do the same thing at the same time. As more and more investors moved to a portfolio insurance approach, this meant that they all would respond similarly at the first sign of a steep market fall. Of course, as the market continued to fall, more automatic computer trading kicked in trying to sell short. Consequently, everyone "ran for the same exit door at same time" and market trades were delayed by forty-five minutes because there were not enough buyers to determine an accurate price.

3. Currency Collapses: World financial history is replete with examples of governments defaulting on their obligations, especially when the debt is incurred to fight a war or when there is a change in the ruling elite. For example, some people are still trying to cash in bonds issued by Tsarist Russia in World War I.

In today's world, international finance has had mixed relations with developing countries. On the one hand, the advanced industrialized countries take some responsibility for a history of colonialism and proclaim a commitment to assist less-developed countries. In addition to the World Bank, there are a variety of regional banks (e.g., The Inter-American Development Bank for Latin America and counterparts for Asia and Africa) whose mission is to provide long-term financing for development and infrastructure projects.

At the same time, a series of private banks have made loans to countries and private companies throughout the developing world. In the 1970s and 1980s, a number of American banks made loans to South American countries that were then reloaned by local governments to finance private projects. When these projects turned out to be riddled with corruption, the Latin companies could not repay their government loans, which meant that the governments could not repay their loans to the international banks.

The first Latin crisis exploded at the end of the 1980s and threatened to lead to bank failures in America and Europe. To avoid a potentially destabilizing series of defaults, money was supplied by the IMF and World Bank to countries, and participating banks were forced to take between 30 and 50 percent losses on the face value of their holdings. This contained the losses, maintained the financial stability of the Latin countries, and left the banks with much stronger assets.

This experience did not reduce the tendency of financial institutions from trying to make money off of loans to less-developed countries. In 1994, there was the "Tequila crisis" in Mexico as President Carlos Salinas massively increased public spending just prior to the upcoming Mexican election. By paying for this bonanza with bonds that were indexed to the dollar, a devaluation of the peso led to devastating consequences for the government. Only a massive intervention by the United States and the IMF led by Treasury Secretary Robert Rubin and his undersecretary for International Affairs Lawrence Summers (with the assistance of his deputy Timothy Geithner) prevented a complete rout of the Mexican economy.

There's more: The Russians defaulted on their bond obligations in 1998, and Argentineans were also forced to go into default in 2001, when their attempt to maintain parity with the dollar (a policy that had successfully stopped runaway inflation) failed.

In Asia, the Thai government was a victim of its own success. After a period of overbuilding using foreign loans, the government could no longer support its currency (the "baht") in relation to the dollar. The collapse of the Thai economy due to the devaluation and economic decline quickly spread throughout Asia to South Korea, Hong Kong, Malaysia, Laos, and the Philippines.

The upshot of this is that there is a lot of "hot money" that can move in and out of countries quickly. While outside money can be used to finance economic expansion, the debts are usually denominated in dollars, which exposes the country to "exchange rate" risk. When some event undermines the confidence in the local currency, speculators sell the currency short, and foreign investors start to take their money out. As the value of the local currency sinks, the repayments become much more burdensome, and the country needs IMF assistance to avoid an economic collapse.

Iceland's attempt to become a worldwide financial center in the early 2000s is a perfect example of money flowing in and out of a country. For a few years, the economy boomed as local banks attracted foreign capital from many countries, especially Britain. A country with a population of just 300,000 and its own currency was building new office towers and hotels. Executives traveled the globe and could easily afford the finest hotels and restaurants because of the strength of the krone. That is, until 2008, when the crisis hit, and foreign money left Iceland, the banks collapsed, and the krone lost over 60 percent of its value.

4. The Leveraged Buyout Craze and Downfall of Drexel Burnham Lambert: In the mid-1970s, Michael Milken started a revolution in corporate finance and governance. In business school, he had seen studies that showed that a portfolio of many noninvestment grade bonds (called "junk bonds") had higher overall returns than a portfolio of only investment grade bonds. Yes, there were more defaults in the first portfolio, but the added interest payments from the nondefaulting company more than made up the difference.

After an initial success selling these noninvestment grade

bonds, Milken realized that if he expanded the market he could make lots of money. Over time, the network of buyers for his securities grew as he formed alliances with merger and acquisitions specialists, especially the firm of Kohlberg Kravis Roberts. A wave of leverage buyouts (LBOs) ensued in which a series of bids were made by such "raiders" as T. Boone Pickens, Nelson Peltz, Carl Icahn, and Kirk Kerkorian. The logic was that these firms were being poorly managed and that new aggressive leadership could increase profits and rid companies of underperforming divisions.

A whole series of measures and countermeasures followed the announcement of a possible LBO. Rumors alone were enough for management to seek a "white knight" and pay "greenmail" to raiders to go away. In some cases, firms would load up on debt so that they would not be as attractive to raiders who relied on debt to make their acquisitions (called a "poison pill defense" because the raiders would be stuck paying off the debt if they bought the company).

There is a lot of dispute about the consequences of the LBO craze. On the one hand, there are those who argue that management had become lazy and needed to become more aggressive. On the other hand, a lot of the restructurings that followed an LBO would lead to a reduction in the number and pay of lower-level employees. If a union were present, there would be an attempt to weaken it or even decertify it. Certainly one of the consequences of this practice was to make managers much more conscious of short-run profits. Critics argued that this was at the expense of the long-run health of the company.

An LBO attack often led to a sharp rise in the stock price of the target company. Therefore, anyone who knew about an unannounced LBO might be able to get a windfall gain by buying the stock before the official announcement. The downfall of Milken and Drexel would come because of this aspect of their multibillion-dollar empire (Milken made $500 million in his last year at the company).

In April 1990, Milken pled guilty to six counts of security fraud and paid fines and restitution of $600 million. Some observers were surprised at the deal because they thought the case would be very difficult to prove. Nevertheless, the government was about to go after his relatives, so Milken (who was the model for the Gordon Gekko character in the film *Wall Street*) agreed to plead guilty. He would eventually only serve twenty-two months in jail and was prohibited from ever working in the securities trading business. Since his release, he has invested wisely and was estimated to be worth $2.1 billion in 2007.

The viability of the LBO strategy turned out to be limited. The early studies showing that a portfolio of junk bonds was a good investment were based on experiences when junk bonds were a limited market. At first, Milken made tons of money using junk bonds for corporate takeovers. Milken's strategy benefited from the fact that a lot of companies were poorly managed and undervalued. Over time however, the newer projects did not have these advantages, and the bonds failed at a higher rate than previous junk bonds. With these higher default rates, a portfolio of junk bonds was no longer a good investment. So once again, a limited strategy when pursued on a much larger scale turned out to be less effective than initially thought.

5. The Collapse of Long-Term Capital Management (LTCM): This was the hedge fund that had everything. Its leadership included two Nobel Prize winners in economics and one of the leading traders from Wall Street. Its secret to success was that it was able to identify items that were mispriced; in particular, they would find situations where two assets that should, in theory, have the same price had slightly different prices and bet that the prices would converge. For example, U.S. Treasury bonds that would mature in twenty-nine years would be more expensive than treasury bonds that would mature in thirty years.

Formed in 1994, LTCM immediately attracted attention by generating 40 percent returns in its first two years, but secrets don't last, and trading opportunities became harder to identify. Furthermore, the ability to generate high returns was based on the high levels of leverage—they financed some of their purchases by only putting up three cents on the dollar and borrowed the rest.

In 1997, the high stock price gains beat the returns of LTCM by a significant margin so there was some pressure on the company to perform better in 1998. At one point they had 7,600 different "positions" to balance bets from different sides. They calculated that the chance of the company losing all of its capital was one in ten to the twenty-fourth power.

Yet, in August 1998, LTCM thought they had a surefire winner and bet a lot of money on several trades about market volatility (they thought it would be low) and the relative value of U.S. Treasuries (they thought it was too high). At that precise moment, Russia decided to default on paying its bondholders, which caused volatility to rise and people to buy U.S. Treasuries as a safety net.

One of the principals, John Meriwether, thought that they were about to hit a home run and opined that "we dreamed that a situation like this would develop." This was not meant to be. At the end, LTCM had about $5 billion in assets and investments of $1 trillion. With the markets not moving LTCM's way, the creditors (who made up the difference between $5 billion and $1,000 billion) demanded more collateral as the losses mounted.

When they could not meet this demand, the Fed looked at LTCM's books in horror, worrying that the whole financial system was at risk if LTCM was declared bankrupt. The reason for the Fed's concerns was twofold. First, if LTCM had to be liquidated immediately, many markets would be thrown into chaos by a forced sale of LTCM's contracts. Falling prices would then impact other companies and potentially undermine their viability. Second, all of the institutions that lent LTCM money would be at risk of only getting back a small fraction of what they had advanced LTCM, and these losses might have undermined these institutions.

With a public guarantee, fourteen banks agreed to put up extra capital in return for 90 percent of the company. Many months later, all of the positions were sold and a small profit was realized.

LTCM made two classic mistakes—they did not adequately manage time and they underestimated the effect of unusual events. Because of their heavy reliance on loans, they could not wait for the market to turn in their favor. The company went under because it could not post enough extra collateral to satisfy their lenders. If they could have waited longer, their bets would have turned out to be profitable.

Finally, it should be noted that the partners of LTCM were so confident in their approach that the top sixteen partners had $1.9

billion of their own money invested in the company when it crashed. At the end of 1997, they had actually returned money to their investors to become leaner and to keep more of their profits just for themselves.

6. The Bursting of the NASDAQ Bubble: From 1985 through March 2001, there was an amazing run-up in the prices of high technology stocks. At the height of the craze in the late-1990s, companies would go public and have the stock prices skyrocket to astronomical levels. The owners became instant multimillionaires as the value of new firms with few sales and no profits were suddenly valued at tens of billions of dollars. These "next new things" were valued many times that of old-line companies with billions of dollars of sales and tens of thousands of employees.

Hi-tech companies with a successful business model and with profits would naturally be worth even more. Cisco Systems, for example, once had the highest market value of any company in the United States, reaching $400 billion.

Wild theories justified these dizzying prices. Books with titles proclaiming that the Dow Jones average would soon reach 36,000, 40,000, or even 100,000 became bestsellers. When Kevin Hassett, the coauthor of *Dow 36,000,* was asked to justify Cisco's stock price, he quickly showed that if Cisco's profits grew by 30 percent a year for the next twenty years, then the stock price was quite reasonable and perhaps even a little low.

Unfortunately, no company can grow like that: If Cisco's profits increased by 30 percent a year for decades, it would fast be approaching the value of all corporate profits in the U.S. economy. Also, if multiple companies had their profits grow like that, corporate profits would fast be approaching the total value of all incomes in the economy.

Everyone seemed taken with "new economy" paradigm in which the old rules didn't apply. Those who had read Kindleberger and said that these stock prices made no sense were ignored. Those who thought this was crazy and shorted technology stocks (bet that their prices were going to go down) had the right idea, but if they moved too soon, their exposure would increase dramatically and they might be wiped out before they were proved right.

The run-up in prices shows the potency of herd psychology.

The excitement of the gains fostered greater enthusiasm as more people wanted to be part of the action. As each new wave of participation drove prices higher, the naysayers were being proven wrong. Of course, as the bubble grew bigger, the day of reckoning loomed closer, and the size of the correction would have to be larger.

Many people were taken in by the general euphoria. As someone who lived in Seattle in the 1980s, I got on the Microsoft/Cisco bandwagon very early and watched with awe as their stock prices soared (at its maximum, my Cisco stock was 140 times the price that I had paid eight years earlier). I was careful not to get into companies with few employees and no profits, but I followed my broker's advice in buying a series of firms that would crash and burn—e..g., Enron, Tyco, Global Crossing, and a few other stocks that were based on lies.

Finally, I knew that prices could not go up without end but did not want to pay the capital gain taxes I would owe if I sold. I was a bit guilty about making so much money without "earning" it. So I was not averse to losing some of these gains and came up with a clever scenario of how tech prices were going to return to normal: Prices would fall from 25 to 35 percent and then increase at a very slow rate for the next ten years.

I had no good reason to pick how much stock prices would fall (Cisco would eventually go from 94 to 11). That was approximately the level of my capital gain exposure so it reaffirmed my decision not to sell. In retrospect, my holding on to what I knew to be overpriced stocks reflects a wider pattern of behavior of people who tend to underestimate the downside risk. Studies by behavioral economists have shown that people feel very strongly about losing what they have and discount the likelihood of events that would cause such a loss.

7. Fraud—Enron and Related Misrepresentations: When Willie Sutton was asked why he robbed banks, he curtly replied, "Because that is where the money is." In many ways, the history of finance is also the history of swindlers and of people (often royalty or governments) not paying their debts. Both sides of the financial divide have not always followed the proscribed rules because the temptation to take the money and run is always high.

Over time, the advanced economies have developed elaborate

rules and monitoring procedures to avoid financial misdoings. The requirements that large firms issue quarterly statements and that annual reports be certified by accredited accounting firms were meant to ensure that companies could not misrepresent their financial situation. As a result, most of the worst practices have been pushed to the margins of society—e.g., loan sharks, payday loans, and pawnshops.

However, accounting is quite complicated and, when the stakes get big enough, there is a temptation to manipulate the books to report higher profits. One of the immediate effects was that yearly bonuses and the value of stock options would rise. Indirectly, a higher stock price permitted companies to make acquisitions by trading stock for other companies. In the age of skyrocketing stock prices, a small company could even buy a larger company by giving the holders of the target company new stock in the acquiring company (e.g., AOL bought Time Warner, and WorldCom acquired MCI Communications).

The highest profile case of stock manipulation involved the Enron Corporation under the leadership of Kenneth Lay. The company grew by leaps and bounds from a Nebraska-based gas company to a multidivision giant that was eventually recognized by *Fortune* magazine as the country's most innovative company for six consecutive years (1996–2001). In addition to owning and trading energy supplies, it branched out into buying and selling broadband access, plastics, petrochemicals, paper, steel, and two dozen other products.

In 2001, the empire built by the "smartest guys in the room" (which became the name of the 2005 movie about the rise and fall of the company) came tumbling down as it was forced to file for bankruptcy in November of that year. It turns out that their stellar profit record was built on accounting irregularities that hid losses in "special purpose entities" (which reappear in the sub-prime mess). A number of executives were sent to jail and their accounting firm, Arthur Andersen, was convicted of destroying documents and lost its license, leading to its demise. At its worst, Enron manipulated a California energy crisis that led to huge increases in energy prices (manipulated by holding power off the market), rolling blackouts, and the recall of Governor Gray Davis.

Unfortunately Enron was not the only case of "creative" accounting. Bernie Ebbers of WorldCom is another executive who took a small company, used the inflated price of its stock, and effectively bought another larger company—in this case, MCI Telecommunications. Yet shortly after the acquisition, the industry went into a downturn, putting great pressure on the new company's business model. In order to keep its stock price high, the company resorted to hiding losses. Eventually, the truth had to come out and the company filed for bankruptcy in 2002. Verizon bought the MCI division in February 2005. Months later, Ebbers was convicted of fraud and sentenced to up to twenty-five years in jail.

Other examples of companies that would admit to misrepresentation and stock price manipulations include Cendant, HealthSouth Corporation, El Paso Energy, Dynegy, Global Crossing, and ImClone.

Lessons Learned from the Last Thirty Years of Financial Expansion

The funny thing is that, even though financial crises have happened before, most people are shocked when they hit home. Writing about crises from the 1850s to 1930s, Keynes opined that "markets remain irrational longer than you can remain solvent." On the other hand, the modern financial leaders convinced themselves that "this time it's different" and that the new innovations made panics a thing of the past.

The biggest failure over the last thirty years was the failure to regulate. Alan Greenspan among others had a deep faith that market actors were better at determining and evaluating risk than government bodies. This view is a complete misreading of financial history that dismisses writers like Minsky and Kindleberger, who warned of the failure of the market to regulate itself.

Against all evidence, this view assumes that financial leaders will never risk the viability of their own company. At a certain level, this is certainly true, but because finance deals with time and uncertainty, it is all too easy for their judgments to be wrong. We have seen over and over again how a collective euphoria has resulted in prices losing touch with reality.

The second intrinsic problem with finance is that it mainly uses other people's money, which skews the balance between rewards and punishments. Midlevel executives faced the following choice: They could receive bonuses of a million dollars by joining the securitization/over-the-counter frenzy or they could be "responsible" by limiting risk that might cause them to lose their jobs. Unless they were either prohibited from taking the risk or very sure of negative consequences of the risk, it is not hard to see what choice they hoped their firm would take.

The following are ten other lessons and associated policy suggestions from the last thirty years; all of them revolve around misaligned incentives that encouraged people to take riskier actions with large upside potential:

1. People need skin in the game: The originate-to-distribute model permits/encourages reckless mortgage lending.

Here is how the bankruptcy court described the actions of New Century (a bank specializing in subprime mortgages): "[it] had a brazen obsession with increasing loan originations, without due regard to the risks associated with that business strategy." Further, management chose to "feed eagerly the wave of investor demands," and "turned a blind eye" to risky loan practices that led to a surge of payment defaults as early as 2004.

They acted this way in part because they and other actors in the subprime mortgage mill thought they were passing on the risk to other investors. If they had to keep part of the mortgages themselves, they probably would have looked more closely to see the quality of the underlying loans.

Policy Suggestion: All financial institutions must keep a share (5 to 20 percent) of the mortgage-backed securities (MBSs) that they create. Although firms ended up with a lot of unsold MBSs when the crisis came, this was unintended and did not enter into company's decision-making process. In addition, holders of credit default swaps insurance contracts should have to take a "hair cut" (not get all their owed money) if the firms that sold the CDSs have to be bailed out by a government rescue plan.

2. Financial transactions need to be on the books.

The shadow banking system made a mockery of regulated capital requirements. In 2008, it looked like the superbanks had more than enough capital, but this appearance did not include all sorts of high-risk investments in CDSs, CDOs, and SIVs. As firms continued upping the amount of write-offs for bad debts, market players realized that there was much that they did not know and lost confidence in many institutions.

Policy Suggestion: All markets must be regulated and conducted in the open. Further, any contingent liabilities (e.g., back-up funding commitments to SIVs) must be quantified and subject to added capital requirements.

3. Institutions can't be both too-big-to-fail and outside of public regulations.

As long as financial executives were confident that the government would bail them out, they could follow a high-risk, high-reward strategy with a certain comfort that their jobs and institutions would not be endangered. Prior to the progressive relaxation of financial rules since 1980, no one firm was nearly large enough to fit the too-big-to-fail threshold. The financial institutions can't have both autonomy and gigantic size simultaneously without facing much tighter supervision.

Policy Suggestion: Some have argued that the genie is out of the bottle and that financial consolidation is something that cannot be reversed. Interestingly, few argue that large superbanks are more efficient in allocating savings throughout the economy. At the minimum, capital requirements and fees should be higher for firms that are deemed too big and too interconnected to fail. This would represent a quid pro quo for the implicit guarantee that they receive. At a maximum, the alternative is breaking up large institutions into smaller entities that would not be too big to fail.

4. Bonuses were not aligned with the long run viability of the investments.

Wall Street thought that their compensation system—in which pay was relatively low but bonuses were very high—would motivate workers to be successful. But because capital valuations are often not accurate, apparent profits may never actually exist. Yet, bonuses were paid on the assumption that the underlying assets were strong and would meet their payment schedules. This pay-now and hope-for-the-best-later practice was another factor that fostered high-risk investments.

Policy Suggestion: Pay norms get set over an extended period and it will be difficult to rein in high CEO pay and high financial trader pay.

The previous attempt to rein in salaries of $1 million and over had the perverse effect of making bonuses a larger share of compensation. At a minimum, however, stock options should be valued and treated as a cost in the year in which they are issued. Second, there should be a prohibition against repricing stock options after they are issued. Third, companies should be forced to list in their public filings all options granted and bonuses given during years in which company earnings are negative. Fourth, since the largest component of high pay is in company stock, new "clawback" rules should allow companies to take back part of bonuses from several years earlier if projected profits don't materialize.

5. Evaluators can't be paid only if they please the client.

There is a clear conflict of interest for accounting firms, rating agencies, and home appraisers: Instead of being neutral evaluations, their livelihoods depend on pleasing repeat clients. In this situation, the reliance on professional ethics has proven to not be enough.

Policy Suggestion: We must try to find efficient ways that also permit new companies to enter and to change the balance between buyer and service provider. One option is to have supervisory bodies randomly assign service providers to clients while also ensuring that the providers are rated by the quality of their work.

6. The search for a little extra yield often backfires.

Ultimately, in a competitive market, you don't get something for nothing—higher yield means higher risk. In this case, higher yield underestimated the amount of risk embedded in the security. German financial economist Martin Hellwig describes the situation in 2003 as "yield panic" as investors sought alternatives to stocks: "Given the hunger of investment banks for the business of securitization and the hunger of investors for high-yielding securities, there was little to contain moral hazard in mortgage origination."

Policy Suggestion: In offering statements, new bonds must explain the risk premiums implied in the yield of the bond. A table should also be required that shows how alternative default scenarios would affect prices and yield.

7. Too much leverage is very dangerous.

One of the main strategies to increase profits is to use borrowed money. Unfortunately, the more leveraged you are, the quicker losses mount up. All of one's capital can disappear and the borrower may have to come up with additional money to pay his or her loan. Supposedly we learned this lesson once before—many people blame the precipitous stock market decline of 1929 on the use of borrowed money in making purchases (buying on "margin"). At the time, people were only required to put up 10 percent of the stock purchase cost versus today's Federal Reserve mandated standard of 50 percent.

The big financial institutions in 2007 were operating with very low capital bases—the median leverage ratio of commercial banks was 35:1, while it was 45:1 in Europe. Martin Wolf of the *Financial Times* describes this situation as follows: "[A]llowing institutions to be operated in the interest of shareholders, who supply just 3 percent of their loanable funds, is insane."[43]

Policy Suggestion: Capital requirements should be raised and they should be higher for large bank-holding companies.

8. Too much complexity leads to mistakes.

Is it any wonder that in 2003 Warren Buffett called derivatives (CDOs, CDSs, and the related instruments) "financial weapons of mass destruction"? He made this statement before any of the problems arose; he just knew that they were subject to be misused by people who would not understand the consequences when the market turned from hot to cold. Further, he had seen Enron create over 7,000 special-purpose entities to hide their losses and knew that too much complication can easily be a road to ruin.

The rating agencies incorrectly evaluated thousands of securities, giving AAA ratings (extremely low probability of default) to thousands of derivative bonds. It was not that the models were conceptually wrong, it was that they used the wrong "parameters" in calculating the likelihood that any single mortgage would fail, and the likelihood that one mortgage failing would lead to other failed mortgages. Their biggest mistake was that they did not err on the side of caution. They used the default experiences of mortgages that were much different from the new ones that were being created.

They fell into this mistake for four reasons. First, the rating agencies were rewarded handsomely by pleasing clients. Second, they were

[43] Available at: http://www.ft.com/cms/s/0/eed3ba7c-659d-11de-8e34-00144feabdc0 .html?nclick_check=1

shielded from liability for their mistakes (previous attempts to sue them for misrating bonds that failed had been dismissed). Third, they underestimated the probability of unusual events that would lead to a huge number of defaults across the board (this is the same mistake that doomed LTCM). And fourth, they figured that if they did not please a client, a competitor would.

The rating agencies play a pivotal role because many institutional investors can only purchase bonds that are rated AAA by one of the three named agencies. This government-provided market, combined with their shield from being sued, is almost a license to print money. Without any real downside consequences of mistakes, this system relies totally on the "professionalism" of the organizations to do a good job.

Policy Suggestion: The worst abuse of where the agencies only got paid after they gave a preliminary rating has been stopped. Nonetheless, more has to be done to create new rewards and punishments for these companies. One possibility is to break the tight connection between the agencies and their clients who want to have their bonds rated. One possibility is to create a new board that would set fees and produce annual reports on the default rate by bond rating of the bonds rated by each company. Perhaps part of their fees could be withheld until the end of the year and only be rewarded on the basis of compliance with minimum accuracy standards. This approach might even include "clawbacks" for large mistakes from previous years.

Further, while it may seem odd that experienced investors have to be protected, even the Bank for International Settlements (the Swiss-based organization that serves as the bank for the central banks of the world) argues for a need for "some form of product registration that limits investor access to instruments according to their degree of safety."[44] They use the analogy of prescription drugs to keep dangerous instruments out of reach for virtually every class of investor. Another idea is to limit involvement in CDSs and related instruments to those with actual ownership of the "insured" instrument.

9. The decision-making process can be very poor and this is why rules matter.

People make bad decisions, especially in evaluating downside risk; regulators can decide not to regulate; safeguards can be ignored. All too

---

[44] Available at: www.bis.org/publ/arpdf/ar2009e.pdf?noframes=1; p. 126.

frequently financial leaders felt that they had to move with the herd—given that other firms were making lots of money with new investment schemes, everyone felt compelled to join in. While we understand this premise when it involves children, apparently rules are just as important in reining in the "animal spirits" of financial CEOs.

Policy Suggestion: Companies should be required to file yearly statements detailing their risk management procedures including reports from compliance departments on their activities during the previous year.

10. The best-laid exit strategies can fail if everyone is trying to leave by the same exit.

There were many strategies used to protect investors from an investment loss—e.g., insurance in the form of a CDS or from a monoline insurer, and hedging by having a short position in an instrument that will decline in parallel with your investment. Unfortunately, when losses are widespread, the companies that provided the insurance often don't have the resources to pay off (e.g., A.I.G.).

Policy Suggestion: The role of the Federal Reserve should be expanded to give it responsibility for identifying systemic risks, including financial strategies that might fail during systemic breakdowns. A yearly report should be issued and filed in the Federal Register for ninety days with a call for comments, before the Fed chairman would have to testify in front of the Senate and House Banking Committees about the report and to respond to any relevant comments.

Conclusion

In Oliver Stone's 1987 film *Wall Street,* the lead character, Gordon Gekko, delivers the memorable line, "Greed is good." Michael Douglas's oily delivery makes it sound particularly devilish. Yet our system is firmly rooted in greed—euphemistically labeled "self-interest"—and there exists ambiguity as to whether this is a good or bad thing.

In the current meltdown, a common criticism is that the crisis is rooted in "excessive greed." Well yes, what else is new? The "greed" label, though, seems to have greater resonance because financial wizardry does not seem to provide a palpable product or service that improves our lives. Moneylenders like Shylock have been attacked as vicious parasites, but are the recent financial actions that different from those of automakers who made lots of money selling gas-guzzling SUVs? Or from drugmakers who copy each other's patented drugs or convince consumers to buy drugs for syndromes that never existed before? Or from meat producers and packagers who treat animals badly and use drugs liberally to keep them healthy and make them gain weight quickly? Or from cigarette producers? Or producers of machine guns for civilians?

For better or worse (mostly better), our free market economy relies on profit-making to guide economic decisions. If there were money to be made in finance, than smart people were going to go out and make it. This response to profit signals is the key mechanism that adds dynamism to our economy. The system does not distinguish between profits in manufacturing from profits in services or from profits in finance.

However, greed in finance still seems less justified because financial professionals don't seem to produce anything, and the public is deeply skeptical of their pay packages.[45] The bailout has only strengthened these feelings because it appears the government has been too quick to help financial executives rather than ordinary people. Each financial company announcement of bonuses is greeted with howls of protest, yet no one seems willing to stop them. The best that the administration could do when Goldman Sachs announced record earnings and bonuses in October 2009 was to try to shame the company into reversing itself by having the president and other advisers criticize these actions.

As history shows, greed unchecked leads to wild swings of optimism and overextension followed by collapses. Over time, we developed a balance of government guarantees—e.g., federal deposit insurance—and oversight to minimize wild financial swings. The success of this system

---

[45] Another financial area that has been questioned by many is the reshuffling of companies through mergers and acquisitions (M&A). This has not been in the news lately because M&A activity has virtually stopped during the downturn. Nonetheless, part of the crisis of 2008 was due to the large number of defaults on loans that were made by private equity firms in 2004 through 2008 to purchase companies and that were securitized in CLOs (collateralized loan obligations). Many have criticized this reshuffling of company ownership with the use of debt as simply a way of draining dollars from companies for the enrichment of deal makers. Steven Davidoff in *Gods at War,* however, tracks six waves of mergers and acquisitions over the last thirty years, and finds that the benefits to company performance have outweighed the costs.

led people to lose sight of why it was developed, and with the urging of a new set of financial leaders, finance became progressively deregulated.

The advocates of deregulation argued that we were in a new world in which stockholder activism would police financial excess. The self-correcting economy (short and mild downturns) that worked so well from 1945 through 2007 provided added comfort that we could handle shocks to the system with minimal disruption. Finally, it was argued that the development of Europe, China, India, Russia, South Korea, and other countries created alternative economic engines for the world economy if there were troubles in the U.S. economy.

In the end, none of this worked. All of the minicrises from 1982 to 2005 look now like a series of tests of how much financial excess our economy could absorb. The spectacular run-up in stock prices from 1982 to 2000 convinced us that meteoric financial gain was a normal part of life. While the collapse of the dot-com bubble was painful, the lesson was short-lived as people became enthralled with rising real estate values. Finally, instead of being a buffer against American financial excess, the world became tied to exporting for U.S. consumption and followed the U.S. lead in seeking huge profits in financial schemes.

So, once again, a full-blown financial crisis erupted. It was driven by new innovations (e.g., MBSs, CDOs, and CRSs) and reckless lending to unqualified borrowers. Given that these loans were the basis of the securities, it is somewhat astonishing that so many financial actors found a way to ignore the weaknesses of the underlying loans. This is why I called this combination of mistakes "brilliant idiocy" in the last chapter. By contrast, those commentators who say that the crisis was based on rising inequality rely on an oversimple narrative of rich people making too much money and poor people being lead astray.

Because financial institutions have such a small capital cushion, the initial losses in the subprime market quickly migrated to other markets and undermined other parts of the economy as a vicious cycle of rising unemployment and falling demand put pressure on all producers. And in an unexpected twist, most other countries experienced larger economic declines and greater unemployment than did the United States.

In a series of breathtaking moves, the Bush and Obama administrations have mobilized a multitrillion dollar rescue package. While some of the money has been directed toward consumers (e.g., the stimulus package and assistance for distressed mortgage holders), the bulk of the money has been set aside to help crippled financial institutions. Without this intervention and a relaxing of certain accounting rules, the majority of the major financial institutions that existed in 2006 would be insolvent (their assets at current market prices plus their capital would be less than their liabilities) and would have been closed.

The specifics of the financial bailout have changed a lot since the initial three-page document produced by Secretary of Treasury Paulson in September 2008. This constant shifting was caused by a lack of certainty about how to fix the problem. Should the mortgage holders be helped so that they could repay the loans and hence increase the value of bonds based on the mortgages? Should capital be given to banks in order to make them solvent more quickly? Should the toxic assets be bought and removed from the books of the financial institutions? Or should the toxic assets be sold through some price-seeking mechanism in which some private parties were encouraged to bid on assets with a significant government guarantee?

The real sticking point was the price of the toxic assets.[46] Banks have been propped up and don't feel compelled to sell these toxic assets at too low a price. After passing the government stress tests in April, they felt greater confidence in their ability to survive and turned down the 2009 market price of 25 to 35 cents on the dollar for these assets; further, the plan for a Public-Private Investment Plan (PPIP) to purchase these assets was not workable, either. As of November 2009, no one was forcing them to sell and they were willing to wait until the economy rebounds and the assets become more valuable.

In essence we lurched toward recovery based on a huge injection of money into the economy by the federal government. It may be that the specifics didn't matter: the stock market started its upward trajectory in March 2009. Since the summer of 2009, monthly job losses have been declining, and almost went to zero in November (the time of writing these words).[47] No one knows for sure what will happen in 2010, but the signs are positive that "green shoots" will mature and a positive feedback loop will develop.

Many people had trouble figuring out where the impetus for recovery

---

[46] Throughout 2008, losses were spreading out to securities backed by credit card debt, commercial real estate loans, and leveraged buyout loans, but these losses were anticipated and were not a shock to the system.

[47] Available at: http://www.reuters.com/article/marketsNews/idUSNYS00511420090603

was going to occur given that the auto and housing markets were so weak. But this is the old way of thinking that relies on specific major manufacturers to lead the way. As will be discussed in chapter 5, the economy is driven by a division of labor in which workers today are primarily engaged in producing goods and services for the needs of the market.

The notion that there can be inadequate demand fails to appreciate the elastic appetite that consumers have for new and different products. In the past ten years, we have worried that consumers have not saved enough (this question is addressed in chapter 7). While unemployment is high and many people are paying down their debts, our high level of income inequality (see discussion in the next two chapters) means the richest 40 percent have the high share of all incomes (73 percent) and are responsible for 62 percent of consumer spending.

The crisis represents a turning point, and we are not going to make the same mistakes again soon. In particular, it is unlikely that investors will soon put lots of money into instruments of unknown quality. We are currently constructing a financial architecture that will be better able to have financial institutions perform the role of mobilizing capital and distributing it to those who can best use it. In the end, the system has great capacity for growth, and the massive government response to the crisis was the key in permitting the factors for growth to coalesce and take us out of our economic decline.

CHAPTER 3

The Barbell Myth: All of the Income Gains in the Last Thirty Years Have Gone to the Rich

DAVID CAY JOHNSTON WRITES in *Free Lunch* that for the bottom 90 percent of Americans on the income ladder, "annual income has been on a long, mostly downward slide, for more than three decades." Jeff Faux, the former president of one of Washington's most important progressive economic think tanks, writes in *The Global Class Struggle* that "in the last twenty years, [there has been a] dramatic erosion of the ability of [most Americans] to maintain their living standards."

These two quotes are representative of a view (held mainly by those in the left wing of the Democratic Party) that the vast majority of Americans have gotten only a miniscule share of the growth dividend of the last thirty years. In the *Squandering of America,* Robert Kuttner, a prominent liberal economist, calls the period from 1980 through 2006 "a silent depression" and argues that the only growth that occurred during these years was due to asset bubbles in stocks and houses. Further, to the degree that people's consumption standards increased, it was because they were increasing their debt and working longer.

According to this view, even when the crisis of 2008 is over, the rebound will be quite weak unless major changes are made. Since President Obama is putting most of his social policy emphasis on health care reform, the Left is convinced that the downturn is going to be longer and the recovery weaker than most analysts predict.

For them, the "economic glass" is between 60 and 80 percent empty; by contrast, in this chapter, I show that the middle class had significant income gains since 1979 and can be expected to be the backbone of strong growth after the crisis is over. While income inequality has indeed increased over these years, I show in the next chapter that somewhere around 80 percent of the population is participating in our economic prosperity. Both of these facts suggest a strong rebound.

The past decade is often contrasted with the "golden age" of the fifties and sixties when all of the defining images were predominantly positive—the blissful complacency of Ozzie and Harriet in the 1950s, the sophistication and charm of Jack and Jackie at the beginning of the 1960s, and the youth revolution of the late 1960s proclaiming that everything was possible and previous limits on acceptable behavior were cast aside. These years are remembered as a time when one paycheck was enough to support a middle-class lifestyle and home ownership.

It is not surprising then that Robert Kuttner and others call for the return of managed capitalism along with a major expansion of government programs and regulations to encourage unionization and to limit corporate power.[48] President Obama has expressed sympathy for the plight of the middle class and has established a task force led by Vice President Joe Biden to propose ways to improve middle-class living standards.

Consequently, this chapter addresses two related issues. First, I explore the "nostalgia myth," which holds that life was better in the 1960s than in the 2000s. Second, I undertake a careful analysis of how the economic growth was distributed, arguing that in fact not all of the growth since 1979 went to the richest 10 percent of families.

Instead, data will be presented that show that there was substantial growth of the standard of living for those in the middle of the income distribution. As the quotes from David Cay Johnston and Jeff Faux show, many commentators believe that the middle-class standards of living have declined since 1979. This position is based on three studies using different data sources and methodologies. They are often cited to

---

[48] On the other side of the political fence, conservatives like Dick Morris (who for a brief time was an adviser to President Clinton) see Obama using the need for massive government intervention as a vehicle to jump-start the economy in order to institute European-style socialism. http://www.realclearpolitics.com/articles/2009/01/the_obama_presidency_here_come.html

prove the conclusion that living standards have declined. In Appendix 3, I will rigorously show that each of these studies is based on flawed methodologies.

Looking at the Past: Was the Grass Greener?

Many little things separate how we live today from how we lived in the recent past. For example, thirty years ago, no one would have thought to pay more than 25 cents for a cup of coffee, or anything for a glass of water. Today, the premium coffee market with specialty coffees selling for $3 to $5 a cup, has sales of $29 billion, and bottled water is a $13 billion market. We can afford to spend money in this way since we have more disposable income and because we spend less on more important basic necessities.

Let's start with a few key statistics from the year 1960 (the middle of the golden era):

- In 1960, inflation-adjusted GDP per person was just 36 percent of where it stood in 2008;
- The overall poverty rate was 23 percent;
- Half of the workforce did not have a high school diploma and only 10 percent had a four-year college degree;
- The poverty rate for those sixty-five years old and older was 35 percent, even though older men were twice as likely to work than they are now; and
- Fewer adults owned their own home (62 percent in 1960 versus 68 percent in 2008).

In 1960, there were no cell phones or personal computers, and long-distance phone calls were expensive.[49] Air travel for pleasure was rare,

---

[49] Do you know "Gwenn Commings"? That was the name you used on a person-to-person collect call. The recipient would answer, "No, she is not here now but will be back at 6:00 P.M." This is how you could find out when you expected your friend to arrive without having to pay for a long-distance call (Gwenn Comming = when are you coming?).

and television shows were, for most of the country, on one of three main networks. The penetration of color TV was just beginning, and the reliability of TV sets improved significantly compared to just five years earlier when home visits from the TV repairman were common.

At that time, a person's living situation was quite different. Many people lived in three-generation households (children, parents, and grandparents), and few young adults left home until they married; only 13 percent of households were composed of a single person living alone (predominantly young people just starting out or old people at the end of their working lives) compared to twice that rate today. Because houses were smaller, 12 percent of all units were considered overcrowded (more than one person per room) in 1960 versus less than 6 percent today. Among other things forgotten from this nostalgic tableau were the poor treatment of African-Americans and the limited opportunities available to women.

The point of these examples is not to portray the fifties and sixties as periods of distress but to emphasize the importance of expectations. After World War II, there was widespread concern that our economy would fall back into the depression conditions of the thirties. One of the reasons for establishing the generous GI Bill college benefits was to prevent flooding the labor market with too many new workers. When the postwar depression didn't happen, many people were buoyed by the economic growth that was only interrupted by short recessions.[50]

Figure 3.1 represents the growth of GDP per capita from 1929 to 2008. Starting at about $8,689 (2008 dollars) per person in 1929, it rises to $46,836 over these seventy-nine years; this represents an increase of 440 percent. This gain incorporates the first ten years of the Great Depression, a time in which real GDP per person did not surpass its 1929 level until 1939.

---

[50] My family history is an indication of growth during this period. Both of my parents came to this country in the late 1920s; my father had not finished elementary school whereas my mother attended a few years of high school. After struggling through the Depression by combining resources with their siblings, their circumstances improved greatly after the war. Up until 1954, we lived in a one-bedroom apartment for two adults and two children. We then made the big move to a more comfortable life in a three-bedroom apartment in Queens, New York. This was just the beginning of our movement up the income ladder (on the basis of my mother's success). Education was always important in our family, and both my brother and I graduated from Princeton after attending the same public high school in New York City; my brother eventually became an M.D. while I earned a Ph.D.

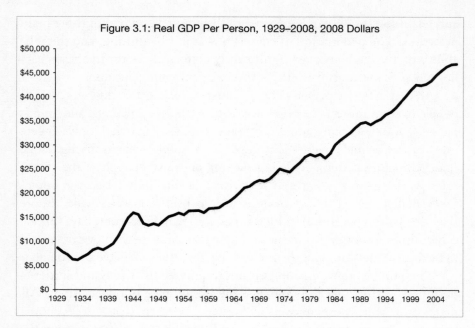

Figure 3.1: Real GDP Per Person, 1929–2008, 2008 Dollars

National Income and Product Accounts

Economists who study economic growth have attributed much of the gain to the increases in the education of the workforce. As Figure 3.2 shows, there has been a steady upward shift in the educational attainment of the workforce. In 1960, 50 percent of workers did not have a high school diploma, almost 30 percent had a diploma but no postsecondary education, and about 10 percent had some college education but not a four-year degree. Only 10 percent of workers had a bachelor's or graduate degree. Today, these numbers are completely reversed: almost 60 percent have postsecondary education (half with a four-year degree), about 30 percent still have as their highest attainment a high school diploma (or GED equivalency degree), and only about 10 percent are high school noncompleters.

In addition to a better-educated workforce, productivity growth— resulting from scientific advances and machines used in production, and better communications and processing of information—is seen as the other pillar of economic growth. From 1947 to 1973, productivity per labor hour in the nonfarm private business sector grew 2.8 percent annually. With the postwar boom, real GDP doubled from 1945 to 1968, causing fears of a new depression to melt away. However, a new concern arose—

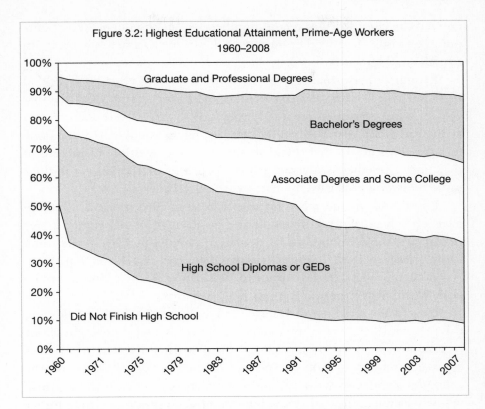

Figure 3.2: Highest Educational Attainment, Prime-Age Workers 1960–2008

Census and various March Supplements to the Current Population Survey

that the increased use of machinery (called "automation") would undermine the demand for production workers in the manufacturing industry, resulting in a rising number of "structurally" unemployed Americans. What these critics failed to see was that greater productivity would generate demands for new and more services as well as a desire for a higher quality and greater variety of goods.

The 1960s were followed by a twenty-two-year period of slow productivity growth of only 1.4 percent per year. Finally, the productivity slowdown ended as mysteriously as it began when yearly productivity growth jumped to 2.4 percent a year through 2007. GDP per capita growth was much steadier than productivity growth because of population dynamics. In the fifties and sixties, high productivity growth was matched by the baby boom, resulting in equally high population growth. During the subsequent productivity slowdown, the number of workers in the labor force increased as baby boomers aged and women entered the labor force in record numbers. As a consequence, total output grew faster than worker output per hour due to a steady increase in overall employment.

Economic performance over the entire sixty-plus years since the end of World War II is unparalleled in American history. From 1854 (the first year of good economic records) through 1945, there were twenty-two economic cycles with the contractions lasting an average of twenty-one months. This means that the economy was in a recession 42 percent of the time. Nonetheless, overall growth over this period was strong because these downturns were offset by strong periods of growth.

From 1945 to the recession that started in December 2007, there have only been ten recessions lasting an average of ten months; this means that the economy was in recession only 14 percent of the time. Only briefly, in 1982, did the unemployment rate rise above 10 percent. As compared with 150 years prior to World War II, the economy in the post–World War II period was much less volatile.

Clearly, the recession that started in December 2007 is not following this pattern. But as were shown in the first two chapters, the depth of this recession was caused by a financial breakdown caused by a series of colossal misjudgments on the part of investors and financiers. As the economy spiraled downward, added pressure was put on the already-tattered balance sheet of the major financial institutions. Once this is cleared up however, our economy will return to the steady growth path of the previous five decades.

Rising Inequality

While economic growth has been consistent over the last several decades, it has not always been equally distributed across all of the rungs of the income ladders. If we think back to the end of the nineteenth and beginning of the twentieth centuries, it was a time of strong economic growth but with great inequality. The "robber barons" lived in luxurious mansions with teams of servants. Immigrants were flooding into the country in search of opportunity and found low wages and bad working conditions. In *The Jungle,* Upton Sinclair documented what it was like in the meat stockyards of Chicago. While he focused on the workers, the public reacted to the food safety issue, which led to the quick passage of the Meat Inspection Act and the creation of the Food and Drug Administration.

Income data were very spotty before the 1950s. The best estimates show that there was a "great compression" from the Depression through the 1950s. From 1950 through the beginning of the '70s, income and wage inequality remained remarkably steady. In fact, the lowest rungs of the population experienced slightly more improvement in their living standards than any other group. As everyone moved up in tandem ("shared prosperity"), the field of studying income distribution seemed to be at a dead-end as researchers proclaimed that there might be an iron law determining how much each group on the income ladder earned.

After the inflation of the 1970s and the decline in productivity growth, the nature of the economy changed dramatically. Back-to-back recessions in the early 1980s led to large losses among blue-collar workers, and once again raised the specter of an underperforming economy. Robert Kuttner, writing in the August 1983 issue of *The Atlantic,* talked about a "shrinking middle class." His work was impressionistic and did not cite hard data. The supporting data appeared in two studies later that year. First, Bruce Steinberg, writing in *Fortune,* posited a segmented retail market in which discounters and luxury marketers did well, while those who appealed to the broad middle class struggled. Second, in the second edition of *Social Stratification in the United States,* I used census data to show that fewer families had incomes in the middle of the distribution when comparing 1983 and 1979. When my results were reported in *The New York Times* in December 1983, the inequality debate started in full force and it has continued to this day.

Many people use 1979 as the starting point (others use 1973) of the rise in inequality because it marks a good turning point in the economy—it was the last business cycle peak before the two recessions of 1980 and 1982. There are other reasons for this starting point: inequality rose sharply during the early '80s, and the strengthening of the dollar during the decade began a period in which America ran a large balance of trade deficit (i.e., the value of imports was greater than exports).

As Table 3.1 shows, income growth at the upper rungs of society was indeed higher than at either the middle or lower end of the scale. Nonetheless, there was growth at every step on the income ladder, with 15 percent growth at the median.[51] Slower growth at the bottom 50 percent

---

[51] There are some reasons to believe that the growth should be even higher than the numbers presented in Figure 3: Robert Lerman ("U.S. Income Inequality Trends and Recent Immigration." In *Inequality, Welfare and Poverty: Theory and Measurement,*

of the income distribution is contrasted with larger gains for those at the top. Those who decry growing income inequality during this period are not wrong.

TABLE 3.1

CHANGE IN REAL HOUSEHOLD INCOME (2007 $),
BY PLACE ON INCOME LADDER

Percentile	1979	2007	% Change
10	$10,926	$12,162	11.3
20	$18,632	$20,291	8.9
50	$43,814	$50,233	14.7
80	$77,190	$100,000	29.6
90	$99,918	$136,000	36.1
95	$124,728	$177,000	41.9

Census Bureau, "Income, Poverty, and Health Insurance Coverage in the United States: 2007"

However, it should be noted that some researchers feel that these numbers understate the amount of real growth because inflation is poorly measured (see discussion in accompanying box). If the critics are right and there has been more growth and less inflation, then all of these numbers should be several percentage points higher.

Volume 9 of Research on Income Inequality, edited by John A. Bishop. Elsevier Science Ltd. 289–307. 2003) argues that the flow of immigrants skew the data downward and that one should compare citizens to citizens and immigrants in the United States to the situation in their former countries. Second, Gary Burtless and Pavel Svaton argue that the rising costs of health insurance covered by employers should also be included in one's incomes and that this would disproportionately increase the incomes of lower-income people. See "Health Care, Health Insurance, and the Relative Income of the Elderly and Non elderly," (Center for Retirement Research, WP 2009–10, March 2009).

INFLATION

ALL ADULTS HAVE MEMORIES of prices from decades earlier; my mother-in-law regales me with stories of skiing in Germany in the 1930s costing $5 for the weekend and when she could buy a week's worth of groceries in the United States in the 1950s for under $10. Given today's prices, she wonders whether we are better off.

While prices rise, people's salaries and incomes rise as well. So, the key question becomes, Which side is winning this race? A few researchers sometimes present data as "how many minutes and hours of a typical worker's salary does it take to pay for certain standardized goods?" This is a simple way to take money out of the equation but is difficult to apply more generally because new goods appear and "old" goods may incorporate many new features.

So, government officials and researchers have developed elaborate procedures to determine pure "price inflation" from "real" changes in our standard of living. This matters a lot because many of our policies—e.g., how much Social Security recipients get—are based on supporting a standard of living and not just some arbitrary amount of dollars.

Over the last thirty years, there have been many criticisms of the official price adjustments and the procedures have changed many times. In 1995, the Boskin Commission studied these issues and felt that the current approach overestimated inflation by approximately 1.2 percentage points each year. The details are complex and the U.S. Bureau of Labor Statistics (BLS), which is responsible for determining the Consumer Price Index, changed their methods. The BLS also developed a research index (CPI-U-RS) that applied the new techniques to develop consistent price adjustments over the last decades. All of the data reported here use this index to adjust "nominal" dollars of each year to "real" dollars based on the most recent year for which data are available.

Some researchers think that the current adjustments

overstate inflation and understate real growth. Other researchers think that there are factors such as added congestion and poorer service, which mean that inflation is overstated. Clearly, the best option is to use the BLS-recommended CPI-U-RS.

The final issue with inflation is whether people at different parts of the income ladder have different effective inflation rates because of the exact bundle of goods that they tend to consume. As is argued in Appendix 3, the position that poor people have higher inflation rates than average is not supported by good data. In fact, an intriguing study by Christian Broda and John Romalis uses bar-code data from stores linked to survey data to show that the goods of low-income customers were composed heavily of mass-produced items that were imported from low-wage countries and, hence, actually rose less in price than the items consumed by middle- and high-income people. With arguments on both sides about the proper inflation adjustment and whether inflation varies by income, the prudent course is to use the recommended CPI-U-RS for all income and earnings analyses.

Has All of the Growth Gone to the Top 10 Percent?

It is a bold statement to say that the bottom 90 percent of the population did not receive any of the growth dividends from almost thirty years of economic growth. From 1979 to 2007, real GDP per person rose by 66 percent. Another way to describe this growth is to say that 40 percent of the output today (adjusted for population size and changes in prices) would not have existed if productivity had remained flat. So, if all of this growth went to the top 10 percent, then its current share would be 40 percent (the growth dividend) plus its share of total output in 1979. The result of adding these two components is that the top 10 percent would have just less than 60 percent of all income.

By contrast, a variety of surveys on incomes in 2007 reveal that the top 20 percent control about half of all income and that the top 10 percent control about 35 percent of all income. This is a far cry from 60 percent—the figure that we would have if all the growth went to the top 10 percent. Furthermore, think for a moment of the popularity of various electronic gadgets—cell phones, iPods, PDAs, large-screen HD TVs, computers, DVDs, etc. These are available to a large percentage of the population, but they would not be affordable to such a large share of the population if the bottom 90 percent had the same real income that it had in 1979.

Further, the data in Table 3.1 are inconsistent with the statement that all growth went to the top 10 percent. In fact, it should be noted that even at the 95th percentile the income gain was 42 percent, 24 percentage points below the corresponding 66 percent gain in GDP per person. Could it be that the top five percent of the population raked in the lion's share of our nation's growth? Or are there factors that are not included in this comparison that skew the numbers?

One explanation for incomes not growing as fast as overall economic growth is that corporate profits are taking up a bigger share and leaving less money available for personal income. Figure 3.3 debunks this argument by showing that neither the shares of corporate profits nor after-tax corporate profits have been growing steadily since 1979. Instead, the share of corporate profits out of national income has moved around a lot in accordance with the business cycle, and it is only since 2003 that corporate profits, and especially after-tax corporate profits, rose sharply.

In the twenty years after World War II, corporate profits represented a relatively high share of national income. This is a bit deceiving because the corporate profit tax rate was high, resulting in much smaller after-tax profits as a share of income. In the 2001 recession, the profit share started quite low and then moved up sharply with the expansion. By 2005, the corporate profit share of overall income had grown to a level that had not been reached in fifty years. The rise in after-tax corporate profit share is even more dramatic with the 2006 and 2007 levels being the highest ones ever.

The unusually high corporate profit share in 2007 is two to three percentage points higher than might be expected (two points higher than the 1997 level). At the same time that profits were high, the share of profits that went to financial corporations reached record levels. Since we now know that these profits were partially ephemeral, the rise in the corporate profit share was not caused by driving wages down but by new ways of financing and securitizing mortgages.

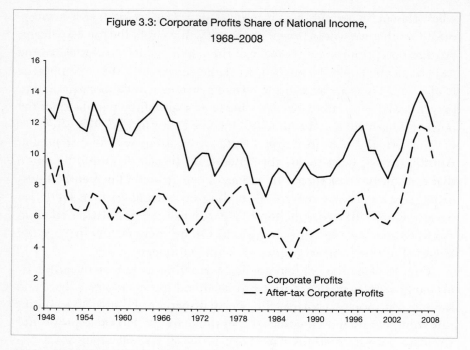

Figure 3.3: Corporate Profits Share of National Income,
1968–2008

National Income and Product Accounts

Changing Demographics

One of the reasons for the productivity-income growth gap is that in many ways this is comparing apples to oranges. While it might seem natural to use GDP per capita growth as the basis of productivity growth, it is not appropriate if the goal is to link productivity to changes in household income. In fact, the number of households has grown at a much faster rate than overall population growth. The increasing number of single-parent households, more single young people living outside their parents' homes before they marry, more elderly widows, and fewer children per family have all contributed to a faster growth rate in the number of households relative to population growth.

Consequently, the growth of income per household (the demographic unit on which income is based) is much lower than the growth of income per capita.[52] For example, if a husband and wife are both

[52] I originally developed this analysis in "Does Productivity Growth Still Benefit Working Americans? Unraveling the Income Growth Mystery to Determine How

working and each makes $50,000 a year, their annual household income is $100,000, but their per capita income is $50,000. If they get divorced, average household income drops to $50,000, while per capita income stays at $50,000. This drop in the size of the average household is why, from 1979 to 2007, real personal income per household rose only by 47 percent and by the 66 percent of GDP per person.[53]

If all households shared equally in the available growth, then the real median household income would also have grown by 48 percent. Another consequence of the demographic shift is that the new households that have been formed are often low-income households. For example, in 2007, the median income for couples was $71,000, while the median income of all single-adult households with or without children was $29,000. Similarly, the share of adults living in married couples fell from 76 percent in 1979 to 68 percent in 2007.[54]

Finally, there are the benefits to workers who are included in GDP data but are not included in household income as reported in census surveys. Because of rising health care costs, the employer share of health insurance premiums alone rose from 4.2% to 9.0 percent of earnings. Over this same period, the combined FICA and Medicare taxes for employers rose from 6.13% to 7.65 percent.[55]

To summarize, it would appear that median incomes should have grown by 66 percent instead of the 15 percent growth reported by the Census Bureau. In reality, available income growth per household was

Much Median Incomes Trail Productivity Growth," The Information Technology & Innovation Foundation, June 2007.

[53] Personal incomes were deflated by the price index for personal consumer expenditures. This index shows more inflation and less growth than the GDP price deflator because of high productivity gains in investment versus consumer goods.

[54] Adults here are defined as people over eighteen years old who are living on their own and not in group quarters or in their parents' homes; married couples include cohabiters—two persons of opposite sexes sharing living quarters (in 2007, the two adults were identified as the "reference person" and the "unmarried partner").

[55] The issue of who benefits from the rise in Social Security and Medicare taxes is complicated. From the point of view of today's economy, various taxes including these are collected to provide money and services to the elderly. The size of this effect has been growing as the share of the population over sixty-five grows, as cash benefits rise, and as Medicare costs explode. Over the longer term, current workers are given the promise of benefits in the future for their contributions today. It is only in this sense that the rise in employer social insurance taxes on workers' pay can be attributed to those employers today.

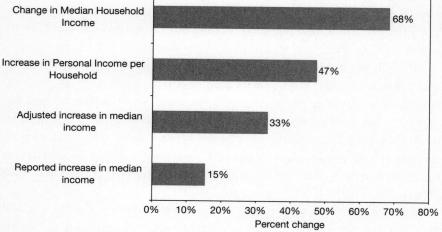

Figure 3.4: Different Ways of Tracking Household
Income Gains, 1979–2007

March Supplement to the Current Population Survey

only 48 percent (see Figure 3.4). Further, if the effect of demographic changes and rising benefits are estimated, median income grew by 33 percent. An apparent 51 percentage point difference (66 minus 15 percent) has been transformed into a 14 percentage point difference (47 minus 33 percent).[56]

Demographic changes are the most important factors in explaining where productivity growth went. It is a sign of progress that most young couples and most retired couples live on their own. In addition, the long-term trend has been for older children to pursue their independence by forming their own households (sometimes with nonrelated roommates). In the last ten years, there has been a slight trend of older children returning to live with parents—and this has led to headlines deploring the poor shape of the economy—but it has been a modest one. In addition, divorce and the rise of single parent households in the United States and in all of the advanced economies

[56] All of these analyses are presented for the population as a whole. In the next chapter, I will focus on prime-age adults (26–59).

of Western Europe raises the number of households, while the number of children per family has declined in all of these economies.[57]

What Happened in the Economic Cycle from 2001 to 2007?

So far, all of the comparisons have been decades apart. If the comparisons went back even further, the growth would be greater. However, the economic recovery from 2001 through 2007 was different from other recoveries in that there was no growth in median income (in 2007 dollars, the median census income was $50,557 in 2000 versus $50,223 in 2007). Some commentators have focused on this number as proof that the middle class is declining, and dismissed the experience of the prior years.

There are several reasons, however, why this period is anomalous. First, these years followed an unusually strong period in median income growth: From 1993 to 1999, real median incomes rose by 14.7 percent ($44,143 to $50,641). The huge demand for labor during the Clinton years resulted in high wage growth for people in the bottom half of the earnings distribution. By contrast, the economic growth from 2001 to 2007 was much weaker (just a 9.9 percent increase in real GDP per capita) with labor markets never being as tight.

Second, employee benefits grew dramatically during these years, meaning that workers got a higher share of their compensation indirectly and not counted in CPS income figures. In terms of retirement, the stock market decline led to massive underfunding of employer pension accounts, and companies were forced to increase their contributions dramatically. On the health insurance front, employee contributions were rising close to 10 percent per year.

Third, during these years, the profits and pay of the financial industry were reaching levels never seen before. The fees embedded in new mortgage and other financial products meant that there was less money available for other purchases. During these selected years, a lot of economic growth was indeed captured by the top 1 percent of earners.

---

[57] While many people think that it would be better if people made the best choice for a life partner on the first try and that families had more children, this, however, has not been the world created by people making their own choices in affluent societies where independence is very much prized.

Because of these three factors, the apparent stagnation of median income during the last full economic cycle does not portend a new pattern of growth in which the middle class receives none of the growth dividend. When the recovery starts and there is slower growth in employee benefits, and when the size of the financial sector contracts, median income should resume its slow path upward.

Conclusion

Over the last fifty years, we have witnessed remarkable changes. Many of these changes have been disruptive, and some wonder whether the change has been for the better. It is very difficult to turn back the clock or to selectively control how change will occur. The youth revolution of the late 1960s was filled with a lot of irresponsible behavior. Nonetheless, some of the achievements of that period were the expansion of personal autonomy, the rising awareness of the importance of environmental stewardship, and the opening up of opportunities for women and minorities.

Without a doubt, our standard of living is much higher for the vast majority of the population than it was decades ago. The General Social Science Survey, conducted every two years since 1994, has always asked respondents, "Compared to your parents when they were the age you are now, do you think your own standard of living now is much better, somewhat better, about the same, somewhat worse, or much worse than theirs was?" The answers have been remarkably consistent: Between 62 and 68 percent say that they live better than their parents and only 10–15 percent say that they live worse.

This question was also asked in a February 2008 Pew Survey. Even though respondents were quite dissatisfied with the state of the economy, 65 percent still said that they lived better than their parents, while only 15 percent said worse. The reason for this is that people seem to greatly prize new consumer options that were not available in the past. As an example, cell phones and the Internet were not available to their parents and they cannot imagine their own lives without these conveniences.

There are a few lone voices that try to prove otherwise (see Appendix 3 for the critique of how they use data). The irony is that economic growth has not "sated" people's appetite for consumer goods. Each time productivity ratchets up another notch, the availability of new temptations and new options on old products (e.g., the transformation of televisions from black and white to color, from large screen to larger screens, from high definition with surround sound to home entertainment centers) have raised the bar of what people want and expect.

There also can be no doubt that there is greater inequality. While we may be fascinated with the lifestyles of the rich and famous, the growth of income for those who live in upscale suburbs (a place where people's incomes tend to be at the 90th percentile of the income distribution) has been faster than for those who live in close-in suburbs and has risen even faster than for those who live in rural areas and central cities.

In the end, many rungs of the income ladder had substantial income growth over the last several decades. The middle class and the upper middle class are alive and well. This is a positive finding and bodes well for our future. In terms of our recovery from this downturn, the middle class will be the backbone of the positive growth loop of more consumption leading to more production and employment leading to more consumption.

CHAPTER 4

The Myth of the Declining Middle Class

What we're seeing is the death of the conventional middle-class life and an increase in the population of working poor.
—Jim Jacobs, president, of Macomb Community College discussing the decline of the auto industry in Michigan[58]

THE PREVIOUS CHAPTER SHOWED that the claims of declining standards of living were wrong, and that there was more growth in median income than was evident in the data from the annual census socioeconomic survey. Other claims about poor socioeconomic performance over the past thirty years include assertions that people are falling out of the middle class and that the only way others stay in is by working longer hours. The commentators who support these positions talk about the eras of Reagan, Bush I, Clinton, and Bush II as if they were periods of rising inequality, economic and social stagnation, briefly punctuated by income gains, fueled by debt and the stock market and housing bubbles.[59]

---

[58] Quoted in Peter Whoriskey, "Autoworkers Pick Up Skills but Downshift to Lower Pay," *Washington Post,* July 4, 2009, p. A1.
[59] Thomas Frank speaks of "the atavistic economic policies of the Reagan, Clinton, and Bush years" in the foreword to Dean Baker's *Plunder and Blunder: The Rise and Fall of the Bubble Economy.* Sausalito, CA: PoliPoint Press, 2009): viii.

This chapter addresses issues affecting middle-class standards of living. For a long time, we have prided ourselves as being a nation with a prosperous middle class as the engine of economic growth. If the middle class has shrunk because more people have incomes below the minimum cutoff point, then we likely can't say that the economy will be in good shape after the recovery. On the other hand, a growing prosperous class, even if temporarily batted by the recession, foreshadows a robust recovery.

Consequently, this chapter continues the debunking of doom-and-gloom claims about the middle class by showing that more people are in higher-income households than in the past. Yes, the middle class has shrunk, but this is due entirely to a greater share of the population moving up rather than down. Further, while wives are working more, the incomes of couples adjusted for inflation are up significantly and only between one-half to one-third of this increase is due to working longer hours.

The rest of this chapter addresses how much income the typical middle-class family has. Surprisingly, this is not a straightforward question even though most people would agree that the appropriate measure is to use a median figure (the income level at which half are above and half are below) as a reflection of typical income. Because of some data quirks and the life-cycle effect, I show that typical family income can be reported in different ways and with very different results—from $50,000 to $78,000.

The last series of analyses utilize an unusual data set that permits the examination of people over their lifetimes, revealing patterns of mobility, volatility, and multiyear incomes. These new data (called a "longitudinal" panel because the same people and their children are repeatedly interviewed in a range of years) provide a motion picture of someone's life versus the snapshot at a single moment: Incomes over time reflect dynamic arrangements, while static snapshots at a point in time might mask the real quality of life reflected by one's average income.

These longitudinal data show that many people have long-term incomes of over $100,000 a year—a level that permits a minimum level of discretionary expenditures in most parts of the country. This large base of families with reasonably high incomes provides the underpinning of our mass-consumer market as evidenced by crowded suburban malls. If one only relies on single-year surveys, it is very easy to underestimate the strength of the economy.

Defining the Middle Class

In 1978, I wrote:

> [T]he term "middle class" is a misnomer. Since it includes prac-
> tically all of the U.S. population, it loses its descriptive function.
> In fact, it obscures vast differences in lifestyle, community,
> working conditions, and political outlook.[60]

Nonetheless, the term is evocative. In 1983, I presented data on the "shrinking middle class" and I continue to analyze the declining middle-class theme in this chapter.

People tend to live in communities with others like themselves, and they develop a concept of the income required to support their spending levels in comparison with others in these communities. For example, many who live in upscale suburbs assume they need a family income of at least $100,000 a year as the minimum to obtain their desired standard of living. At the other extreme, those who live in relatively poor neighborhoods require $40,000 as their minimum to maintain their desired lifestyle.

The government does not define the middle class, and publishes no official definition thereof. As a result, commentators use the term loosely and define it differently. One study described moderate income as those with household incomes between $20,000 and $40,000 and middle income as between $40,000 and $60,000; everyone in households with incomes above $60,000 was considered in the upper-income strata.[61] By contrast, advertisers often define their target middle-class audience as those with incomes between $50,000 and $150,000 annually. Finally, at one dinner conversation among a group of professionals in Washington, D.C., one woman proclaimed that she was not part of the "upper" middle class but part of the "middle" middle class, even though she and her husband had an income above

---

[60] *Social Stratification in the United States: An Analytic Guidebook,* Baltimore, MD: Social Graphics Company, 1978.

[61] As stated by S. R. Collins, K. Davis, M. M. Doty, J. L. Kriss, and A. L. Holmgren, in "Gaps in Medical Insurance: An All-American Problem," Commonwealth Fund, April 2006.

$250,000, no children, and four properties in three countries worth $2 million.

The term "middle class" arose in the nineteenth century to depict the socioeconomic groups above the working and peasant classes, but below the landowning class. The middle class consisted of small shop owners, independent artisans and professionals, and sometimes clerical workers (in the tradition of Dickens's Bob Cratchit, whose literacy set them apart and promised upward mobility). Even today, there is a high-brow usage of the term "middle class" that distinguishes "proper" social behavior from that of the lower and working classes.

By the early twentieth century, the advance of industrialization brought prosperity to more people. Breakthroughs in mechanizing agri-culture and the invention of the assembly line promised to put a "chicken in every pot" and "a car in every garage." Rising living standards for average workers and the expansion of political rights brought a greater sense of dignity and prosperity to the masses of working people.

Following the interruption caused by the Great Depression and World War II, economic progress resumed for many workers. Living standards rose, home ownership expanded, and more families had cars in their new suburban neighborhoods. The ranks of this ill-defined middle class swelled as unionized blue-collar workers began to live the American Dream.

The rise of middle-class America was etched in the nation's changing physical landscape and reflected in the symbols of its pop culture. The Levitt brothers built thousands of 1,000-square-feet, stand-alone homes on Long Island. Others did the same across the country as people fled the cities for the open spaces of suburbia. Meanwhile, Americans gathered around their new television sets for Lucy and Desi, the Cleavers, *Father Knows Best,* Loretta Young, and Ozzie and Harriet—all of them, a semi-idealized reflection of life in postwar, middle-class America.

Part of the attraction of the term "middle class" is that few people want to consider themselves poor or part of the lower class, even if their incomes are low—"poor but proud" is not a desired American state. The result is a concept that elevates lower-income families when self-defining their status, and includes those with higher incomes who feel they are not in the upper strata of society. For example, those with high incomes know many people who have more income. Since their social circles and aspirations are so narrow, they do not realize their rarefied status. Consequently, they don't consider themselves rich or part of the "upper class," a term that promises a higher standard of living.

Most people identify themselves as part of the middle class and sometimes add an adjective such as "lower" middle, "upper" middle, or even "middle" middle. For example, in a February 2008 poll from the Pew Research Center, 91 percent of Americans said they were middle class: just 2 percent put themselves in the upper class, while 6 percent identified with lower class, and 1 percent were undecided. Of those in the middle class, nearly half said that they were either "upper" or "lower" middle class.

Furthermore, polls also show that when given the option, many people consider themselves part of the working class as well. This term does not have any of the connotations of being poor or lower class, and is used with pride to mean, "I earn my way." No matter whether they call themselves middle or working class, Americans are very proud of the openness of our economy and the opportunity to reach a comfortable standard of living. Any hint that the economy is no longer providing pathways to success leads to great public angst.

Today's Middle Class

Analysts agree that one's standard of living is best reflected by total family income—a figure that includes all sources of income (e.g., earnings, business income, rental payment, interest and other financial income, and transfer payments such as Social Security, unemployment insurance, and welfare and disability payments) from all members of the family. It is not a perfect measure but it is readily available and can be used with care to discuss changes in middle-class lifestyles.

One complicating factor is the number of members in the family: As family size grows, fixed expenses like housing, utilities, and consumer durables don't rise much. On the other hand, expenses that are tied more closely to individual consumption—such as food—do rise with family size. Few dispute that the same amount of money does not support the same level of consumption in households of different size, and researchers have developed methodologies to align income and size to get equivalent standards of living. For example, in the approach that is used here, a single person with $50,000 of income has the "equivalent income" of a family of three with $86,600 or a family of four with $100,000.

To put these figures in context, consider that for 2008, the official federal poverty line was about $21,200 for a family of four, $17,600 for a family of three, and $10,400 for a single person. Because it takes more than that for families of these sizes to get by in today's America, the federal government gives the poor and near-poor a number of benefits, such as Medicaid, housing, and food assistance.

The poverty line tells us something about our society, but not enough. Researchers at the Economic Policy Institute (EPI) have created a useful concept of "minimum but adequate budgets"—an indicator of what's needed to get by—for different types of families in 400 regions of the country. Each budget estimates all necessary family expenses, including taxes. The researchers found that, in 2004, when the official poverty line for a husband-wife couple and two children was $19,157, the "range of basic family budgets for a two-parent, two-child family is $31,080 (rural Nebraska) to $64,656 (Boston, Massachusetts)."[62]

These numbers are similar to the "minimum but adequate budget" that the Bureau of Labor Statistics (BLS) developed in the 1970s. Their nationwide figure for "minimum but adequate" was approximately 175 percent of the poverty line, while the EPI budget is about 185 percent of the poverty line. The BLS also estimated a "high budget line," which included more amenities and reflected typical suburban living, at approximately 4.25 times the poverty line.

Estimates of socioeconomic conditions are based on the Census Bureau's monthly Current Population Survey (CPS).[63] Each March, the census asks a set of questions about household living arrangements and incomes in the previous year. This survey is then used to compute the share of the population in poverty. But the data are also used to generate median household income, a widely cited number meant to portray how the typical American lives.

For 2007, the median was $50,233, but I don't think that this figure provides a good measure of how middle-income people live, for four reasons: There are changes in earnings over a person's life cycle; the difference between household and "person-based" measures; the impact of family size; and the difference between a single year's income and the average over a longer period of time.

---

[62] Available at: http://www.epi.org/content.cfm/bp165
[63] Census surveys nearly 80,000 households and, from this outreach, calculates the monthly unemployment rate.

First, income measured at a point in time is static and does not reflect how it might change over the course of one's life cycle. For most people a standard of living is something that persists over time (researchers call this "permanent income"). If a wealthy businessman has one bad year, few people would consider this person poor unless the one bad year leads to a long-term trend. Similarly, graduate students spend many years with low incomes, but that's clearly not a reflection of their future income status.

In general, young people start their careers in search of the best niche for themselves, usually at the bottom of the seniority ladder. Their current income does not reflect their permanent income. Complicating matters further, many twenty-somethings get support from their parents even when they are not living at home. At the opposite end of the age spectrum, retired people have fewer direct expenses, have often paid off their mortgage, have homes filled with furniture and appliances, and most no longer subsidize their adult children. Consequently, a retiree's income of $40,000 translates into a much higher standard of living than the same income level would afford a young couple with a newborn child.

Figure 4.1 shows the dramatic difference of median income among age groups; income is under $35,000 until age twenty-two and does

Figure 4.1: Median Household Incomes by Age, 2007

2008 March Supplement to the Current Population Survey

not reach $50,000 until twenty-seven. By thirty-five, median incomes reach $64,137 and rise slowly until they reach their peak incomes of $74,256 at age fifty-two. They then decline slowly through the late fifties and rapidly after age sixty-two, at which point median income is only slightly above $50,000. By age sixty-eight, incomes dip below $40,000; and by seventy-five, median incomes dip below $30,000.

If you accept that the incomes of the young and old aren't representative of their long-term standard of living, you might want to exclude these values to get a better single indicator of the income of the "typical American." One step in this direction would be to limit the analysis to "prime-age" adults—those who are older than twenty-five and have finished their education and those younger than sixty and have not begun to cut back for retirement. The median income of the households of prime-age adults is about $7,000 higher than the median income of all households.

The second reason the census's median income measure is problematic is that it reports income distribution on the basis of households and not persons. This may seem arcane but it has a big effect on median income calculations. Researchers tend to present the income distribution

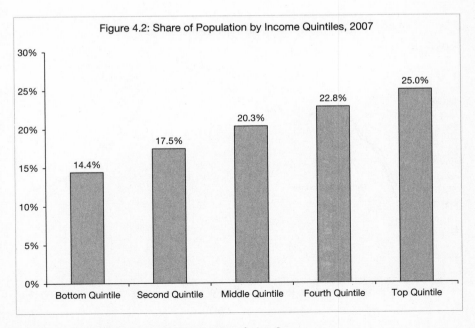

Figure 4.2: Share of Population by Income Quintiles, 2007

2008 March Supplement to the Current Population Survey

by using five ordered groups of 20 percent each—that is, quintiles—of households, from poorest to richest. Each quintile includes an equal number of households, but, as Figure 4.2 shows, the share of the population in each household income quintile varies considerably. Because couples have considerably more income as a rule than single people, and because these couples are much more likely to have children, the share of the population in the bottom quintile was less than 15 percent in 2007. At the other end, the share of the population in the top quintile was 25 percent, and nearly half of the population was in the top two quintiles.

If we reported the family incomes of each person separately, the median income in 2006 would be $5,000 higher than the census's estimate. Taking into account both the household-based population adjustment (Figure 4.2) and the age effects (Figure 4.1) the median income of prime-age people to $61,500 in 2007, over $10,000 higher than the $50,233 reported by the Census Bureau.

Third, we must factor in family size when assessing median income because as was shown in the previous chapter, many more people are living in single-person households. Figure 4.3 depicts median incomes by age both adjusted and not adjusted for the number of people in the household. For example, eighteen- to twenty-four-year-olds tend to

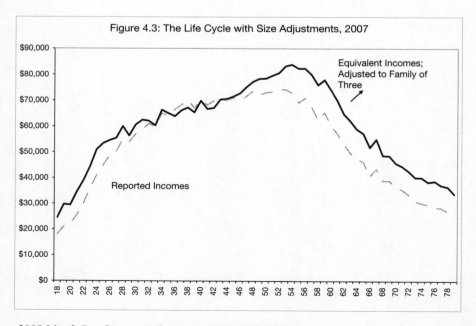

Figure 4.3: The Life Cycle with Size Adjustments, 2007

Equivalent Incomes;
Adjusted to Family of
Three

Reported Incomes

2008 March Supplement to the Current Population Survey

live alone (here, roommates are treated as separate single people) and are rarely married with more than one child. Adjusting for size raises their reported median incomes by 35 percent. For those twenty-nine to forty-four years old, adjusting for size has very little effect. Only 15 percent of them live alone, and 48 percent are in households with more than three people. For those forty-five to sixty-five years old, their children have generally moved out so the number of people in their households shrinks to less than three. Consequently, median incomes adjusted for size now are higher. For those over sixty-five, size-adjusted incomes are 30 percent higher.

Median income rises to $66,000 when combining the effects of person-weighting rather than household-weighting, focusing on prime-age years, and adjusting for family size. Figure 4.4 presents a summary version of how median income varies by age and by different methodological approaches to estimating median income. If the analysis is limited to the more successful household types, then median incomes soar. For example, the median income of prime-age two-earner couples is $91,600, while the median income of prime-age couples in which both individuals have at least a bachelor's degree jumps to $121,200.

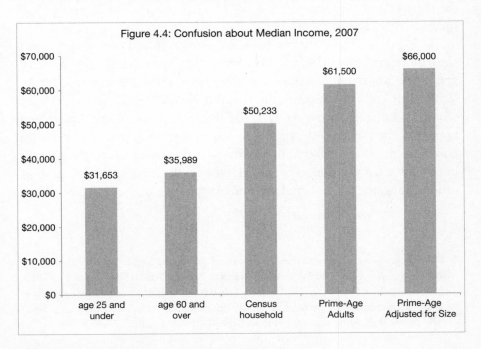

Figure 4.4: Confusion about Median Income, 2007

2008 March Supplement to the Current Population Survey

Instead of just tracking medians, let's set some income boundaries to determine what has happened to the middle class for prime-age Americans. While there are no accepted boundaries, picking a reasonable set of income boundaries will give us some sense of the changes of real income. So, to be a bit more selective—and to avoid relying on the self-classification of 91 percent of Americans who put themselves in the middle class—in defining the income boundaries of the middle class, income groups are defined as follows (income is converted into 2007 family of three equivalents):

- poor and near poor=under $35,000;
- middle class=$30,000–$70,000;
- upper middle class=$70,000–$105,000; and
- well-off=$105,000 and more.

These ranges are based on multiples of the poverty line: two times or less is the bottom category; two to four times is the middle-class group; four to six times is the upper middle class, and six times and above is the well-off category. While the minimum income of $105,000 for the top category may seem low, less than 13 percent of people had incomes this high in 1979.

Using this schema, we can track movements in and out of the middle class more narrowly defined. As Figure 4.5 makes clear, the share of prime-age adults in the middle class ($35,000 to $70,000) declined sharply. While this seems to validate the shrinking-middle-class thesis, let's see where these people went. In fact, the shares of people in the lower and upper middle class shrank, and there was a huge jump of 14.2 percentage points in the share of the well-off category. By this measure, the shrinking middle class was due to people moving up the income ladder, an indication of income gains shared by more people.[64]

---

[64] Nonetheless some commentators cannot resist drawing a negative conclusion wherever possible. For example, two professors of history, Michael Kazin and Julian Zelizer, wrote in a *Washington Post* op-ed, (February 8, 2009) using EPI data showing the same social mobility only focused on the shrinking aspect of the middle class and not the fact that more people are living in higher-income families. They write: "Younger Americans no longer expect to enjoy as good a life as their parents did. Wage earners fear for the future of their jobs and incomes. No family is secure."

Figure 4.5: Shrinking Middle-Class; Growing Affluence

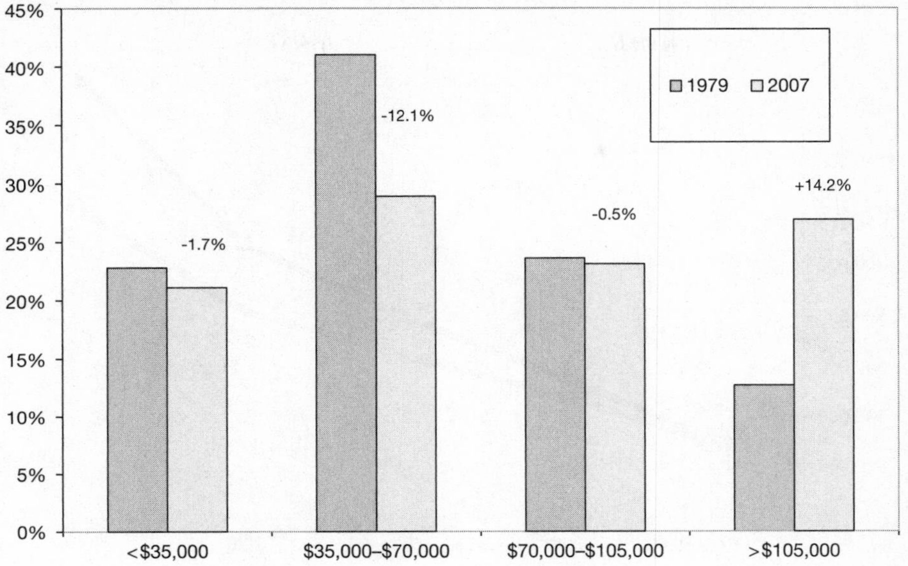

1980 and 2008 March Supplements to the Current Population Survey

Are Couples Working Longer Hours for the Same Income?

Once rising incomes are accepted, some critics change courses to argue that, if people are moving up, it is because they are working longer hours. The "working more" in this claim is certainly true but is often not correctly described. Men's working hours have hardly changed over time while all of the increase in working time is limited to women. So, the working-more-for-the-same-income argument only applies to husband-wife couples.

Figure 4.6 shows incomes of married couples at different points on the income ladder in 2007 compared to 1979, in constant 2007 dollars. As you can see, those with the lowest 10 percent of income had small gains, those at the 50th percentile (the median) gained 24 percent, while those at the 90th percentile gained 42 percent.

These numbers certainly dispel the notion that couples are working more for no added income. But let's look more closely at the effects of

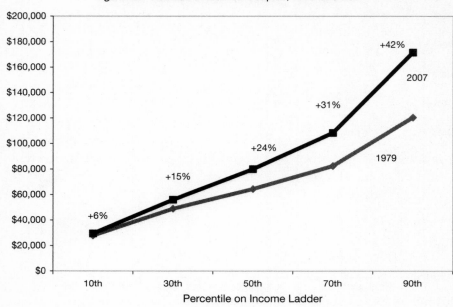

Figure 4.6: Incomes of Married Couples, 1979 and 2007

1980 and 2008 March Supplements to the Current Population Survey

wives working longer. While their hours in the paid labor market are up, so are their hourly wages. For example, for wives in a median income household, they worked 972 hours at $8.50 an hour in 1979. By 2007, these numbers had risen to 1,487 hours at 14.30 an hour.

Now, let's assume we recalculate incomes by limiting wives in 2007 to the number of hours they worked in 1979. That reduces income gains but does not eliminate them. At the median, the gain drops from 24 percent to 13 percent and, at the 90th percentile, from 42 percent to 33 percent; even at the 10th percentile, incomes would be 3 percent higher than they were in 1979 if the working hours of wives had not increased. Thus, husband-wife couples are working more for more income. But even without the greater work effort of wives, median incomes would have risen.

Some say women are forced to work because their families need the money. While that's certainly true in some cases, there are three reasons to doubt that need is the driving force behind women's increased hours. First, the rise in women's hours in the paid labor force dates back to the mid-twentieth century; from 1950 to 1973, women's hours rose more quickly even though male earnings were rising steadily. Second, the same trend has occurred in all other advanced industrial countries, most of which saw male earnings also rise. Finally, third, the rise in hours has been greatest for women whose husbands have the highest earnings.

Consequently, it seems much more appropriate to argue that women are working more for the extra money and because it gives them much more autonomy over their own lives. Their extra time in the paid labor force has created tensions on how to manage family-care needs, and "family-friendly" workplace policies have become of popular interest. Working mothers, even with young children, are a fact of modern life here and abroad.

Long-term Income Paths

Many commentators like to make broad statements on the state of the economy by talking about how many people have gained ground over time—e.g., the candidates Bill Clinton and Barack Obama often said that up to 80 percent of people were worse off than they were in the past. There are two ways to interpret these statements. On the one hand, there is the common-sense interpretation that individuals have lower living standards today than in the past. To assess how incomes change over time, we need a data source that follows the same people over many years. Obviously, this is much more difficult to do than to survey the population at a single moment in time. Data sets that follow people for many years are called "longitudinal panels," and provide a rich source of information. Most of the material in the rest of this chapter is based on the Panel Study on Income Dynamics (see a discussion of this source in Appendix 4).

On the other hand, what the studies and commentators are actually doing is comparing "similarly situated" people at different points in time. This means comparing the median income in one year with the median income in an earlier year: If the median is lower in the later year, then the statement is made that 50 percent of the population is worse off today. Similarly, if the value at the 80th percentile was lower today than in the past, then the statement could be made that 80 percent of the population was worse off.

This latter approach is called a "comparative cross-sectional analysis," and the incomes of the same person are not being compared over time. To illustrate the importance of this point, let us use the example of an escalator, with someone standing on each step. If the escalator raised people twenty feet, then the median person on the escalator would be at the ten-foot level. No matter how long you waited, assuming someone steps on as someone steps off the moving escalator, the median person on the escalator would also be ten feet above the ground level.

Clearly, we would not argue that no one on the escalator has reached their higher level just because the median has stayed the same. In the same vein, we have to understand that earnings and income dynamics work in much the same way. As older people retire, they tend to leave the employment escalator at the top with high earnings. Offsetting this loss is a stream of younger people entering the labor force at the ground level, usually at relatively lower pay. But much like the escalator, the people who remain in the labor force are taking the openings that are left by the retirees and moving up on their careers. Stated simply, there is a difference between a static picture of median income in society at any point in time and the dynamic change of a person's income over their working lives.

Thus, *it is possible for a measure of median income or earnings to stay exactly the same while each individual receives a wage increase every year.* This is not what actually happens, but the escalator model shows that the comparison of similarly situated people—each on a specific step at a certain height—can show no change while each person progresses from the bottom to the top of the escalator.

When we look closely at an individual's income path, there are a surprising number of swings associated with isolated good and bad events. Since these movements can be relatively large, many people have yearly incomes that are very different from their usual level. For example, in any given year, about one-third of the people at the bottom and at the top of the income distribution ladder are there temporarily because of an unusually high or low income year.

The isolated swing in one direction is followed shortly thereafter by a swing in the other direction. In other words, many people with low incomes in one year will likely have much higher incomes the next. Similarly, many people with high incomes one year will have much lower incomes the next. Statisticians call this leveling over time "reversion to mean."

Practically speaking, this shows that the distribution of income based on a single year's data is much more dispersed than the income distribution of the same population whose income is measured as the average of multiple years. For example, over the last five years, the poverty rate for working age adults has hovered around 7 to 8 percent. However, over five years, all of the following statements are true:

- About 18 percent of this population have at least one year in which their incomes are below the poverty line;
- The average poverty rate for all five years of income is less than half the single year number of just over 3 percent; and
- Only 2 percent fall below the poverty line for 4 or 5 years.

If we expanded the time horizon to ten years, the ten-year poverty rate is about 3 percent, but now 25 percent of the population will experience at least one year in which their incomes fell below the poverty line, but only 1 percent of these adults are below the poverty line for at least nine of the ten years.

Table 4.1 (p. 118) shows the real income paths over ten years for four distinct time periods, from 1967 through 2004 (the last year for which PSID data were available at the time of this writing). This analysis is limited to prime-age adults who are never younger than twenty-six (they've finished their education) or older than fifty-nine (they've not cut back work in preparation for retirement). Instead of comparing similarly situated people, this estimate is based on computing a size-adjusted income trend line for each individual. The four periods were chosen to compare similar points in the economy; each begins and ends in the middle of a business cycle.[65]

The first finding from this analysis is that there's a wide distribution of income paths, with a substantial number of individuals having lower real incomes at the end of a ten-year period as compared with the beginning. Second, the number of "income losers," however, is much lower than one gets from comparative cross-sectional analysis. Third, in all of the four periods, the share of income gainers is considerably larger than the share of income losers, and the number of losers is never greater than 37 percent. Fourth, with the exception of the first period, the distribution of income losers and gainers is similar in each

[65] When other ten-year periods were chosen or when incomes were not adjusted for family size, the results were quite similar.

TABLE 4.1
INCOME PATHS OVER TEN YEARS, 1967–2004

	Loss of at least 25%	Loss of 5–25%	+/− 5	Gain of 5–25%	Gain of at least 25%	All Losers
1967–76	15.6	11.5	7.5	15.1	50.2	27.1
1975–84	21.7	14.1	7.9	13.9	42.4	35.8
1985–94	23.3	13.9	7.7	13.2	41.9	37.2
1995–2004	22.6	13.8	6.2	13.8	43.5	36.4

Panel Study on Income Dynamics

of the three ten-year periods. *This implies that since the mid-1970s, the pattern of individual mobility has not changed—i.e., things have not been getting steadily worse.* Fifth, the mobility patterns do not seem to be sensitive to business cycles. The period from 1975 to 1984 included two recessions, with unemployment reaching nearly 10 percent at the end of 1982. Yet, the number of income losers in this period was lower than in each of the two ensuing ten-year periods in which the recessions were milder.[66]

Long-Run Incomes

While analyzing income paths is useful in understanding mobility over one's lifetime, it is always important to understand how the level at which people live has changed over time. Table 4.2 presents the average ten-year incomes of prime-age adults at different points on the income ladder for the first and last ten years of PSID data (the middle two ten-year periods merely represent steps in the movement from the lower incomes at the beginning to the higher incomes at the end), adjusted for family size.

First, there is a big difference in income growth depending on

[66] This confirms my earlier finding that there were fewer income losers from 1967 through 1979 when compared with the period from 1977 through 1989; see Rose, "Declining Family Incomes in the 1980s: New Evidence from Longitudinal Data," *Challenge,* November–December 1993.

whether incomes are adjusted for size. At the median (50th percentile), incomes grew by 28 percent without size adjustments and 47 percent with adjustments. The effect was even bigger at the bottom of the income scale: The tenth percentile had just a 6 percent growth over thirty years, if just reported incomes are used, versus a 25 percent gain if incomes are adjusted for number of people in the family. Starting in 1967, there were 3.3 persons per household, but by 1998 that figure dropped to 2.6 persons. For those at the bottom of the income scale the change was more dramatic. In the first ten years there were slightly more than three persons per family, but by 1995 to 2004 the growth in the number of single adult households lowered the average family size to 2.6 persons per family.

Second, the rising income inequality reported in the census data is reproduced in the longitudinal approach. Over the thirty-plus years of the study, people at the 90th percentile had their ten-year average incomes (both adjusted and unadjusted for size) grow much more than those at the 50th percentile, and people at the 50th percentile had greater income growth than those at the 10th percentile. In effect, those in the top 10 percent saw income rise from just under four times to almost six times that received by people at the bottom 10 percent of the income distribution.

Third, it is also instructive to look at the levels of income in the later period: the median is nearly $78,000 and over 30 percent of prime-age adults have average incomes (in inflation-adjusted 2007$) of $100,000 a year.[67] This median figure is over 50 percent greater than the median income level of $50,233 reported by the census and is even considerably higher than the median prime-age income. The reason for this is that incomes are quite volatile and the upward swings are actually larger in dollar terms than the downward. This asymmetry means that the long-run median is higher than the single-year median.

Finally, these numbers are averages and we know that people's incomes rise and fall a lot over ten years. Another way to look at incomes over many years is to see how often people experienced high and low incomes. Indeed, fully 60 percent of adults had at least one year in which their incomes were at least $100,000. Of this group, 18 percent

[67] When additional analyses were done for longer time periods, the results were very similar. For example, the median average twenty-year incomes for 1985–2004 were $77,864.

TABLE 4.2
TEN-YEAR MEDIAN INCOMES,
BY PERCENTILES

	Adjusted for Size Family of Three, 2007 $		Percent	Unadjusted for Size 2007 $		Percent
Percentile	1967–76	1995–2004	Change	1967–76	1995–2004	Change
10th	$27,452	$34,264	25	$28,250	$30,085	6
30th	$44,334	$60,981	38	$47,986	$55,795	16
50th	$56,926	$83,413	47	$60,784	$77,715	28
70th	$73,066	$110,995	52	$75,858	$104,267	37
90th	$99,471	$171,574	72	$105,147	$164,361	56

Panel Study on Income Dynamics

reached this level just once or twice, which means that over 40 percent of the prime-adult population had incomes of $100,000 or higher for at least three years. At the other end of the spectrum, 40 percent of adults had at least one year with incomes of $30,000 or less. However, one-half of this group only experienced this low level once or twice. In effect, only 20 percent of adults had three or more years with low incomes.

There is probably no better indication of why suburban malls are so crowded (even during the economic bad times) than these income figures. And clearly, the picture one gets from these income levels is light-years away from the implications of the widely reported median household income of $50,000.

Is Volatility Bad?

Jacob Hacker's *The Great Risk Shift* and Peter Gosselin's *High Wire* argue that the rise in volatility creates great uneasiness in people. They focus in particular on the people who lose ground, arguing that people care much more about losing income than gaining income. Hacker shows that the share of people with large losses of 50 percent or more over two years has risen from 4 to 9 percent of the population from 1967 to 2004.[68] Both Hacker and Gosselin then focus on other issues such as health insurance, retirement, and savings to show that ordinary Americans face many more difficulties than they did in the past.

Let's look a little more closely at income volatility and loss. First, many of the downward experiences are reversions to the mean after unusual upward movements. It is hard to see how these "declines" will have great psychological effects given that the higher incomes were not the normal levels that these people experienced over time. Second, some of the volatility is due to wives adjusting their labor force participation to respond to family responsibilities. These voluntary choices are difficult ones but couples are weighing their options when they make this decision and are aware of the trade-offs.

Figure 4.7 uses the same data set used by Hacker and Gosselin, and tracks the share of prime-age adults who have income losses when compared with their incomes two years earlier. The data were only collected every other year after 1997 so the two-year comparisons are made back to 1969 in order to be consistent. However, from 1967 to 1997, the distribution of one-year changes was not very different from two-year changes.

This figure doesn't show the overall number of losers rising over time: If one were to start in 1975 (remember the early finding on the initial strong mobility patterns in the late 1960s and early 1970s), the trend line for the remaining years is flat. It is true the share of those with income losses of greater than 25 percent rises modestly (the finding of Hacker and Gosselin), however, this does not come at the expense of the number of people with income gains (a fact that is conveniently omitted by Hacker and Gosselin).

Further, if we look at personal income paths over five successive years, a loss in the first year does not lead to losses in the following years. Virtually no one loses at least 5 percent of income for five consecutive years (by contrast, one in eight have a rise in income for five consecutive years). Looked at slightly differently, just 3 percent never have a yearly increase in income and 12 percent never have a fall (the 5 percent, plus and minus, are considered those with no income fluctuation and

---

[68] His original book had the gain from 7 to 17 percent but he was forced to change these numbers when other researchers could not reproduce these findings.

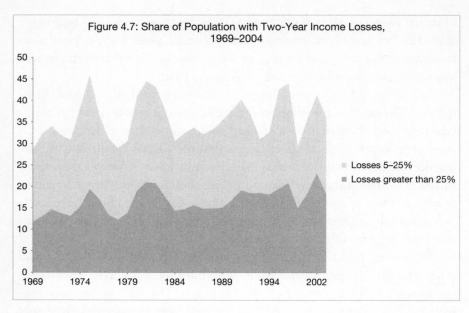

Figure 4.7: Share of Population with Two-Year Income Losses, 1969–2004

Panel Study on Income Dynamics

don't count in either tally). Most people have a combination of two or three up years and one or two down years. A lot of these ups or downs represent the unusually good/bad years followed by a return to one's more normal income level. Unusually good years are characterized by bonuses, working extra overtime, or earning a high commission on a big sale. Unusually bad years are characterized by temporary layoffs, illness, or a spouse taking time off to deal with a pressing family issue.

Rebounding from an Income Decline

An important issue in the volatility debate is the long-term consequence of a decline in income. One measure of the impact of a loss is to calculate how long it takes to recover to one's original income. The results in Table 4.3 are based on comparing incomes in the following ten years after a year-over-year decline of either 5–25 percent (small decline) or 25 percent or larger (large decline). In order to be consistent with the last time period (when the survey changed from annual to bi-annual data collection) the comparisons are done one year after the decline, two or four years later, and at years six, eight, and ten. This approach was used in four different ten-year periods (each following a yearly loss from the income two years earlier in relation to the income one year before).

The data show that approximately 70 percent of those with a small decline (under 25 percent) returned to their former incomes within four years. Only about one in six individuals who suffered this level of income decline never regained their former income level. By contrast, one in three who suffered a sharp decline never returned to their former incomes. Furthermore, only about half of these large losers returned to

TABLE 4.3
RECOVERY TIME FROM INCOME DECLINE, 1969–2004

Loss of 25% or more	Year 1	Year 2 or 4	Year 6, 8, or 10	Never
1969–1978	17.2	32.3	22.1	28.5
1975–1984	14.3	35.9	14.5	35.3
1985–1994	19.7	25.0	21.8	33.5
1995–2004	20.0	29.6	16.0	34.5
Loss of 5–25%				
1969–1978	39.3	36.7	10.1	14.0
1975–1984	27.0	38.3	15.4	19.3
1985–1994	38.2	32.1	13.1	16.6
1995–2004	31.8	38.5	14.1	15.6

Panel Study on Income Dynamics

their former income level within four years. Finally, once again, the ability to recoup one's income loss does not change from 1975 on.

A complementary way to understand this analysis is to trace what happens in the years following a loss. This is important because the mere fact of returning to one's former income may not be an adequate gauge of a person's well-being. First, merely returning to one's former income level may be followed by large declines after this level has been reached. Second, on the other hand, the initial decline may only reflect a return from an unusually high income year.

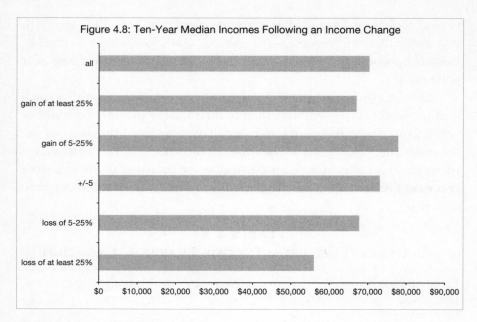

Figure 4.8: Ten-Year Median Incomes Following an Income Change

Panel Study on Income Dynamics

Figure 4.8 combines the experiences of four periods and shows that income over ten-year periods based on prior income changes are not always what you might anticipate. As expected, those with large declines have income significantly below (20 percent) the average of ten-year incomes for all prime-age adults. However, the ten-year incomes of those with losses of 5–25 percent are just 4 percent below average. And surprisingly, those with large income gains of 25 percent follow up this experience with ten-year incomes that are 5 percent below average. These large gainers start from very low incomes and are often followed by stagnating or declining incomes. The group with the highest ten-year incomes (11 percent above the population average) is composed of those who had small gains in the prior two years. These results underscore once again that single-year changes are not the best indicator for measuring long-term well-being with the exception of those who have income declines of more than 25 percent.

Conclusion

As we exit the worst recession since the Great Depression, the key issue is whether we will be in position to grow once the financial collapse is settled. Certainly, if the middle class were in the dire situation that many said they were in before the meltdown, then the recovery will not be robust. But the claims of middle-class decline from 1979 through 2007 are not true: The middle class "shrunk" because many Americans moved up to higher incomes. Notwithstanding the serious challenges that many Americans face, from paying for health care to sending their children to college, more middle-class Americans are enjoying higher living standards than ever before.

In the introduction, I said that doing data analysis was as much art as science. In this chapter, I present a variety of new approaches and show that a number of commonly used approaches were misleading. It is not that there are computation errors, but rather the researchers don't ask the relevant questions.

Nowhere is this more evident than in the presentation of the median income. Yet, I show that the widely cited census figure is not the best number to reflect how the "typical" American lives. It is not a gimmick to exclude young adults and seniors in determining a more realistic median income figure. Their current incomes neither reflect their current living standards (both the young and old) nor their realistic aspirations of how they will live (the young).

All of these numbers paint a mixed picture of how Americans are doing. While the extreme claims of those who see the middle class in economic distress are refuted, this should not be taken to mean that there are no problems. Under all circumstances, inequality has risen considerably, and this is a bad thing for America. Those at the bottom of the income ladder have benefited only minimally from the significant gains in overall production over the past three decades. Polls show that people do not approve of the level of inequality that exists in America today (especially when it comes to the outsized salaries of the CEOs and financial professionals) and support public policies to aid those with low incomes.

However, the key finding from this chapter is the huge growth in the share of households with incomes over $100,000. These are the people with a fair amount of disposable income, and these are the people who are going to power our recovery.

CHAPTER 5

The Hamburger Flipper Economy—The Myth of the Disappearance of Good Jobs

WE HEAR IT all the time. All the good jobs are being outsourced to China and India. Americans don't make anything anymore. It's flipping burgers or the unemployment line.

But the notion that the overall quality of American jobs has declined in recent years is an outlandish claim. By focusing solely on the decline of well-paid unionized blue-collar jobs, the growth of high-end managerial and professionals jobs is missed. If we were indeed becoming a low-paid service economy, the suburbs would be wanting for home buyers, those shopping malls wouldn't be so crowded, and the recovery after the financial crisis would be doomed.

The so-called decline in the number of good jobs because of the decline in manufacturing employment occurred during a time when the economy was growing and educational attainment was rising. For example, real GDP growth per person (our best measure of the amount of economic goods consumed adjusted for inflation and population growth) has nearly tripled (grown by 174 percent) from 1960 to 2008. Accompanying this growth (and one of the major reasons for it) was a massive increase in the educational attainment of those working: As noted in the previous chapter, we went from a labor force in 1960 with over half of the workforce not having a high school diploma, to a labor force today in which over 60 percent has some postsecondary education, and 30 percent has a bachelor's or graduate degree.

So the importance of service employment grew in tandem with

these positive macroeconomic events. Can it really be true that a more educated workforce has worse jobs? Further, how can a bigger economic pie (higher real GDP per person) lead to a larger share of people having low earnings? Showing how the new service economy is composed heavily of managerial and professional worker will go a long way to understanding how growth will resume after the financial crisis is over.

There is a lot of confusion about the nature of service employment. This shift is often presented as a negative trend because service jobs are not thought of as "good jobs." The popularized form of this sentiment is that "we are becoming a nation of hamburger flippers." More scholarly treatments of the issue have argued that "manufacturing matters" because "deindustrialization" (or the "hollowing out of the American corporation") decreases the demand for activities in the high-end service jobs that are closely tied to production—e.g., design, research, selling, etc.

The purpose of this chapter is to show that economic growth, higher educational attainment, and service sector growth are compatible, and that there has been an increase, and not a decline, in good jobs. In fact, the vast majority of people who have bachelor's degrees work in the service sector and, correspondingly, most of the people who live in upscale suburbs are service workers. Recovery will come from here.

Most people don't understand the service economy because they have a narrow conception of services as barbershops, fast-food restaurants, and the like. Although the terms "knowledge economy" and "postindustrial economy" are used broadly, they are rarely carefully defined. In this chapter, I will reexamine the question of what people do and how to classify their work.

By developing "functional" groupings to replace industrial divisions (which are the current basis for distinguishing manufacturing from service jobs), we can put similar activities across firms into the same categories. In particular, we'll classify front-office activities across all industries, along with business and financial services and public administration as a common "office function." As will be shown, these activities represent a very large share of our economy (over half of all earnings). This finding is somewhat counterintuitive because there is a common presumption that the production of goods is more important than paper-pushing activities. But the importance of office work should not be surprising if you just look up at all the large office buildings in downtowns and even in the suburbs.

Tradable Goods and the Functional Division of Labor

Today, we are living at the end of a long cycle of technological innovation, one that has made producing consumer goods relatively easy. Two hundred years ago, the vast majority of people around the world lived and worked on farms. Progressive improvements in the production of food within industrialized countries have reduced the number of people engaged in farming to less than 1 percent of American workers.

In much the same way, the share of employment in the manufacturing sector has declined since reaching its peak in the 1950s. Like agriculture, technological changes have resulted in a significant decline in the number of workers needed to manufacture ever more goods. In its place, the employment in the "services" sector has grown considerably, absorbing all of the increase in employment since 1960 in this country and in every other industrialized country in the world.

A typical day for many people begins with turning on a morning TV talk show while they get ready for work and have breakfast. On the ride to and from work, a local radio station will be broadcasting favorite songs and traffic information. At work, they may do a Google search a couple of times, check in with the online version of *The New York Times,* CNN, *USA Today,* or *Sports Illustrated,* and print out Mapquest directions to a restaurant that was recommended by an online city guide. After dinner, there will be several more hours of watching TV before going to sleep.

Throughout this unremarkable day, few will be aware of how many "free" services they have utilized. Underwriting these cashless transactions is the $350 billion a year companies pay for the opportunity to get your attention for from ten to sixty seconds in order to show you an advertisement for their product. In the jargon of the trade, they are competing for "eyeballs," even though they only expect to influence at most a few people out of each 1,000 they reach with their ads.[69]

The costs of advertising are borne by consumers indirectly in the form of higher prices for the goods that are being advertised. At first glance, it may seem odd that you are paying to be convinced what to

---

[69] Young people are an especially critical target audience because they are more likely to be swayed, not yet having developed brand loyalties.

buy. But from the producer's point of view, advertising is as much a necessary expense as buying the raw materials and fabricating the product. In a very competitive marketplace, it is advertising that helps convince consumers to buy your product rather than your competitor's product. And it is the final sale that validates your decision to create the company and your products.

In our daily lives, we are accustomed to most economic transactions being done with money: We get paid a salary; we buy goods from the store and pay our mortgages; we save money in retirement accounts so that we will have money when we are not working. These everyday events are actually the result of a long historical process that began with money being used only for trading a very limited number of goods and very few people working for wages.

While ubiquitous money facilitates modern transactions, the use of money also adds a layer of confusion about how economies really work.

One way to understand the structure of the economy and to build a functional approach to classifying labor is to start at the margins of the economy and work toward the center. Consider, for example, the plight of the non–Eskimo, back-country inhabitants of the Alaskan wilderness. These people have forsaken the conveniences of modern America for solitude and deep connection to the land. They are mostly self-reliant, doing their own hunting, fishing, and gardening, while building and maintaining their own homes.

Nonetheless, these back-country Alaskans depend on the outside world in many ways. While some may fashion bows and arrows to hunt, the majority buy and use the much more effective firearms. Similarly, it is easier to purchase flour and other staples (e.g., nails, paper, wire, etc.) that are hard to grow or produce and for which there are no easy substitutes. They get these provisions, equipment, and even fuel and parts for their snowmobiles on periodic trips to town. Their mail is delivered monthly by plane, and children are taught during the periodic visits of a teacher; in winter, both the teacher and the pilot stay the night.

Their economic interactions with the outside world are conducted in cash, requiring a source of income, often earned selling furs, food, and/or crafts. This lack of complete self-sufficiency means that they engage in the marketplace by bringing "tradable goods" to earn money to pay for those items that are difficult to produce for themselves. Obviously, people make choices regarding their degree of self-sufficiency, which defines the effort needed to generate goods for trade. The actions of those at the edges of our economy personify the concept of division of labor. The choice these consumers face is either to produce something themselves, forgo consumption, or work at something that can be traded with others for cash to purchase items in town. Choosing to produce for the market represents their work "specialization" beyond meeting their consumption needs.

The distinction between being self-sufficient and producing tradable items is clear for people who live in the backwoods, but it is also a choice made by wage earners in metropolitan areas. We actually have a lot of choices between working more and paying for services. Do we do our own housecleaning or hire a maid or an outside service? Do we prepare our own meals or eat out? Do we take care of our children or hire a nanny? Do we rake the leaves and cut the grass or hire someone to do these chores? While these choices face everyone, the wealthy, not surprisingly, are the biggest consumers of these "maintenance" services.

To further understand economic structures (that we often take for granted), let's continue to move from the periphery to the center. In its turn, small towns have general-purpose shops providing basic necessities such as groceries, gas, tools, hardware, and clothing. These shops are depositories of items needed by occasional travelers or by those who live in the countryside. They are usually staffed by the owners, with a little assistance from hired help. The meager profits, based on the markup from wholesale prices, support the overhead, the owner's salary, and wages for any employed workers.

It is not difficult to understand the economic importance of this sales function. Direct barter or even direct buying from the original producer is much too cumbersome and inefficient. These retail shops provide an intermediary role that facilitates the flow of goods to the country residents, and a destination for the tradable goods that those residents produce. Even though sales workers do not produce anything themselves, they are an integral link in the overall division of labor that ties producers to consumers. In essence, most small retail shops provide a service rather than act as a direct producer.

As towns grow in size and serve ever larger populations and wider geographic areas, the level of specialization grows accordingly. In addition to a growing variety of stores with more specialized goods for sale, there are now barber and beauty shops, hotels, restaurants, repair shops, doctors and hospitals, lawyers, and entertainment facilities (e.g., bars, movie houses, bowling alleys, etc.). The economic functions of the town are now many, serving local residents, business travelers, tourists, and specialized service providers to smaller towns.

The movement to cities is reflected in the size of the enterprises; instead of the solitary producer, there are multiperson work sites and factories. As Adam Smith so vividly described in the production of pins, an internal division of labor is much more efficient than simply reproducing an equal number of independent producers. The larger scale of production makes the use of machinery more economical. In this case, tradable goods are not furs and other items extracted from the land but manufactured output. And the money generated is not just for the isolated individual, but for the collective enterprise.

Within manufacturing enterprises there is much more diversity than first appears to be the case. The process of production may be simple for the back-country Alaskan hunting and selling furs, but grows in complexity as firms become larger. The role of the owner expands to include supervision of their employees, bargaining over wages and working conditions, marketing, raising financing, arranging transportation of the goods to market, and devising strategic short- and long-term planning.

Most of these tasks are required by all producers, including the solitary hunter, but gain in significance as the size of the company grows. In the largest firms, there are separate legal departments, sales forces, and layers of management from the president to the line supervisor. Smaller firms contract out for many of these tasks because key managers are not skilled enough. As a result, a variety of consultants and firms providing legal services, advertising, accounting, etc., have developed to fill this niche. Over the last thirty years, these "business-to-business" services have been one of the fastest-growing sectors of the economy.

As economic activity grows, individuals and even families no longer desire or are able to manage and finance them alone. The separation of ownership and management leads to new kinds of economic units. Companies are now owned by stockholders who, in turn, are represented by a board of directors. These directors are themselves neither the direct managers nor the majority owners of the firm. The solitary producer is replaced by a network of specialists with an extensive differentiation of tasks. The value of the tradable good is now shared by all of the participants including the absentee owners. Instead of the money flowing directly to the single producer, there are now allocations for wages for workers, salaries for managers, profits for owners, and retained earnings for future growth.

The growing complexity of production is mirrored by a more intricate social fabric. The public sector performs a myriad of functions: maintaining a legal and financial system; providing education from kindergarten to postgraduate level; providing for social stability with police, fire departments, and prisons; creating and enforcing overall regulation; and even creating systems to take care of the elderly, sick, and impoverished. In addition to the public administration, nonprofit institutions, membership organizations, unions, religious institutions, and social service agencies perform a coordinating/societal support role in education, health care, and other social services.

Finally, a series of economic and legal institutions have developed to facilitate economic and political transactions: banks provide credit and finances; legislatures pass laws; lawyers write contracts; disputes are litigated in courts; insurance companies pool risks; and other specialized actors facilitate the flow of goods and commerce.

Over time, business and societal coordinating functions are more and more the lifeblood of modern economies. The large downtown office towers are the home of banks, insurance companies, lawyers' offices, and the like. They serve not only their local region, but tend to provide services to concerns in smaller cities. These activities represent one of the largest tradable goods of big cities vis-à-vis smaller cities and the rest of the world. There is a hierarchy among cities in which large cities perform functions for smaller ones that in turn buy more sophisticated professional services from yet larger cities.

This tracing of economic activity from the isolated back-country trapper to the central business office district roughly approximates the evolution of modern economies. There has been a relentless march of an increased application of scientific principles to production (often set in motion by military needs). In eighteenth-century Europe, productivity in agriculture finally reached the point where it could support a large urban population. The ensuing inventions around power devices (steam, then electricity) and structural elements (beginning with iron) permitted increases in the scale of production. Advances in transportation (railroads and steam-powered ships) and communication (telegraph and telephone) facilitated the geographic expansion of markets. And as these technologies were developed and placed into production, nation building (often in midst of war) and new social institutions (banking, insurance, etc.) formed to accommodate new needs.

As capitalism matured, fewer and fewer people were tied to the land and the high level of self-sufficiency that goes with rural life. More consumer functions were commoditized with the growth in the division of labor. With each advance in productivity, mankind moved up the hierarchy from basic consumer necessities to more discretionary items. What were once luxuries (e.g., first sugar, and later automobiles) became basic items in most people's lives. Over time, the highest productivity gains have been made in the production of goods, freeing up labor to provide more consumer services, especially in health care and recreation (e.g., travel, performing arts, spectator sports, athletics including sports clubs, and other entertainment activities).

With each step forward, the size and scope of the market has increased, permitting an ever finer division of labor, in particular, an increase in the relative size of managerial and coordinating activities. More people are engaged in managing a geographically disparate and internally complex production process. Furthermore, the marketing environment is very intense as each firm tries to distinguish it from others and to develop brand loyalty. More and more, the competition is over convenience, originality, and adaptation to changing tastes.

Is There Any Productivity Growth in Services?

The view that services are a drag on the economy is very deeply rooted. William Baumol, in a series of articles in the 1960s, identified "the cost disease," arguing that it was much harder for there to be productivity gains in services.[70] Two of his examples were musicians performing a Mozart concerto and mail being delivered twelve times a day in London in the middle of the nineteenth century. In the first example, it takes the same labor today to perform a live concert, while in the second case, the level of service today seems to be much less.

---

[70] For a full discussion of Baumol's arguments, see James Heilbrun, "Baumol's Cost Disease," Northampton, MA: Edward Elgar, 2003.

Let's look more closely. In the case of the Mozart recital, the original setting was a small, live performance for royalty or other major court figures. Today, to hear the performance live, we could go to Lincoln Center in New York City or another major concert hall. The price is reasonably high, but certainly affordable, for a sizeable proportion of the population. This is not as intimate as the drawing room of a noble or royal home, but it is accessible to a larger share of the population.

Furthermore, there are few limits on the options for enjoying classical music. In the last seventy-five years, there has been vast improvement in how we listen to recorded music—from early phonographic technology, to improvements in phonographic recordings and playback, to cassette tapes, to CDs, to improved CDs, to cheaper and better quality CDs, to digital recording systems, to Sony Walkman players and iPods. At each point in this evolution, there were leaps forward in cost reductions of the equipment needed for listening. Over time, the durability, the added convenience, and the improvement in the quality of sound reproduction meant that the music could be experienced by many more people.[71]

This dynamic process of music enjoyment is hardly defined by the twenty minutes it takes to play a specific Mozart composition. In fact, we should actually expand the horizon to make a real comparison over two centuries. The purpose of the Mozart recital is to entertain, so we should compare the entertainment options and prices available then to those available today. Using this perspective, the modern world has many more options available to a larger slice of the population.

Instead of just looking at the playing of music as an abstraction, we should focus on what is actually consumed and how it is delivered. Baumol has played a trick on us by narrowly choosing an example that was limited to the superelite as one to track economic progress through time.

The other example has similar flaws. The multiple daily delivery of mail in London ("proving" we are getting far worse mail service today) raises the issue of how much service was delivered and to whom. The underlying issue is really communication and not just one form of delivery. These multiple deliveries served a small segment of the popula-

---

[71] Baumol's cost disease does exist in the music industry and is evidenced in the high cost of live symphony orchestras with dozens of professional musicians. These activities are only viable with large charitable contributions.

tion relying on rapid communication. By this measure, technological progress has reduced costs and widened the market many times through new forms of communication ranging from telegraphs, telephones, faxes, answering machines, cellular phones, beepers, e-mail, and instant messaging.

The discussion of these examples shows that goods and services are much intermingled. For example, when we travel by air, we need planes, fuel, and airports. On the other hand, the costs of goods sold in stores is predominantly made up of services—sales, research, advertising, and management.

Technological progress is reflected in the array of new goods and effectively lower cost (as a share of our incomes) of old goods. But there has been a corresponding revolution in traditional services by integrating complementary products (e.g., faxes, phones, computers, etc.). It is absurd to look backward in time and think that somehow services were cheaper and more readily available.

Defining Five Functions

In an economy in which three-quarters of workers are in service industries, the service category is too broad to be analytically useful.[72] A better framework will allow us to avoid the negative stereotype of services with their supposed lack of good jobs. Further, if we are ever to understand what workers with postsecondary education do, we need to break free of the simplistic view of good jobs in manufacturing and dead-end jobs in services.

In the approach developed here, functions are defined as common

[72] The first paradigm shift in economics occurred in mid-eighteenth century in Europe, when agriculture and home production predominated. The French Physiocrats argued that only agriculture added to a nation's wealth and that manufacturing activities were barren (using up as many resources as was added). Starting with Adam Smith in the late eighteenth century, this distinction was dropped, and economists focused on the production and distribution of wealth, treating agricultural and manufacturing equally. By emphasizing the advantages of the division of labor and self-interest, arguments for free markets at home and abroad in goods and labor came to dominate economic thinking. Further, as the Industrial Revolution matured, manufacturing became viewed as the dominant economic activity with agriculture falling to a secondary role.

production activities.[73] Why should we focus on functions? Allocating employment by the primary industry of the firm can often distort or obscure the true nature of the work performed. For example, sales and management employment within manufacturing firms has grown to one-third of all jobs in these companies. With whom do managers and business sales representatives have more in common in terms of the pay and nature of work? Is it the factory workers or other business professionals in finance and management consulting companies? The answer is fairly obvious and our categories should reflect this. In fact, in large manufacturing companies, the administrative and sales offices are often located in separate facilities, far from where the production takes place.

Another example involves outsourcing: consider people employed by one of the world's largest temporary service firms, Manpower. When it places workers in factories for temporary periods of time, these workers are counted as part of the service sector, thus overstating service employment. Alternatively, when a firm like General Motors outsources management and accounting work, these workers may also not appear in the correct category of work.

The unique characteristic of the functional approach is that employment within the same firm is allocated into different categories based on the nature of the work. In a few cases, even the same job category is split between functions. Since construction foremen both do work and supervise others, these employees are split between doing manual work and being part of management. Or, consider communication services that serve both consumers and companies. To be consistent, these workers are split between high-end consumer services and business management.

The five functions are defined as follows.

1. Raw material production ("Primary Production")

The farm function represents all the direct labor in extracting raw materials from the land, sea, forests, and underground. Historically, we have only moved away from the countryside in the last century. As late as 1900, 40 percent of the labor force in the United States was still involved in agriculture. In less-developed countries today, as high as 75

---

[73] I developed this approach while employed by the Educational Testing Service. The original description and supporting data through 1995 were published as Anthony Carnevale and Stephen Rose, *Education for What? The New Office Economy,* (Princeton, N.J.: Educational Testing Service, 1998.)

percent of the population remains in rural settings, barely eking out a subsistence standard of living.

Our solitary Alaskan producer belongs in this category, as would all of the small farmers and independent producers in this country. But even in these industries, most employees work in medium and large concerns, and there is much more mechanization and use of new technologies. Along with the corporate farm, many of the extractive processes have been industrialized. Mining operations are structured very much like many factories while logging, in fact, is officially listed as a manufacturing industry. Nonetheless, these are extractive processes tied closely to natural resource development.

It should be noted that the purpose of this category is to isolate and identify the labor expended on direct production. Farm owners and managers and blue-collar supervisors in the other industries have the joint responsibility of doing the work and overseeing others. As a result, these workers are divided equally between direct productive work and management/supervision, with the latter half being assigned to the office function.

2. Industrial production ("Secondary Production")

This category, representing industrial production broadly, includes direct labor in manufacturing, construction, public utilities, and transporting and storing goods on their way to market. Since these traditional blue-collar jobs often require heavy lifting and physical exertion, they have been mainly performed by men. The isolated artisan has been replaced by large factories and work sites. The first workers to unionize in this country were skilled craftsmen in various trades in the second half of nineteenth century. By contrast, the wave of unionization under the banner of the CIO in the 1930s occurred among the less-skilled workers in these large factory settings.

Nonmanufacturing industrial employment consists of blue-collar workers in construction, public utilities, transportation, and wholesale industries. These industries have a similar work organization as the manufacturing companies and are paid at the level of high-wage manufacturing employees. Longshoremen, truck drivers, utility workers, and warehouse movers all have similar skills comparable to workers in construction and manufacturing.

This category also includes a few non–blue-collar workers, such as aircraft engineers who are intimately connected to the production processes. Furthermore, some CAD-CAM machine operators deal with highly sophisticated machinery and are now classified as technicians and technologists rather than skilled blue-collar workers. Finally, line supervisors are again split between performing production work and supervising, which is part of the fifth function.

3. Low-skilled services

The third category consists of workers with direct consumer contact that do not require highly specialized training or a massive physical capital base. In general, these personal contact jobs require the least skill and can be flexibly staffed by newcomers and part-timers. More than any other function, these jobs fit the image of dead-end jobs with little chance for high pay and mobility up the career ladder. Historically, these jobs have been often been held by women and men with the least education.

The jobs in this function usually have direct personal contact with the consumer, either in sales or services that do not require high skills. Not all of the jobs in this area are low paid. Some salesclerks in hardware stores and upscale clothing outlets earn considerably more than department-store clerks. Within the food service sector, McDonald's workers make just above the minimum wage while the waitstaff at elegant restaurants garner hefty tips at dinner and lunch. Finally, entertainment companies are staffed mainly by ushers and ticket takers, but also include those on the stage or on the ball field. While many in this latter group toil for low wages, the few stars shine brightly and command some of the highest pay in the country.

4. High-skilled services

The fourth function is similar to the third in involving direct personal consumption but the service now requires the effort of more skilled labor. Interestingly, these services, which have a number of higher-paid workers, have historically been organized by the government, nonprofit concerns, and regulated private industries. The two major professional services that fall into this category are health care and education.

The difference between these services and those in function three is highlighted by the nature of their workforces. In low-skilled services and retail, only 11 percent are managers or professionals, and 50 percent are operatives, service workers, or helpers. Education is the most professionalized of all industries with 61 percent of those employed being managers or professionals and only 16 percent being among the least-skilled. In health care, there are doctors and registered nurses but also licensed practical nurses and orderlies: 39 percent of the health care employees are managers or professionals, another 15 percent are medical technicians, with 32 percent falling among the least-skilled.

Personal transportation and communication employment do not fall clearly or easily into any category; they are neither a professional service nor a low-skilled personal service. Because there is so much physical capital requirement (e.g., phone lines, airplanes, trains, etc.), most of these workers have medium skills and moderate pay. Many of these work situations are similar to industrial workers but clearly no physical product is involved. So, the 1 percent of the labor force employed in this category (many more workers are involved in servicing other companies through trucking and business travel and communication) is allocated to this fourth category of higher-skilled services.

Another higher-skill service activity is performed by police and firefighters. Due to their unique characteristic of serving the public good, they have been historically subsumed in the public sector. In this approach, these workers are allocated to the high-skill service, while other public administration workers are included in the office category.

5. Office and other administrative activities[74]

The work of managing the overall affairs of business and government is diverse and grouped into five subcategories. First, the task of coordination and supervision in industries producing a good or performing a service consists of all managers and one-half of line supervisors in these companies. Second, the entire FIRE sector (finance, insurance, and real estate) is included. This is done because these functions fundamentally are about managing assets, be they personal or business. They are part of the large, somewhat hidden, intermediary business expenses of companies, while for individuals they represent a very different kind of "consumption" than either of the other two service functions.

---

[74] Office activites involve more mental than manual labor and could be considered the "brain" functions of the economy, While it is traditional to think of the brains (or "superstructure") as small relative to the body, we are now in an economy where coordinating labor is almost as large as the entire effort of producing goods and services.

The third component of this function represents business professionals employed in the managerial hierarchy. There are almost as many people employed here as in all of FIRE. The majority of these workers are sales representatives, accountants, and the like. But there are also one million science-related professionals who neither work in academia nor for manufacturing firms. These are often computer-related analysts servicing headquarters activities.

The fourth part of the coordinating function includes those employed in public administration. This is a coordinating function at the communal level. The largest component of public employment revolves around educational institutions (which are in the fourth function), with only one-third concerned with more purely administrative activities.

The last component consists of the support staff, primarily the army of clerical and administrative workers. Also included in this group are the janitors and other office help that are neither professionals, nor managers, nor clerical workers. These individuals are the least well-paid and only represent less than one-third of the overall employment in this function.

Before proceeding to the empirical analysis of the functional approach, it is interesting to note that each function is associated with specific types of workplaces and usually a few stands out.

- Farm and mines
- Factory, loading dock, and construction site
- Sales counter and restaurant
- Hospital and school
- Office

Tracking Functional Employment and Earnings

Figure 5.1 reveals several trends about the evolution of employment in the five functional sectors from 1960 to 2007. There is a nice symmetry in the changing employment shares over time: two functional areas declined, one remained constant, and two grew.

First, there was a marked decline in the share of employment in the

Figure 5.1: Shares of Functional Employment, 1960–2008

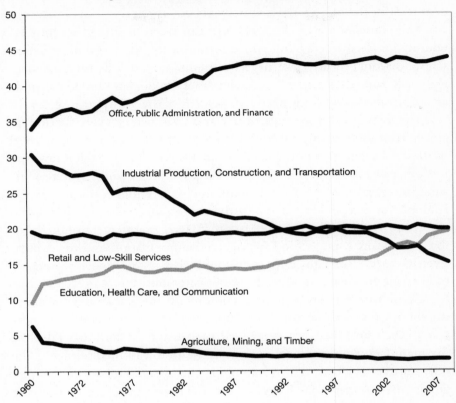

1960 Census and March Supplements to the Current Population Survey

manufacturing/construction function, from 30.5 percent of employment in 1960 to 18.4 percent in 2007. In fact, the absolute number of
jobs in these areas has remained at approximately 25 million since 1979,
despite the growth of the number employed of over 40 million. Certainly, the rate of decline has lessened in the last decade, and the share of
employment in this function will likely continue to decline very slowly
in the years ahead.

The nonmanufacturing part of this group—direct labor in construction, delivery, longshoring, and utilities—had only a minor decline
in its share of total employment. By contrast, the share of low-paid
manufacturing employment fell from 8.1 percent in 1960 to 2.7 percent

in 2005, and the share of high-paid manufacturing fell from 12.6 percent to 5.5 percent over these same years.

The consequence of the decline of this sector is that it has hit less-educated male workers hard. Among those who did not even get a high school diploma, nearly half have been employed in this function over the years studied. Those with a high school diploma but no postsecondary education account for nearly 40 percent of the jobs in this sector.

The other declining functional area was primary production in agriculture and mining. In 1960, 6.3 percent of workers were employed in these jobs, and this figure declined to 1.6 percent in 2007. Considering our past, when a large share of the population worked in agriculture, the current share of people employed in activities connected to the land is breathtakingly small. The astonishing increase in productivity in this sector is most evident in the fact that less than 1 percent of the labor force produces enough food for our entire population and for export. Even twenty years ago, one study found that it took more secretaries than farmers to bring food to the American table.

Third, in what may be a surprise for many, the employment share of the low-skill service sector has remained relatively constant at 20 percent of the labor force. Many people have taken it on faith that a declining manufacturing sector must mean a rise in low-skilled services. The only indirect evidence of this is found in the biennial report on ten-year employment projections. It appears that the fastest-growing job titles are low-skilled service jobs. But this "fact" is based on the anomaly that most job titles are very finely defined—e.g., managers in seven different industry categories—while job titles among service jobs are broad and consequently have many more workers.

Fourth, the office sector rose in importance from employing 34 percent of employees in 1960 to 43 percent in 2007. This sector grew steadily through 1988 and then leveled off with its share of employment varying slightly around 43 percent. Part of the leveling off was the decline in the share of clerical workers associated with the increased use of computers. This decline offset the slight increase in the years prior to 1988. Furthermore, another subcomponent of this sector that had a constant share of overall employment was public administration (2005 employment of 4 percent of the labor force). This means that all the growth in this sector was due to expansion in the employment of managers, sales representatives, stockbrokers, and other professional workers.

Fifth, there was nearly a doubling in the share of employment in high-skilled services (from 9.7 percent in 1960 to 18.4 percent in 2007—a level that almost equaled that of blue-collar employment in manufacturing and construction). Most of this growth was due to the huge expansion in the health care sector. The number of jobs in education grew quickly in the 1960s and then remained fairly steady at 8 percent of overall employment. Similarly, the number of police and fire jobs edged up slowly over these years to 1.3 percent of employment.

Finally, another way to look at the economic impacts of the five functions is to measure the shares of total earnings rather than just employment. Figure 5.2 tracks the earnings in each of the functions, showing the dominance of the office sector. Since 1986, workers in this sector accounted for more than 50 percent of all earnings in the economy. This reflected their increasing numbers, higher than average pay, and the increasing premium of being in these jobs.

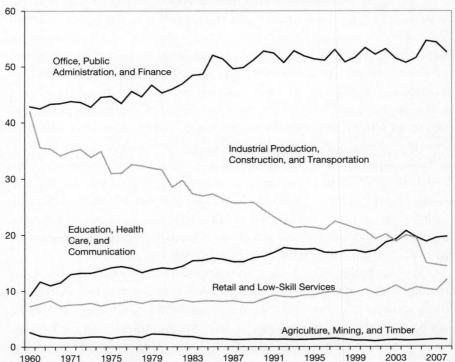

Figure 5.2: Shares of Earnings by Functional Area, 1959–2008

1960 Census and March Supplements to the Current Population Survey

By contrast, the share of earnings of manual workers in manufacturing and related industries was cut in half—from 34 percent in 1960 to less than 17 percent in 2005. This decline is larger than the decline in their employment share because the relative earnings of workers in this sector dropped as well. In 1960, workers in this functional category earned 13 percent above the average of all workers; by 2005, they earned 5 percent less than the average.

What is truly astonishing is the relationship of total earnings in the factory sector versus the high-skilled service sector. In 1960, over a third of earnings were in the former and less than 10 percent were in the latter. By 2005, the share of total earnings in high-skilled services was 18.7 percent while the share of earnings in manufacturing/construction was 16.7 percent.

A Changing Workforce

The changing functional distribution drives the kind of jobs that are available, but, to easily understand this in terms of the good jobs/bad jobs debate, another methodology is needed. The Department of Labor has developed an elaborate occupational code that divides types of work into various categories: managers, professional and technical, administrative support and sales, skilled blue-collar, less-skilled blue-collar, service, and farmers/laborers. These major occupational categories seem self-evident but are less so when looked at more closely. For example, consider the following list of occupations: accountants, musicians, airplane pilots, and stockbrokers. Many people would probably consider all of these professional jobs because of their pay and educational requirements. However, of these, only musicians are officially categorized as professionals, while all of the others are put in different categories: Accountants are placed with managers, airplane pilots with technicians, and stockbrokers with other sales workers.

So, while the official categories appear to represent a hierarchical listing of jobs, it is not, and occupations with high and low skills, and high and low pay, have been lumped together. Thus, for our purposes, we have come up with simpler and more commonsense categorizations. In particular, we have tried to remedy four major incongruities in the official code where occupations with very different pay and educational requirements are combined together. In the official code:

1. Managers at fast-food restaurants and retail establishments are not distinguished from corporate vice presidents; here, they are listed with nonprofessional supervisors.
2. Stock and real estate brokers are combined with salesclerks even though brokers must have college degrees, earn many times more, and work far longer hours than salesclerks. To correct this we include sales reps and brokers with other business professionals.
3. Police and firefighters—municipal employees who fit more in the craft model of organization and skill—are categorized as service workers along with janitors, fast-food workers, and health aides. In this categorization, these workers are assigned to the category that includes skilled blue-collar craft, machine, and repair workers.
4. Medical and science laboratory workers, operators of numerical control equipment, and paralegals are often grouped with managers and professionals. These workers are highly skilled but not to the same extent as professionals; nor do they have the same autonomy, pay, or education. As they more closely resemble other moderately paid workers such as supervisors, craft and repair workers, police, and firefighters, they are included in the same category.

To track the history of the quality of jobs, a simple three-tier division of jobs was created:

- A top tier ("elite jobs") of managerial and professional jobs, including company sales representatives;
- A middle tier of moderately skilled nonprofessional workers ("good jobs"). Job titles in this tier include direct supervisors, nonprofessional self-employed, construction craft and other skilled blue-collar workers, technicians, operators of CAD-CAM (computer-aided design/computer-aided manufacturing) and other intricate machines, clerical workers, police, firefighters, and licensed practical nurses; and
- A lower tier of less-skilled blue-collar and service workers ("less skilled jobs").

As Figure 5.3 shows, economic growth from 1960 through 2008 resulted in a large upgrading of the jobs in the economy. The share of workers in the top tier of occupations made a huge leap from 18 to 32 percent. This is the reason why all of the additional college grads were

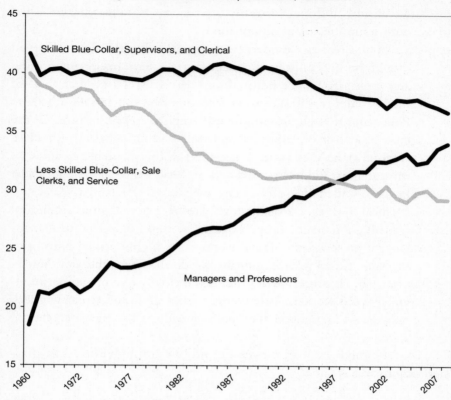

Figure 5.3: Shares of Occupation Tiers, 1960–2008

1960 Census and March Supplements of the Current Population Survey

not forced into jobs for which they were overeducated. By contrast, the largest reduction occurred at the bottom of the occupational hierarchy as the share of less skilled blue-collar, salesclerks, and service workers fell from 40 percent to 30 percent. The share of workers in the middle tier remained at the highest level of the three tiers but edged down from 42 percent to 38 percent.[75]

Although there was a shift to higher-end jobs, the shift in educational attainment was significantly greater. Consequently, there was a large amount of educational upgrading within jobs in each of the three grand tiers. Basically, in virtually every occupation, new hires had higher

[75] Erik Olin Wright and Rachel Dwyer also find an upgrading of jobs in "The Patterns of Job Expansions in the USA," *Socio-Economic Review* (2003)*1*, 289–325.

educational credentials than had previously been required. For example, insurance agents, midlevel company managers, and sales representatives (those who sell to business and not the public) used to only need a high school diploma to qualify for these positions. Now, very few workers in these positions have at least some college, most have a four-year degree, and a few have a graduate degree such as an MBA. Specifically, this meant that in 1960, 54 percent of those in elite jobs did not have a four-year degree and 36 percent had at most a high school diploma. By 2007, the share of those with only a high school diploma fell to 13 percent, and 65 percent of the workers in these jobs had a four-year degree.

The same upgrading occurred in occupations in the other tiers. In the middle tier in 1960, fully 48 percent did not have a high school diploma, while another 36 percent had a diploma but no postsecondary education. By 2007, there were few (9 percent) dropouts in these occupations and another 37 percent with a high school diploma as their highest educational attainment. This meant that over half of these middle-tier workers had some postsecondary education.

Even in the lowest tier, the workers have become better educated. In 1960, 95 percent of these workers had no postsecondary education, and 73 percent did not have even a high school diploma. By 2007, only 23 percent did not have a diploma in these jobs; 45 percent had a diploma; and 32 percent had some postsecondary education.

Conclusion

There have been three major trends in the employment market over the last fifty years:

- The share of manufacturing employment has declined;
- The share of workers with a postsecondary education has increased; and
- The share of elite managerial and professional jobs has risen while the share of low-skilled jobs has declined.

Surprisingly, there is no commonly accepted unifying narrative that easily explains these trends. Instead, many people have talked about the rise of services, emphasizing the low-end services of retail and fast-food outlets.

In this chapter, we saw that the new economy is based heavily on office and skilled-service jobs. This is consistent with the rise in the educational attainment of the workforce and is one of the factors that drove the rise in earnings inequality. In the functional approach, employment in the low-skilled sector has remained virtually steady throughout the period of 1960 to 2007. More to the point, as manufacturing employment and primary production in agriculture and mining have declined, these declines have been offset by increases in office/administrative work and high-skilled services, both of which employ large numbers of managers and professionals.

Looking around, we see that office buildings dominate the downtown landscape of all large cities and have even spread to the suburban areas that spread out as central city land prices soared. We have missed the obvious growth of these activities for three reasons. First, as noted above, our statistical agencies report employment on the basis of industrial categories, which have been developed and refined over the last seventy-five years. The focus on the major activity of a company hides the fact that there is a divide between front-office activities and direct production.

Second, our natural prejudice is to believe that economies must be about producing goods either for consumption or to be used in production. This seems commonsensical because goods production is seen as the essence of economic well-being and a high proportion of the labor force and the GNP have historically been related to producing and bringing goods to market. In the past, the fate of the large industrial giants seemed to dominate economic movements, as evidenced in the famous phrase, "What is good for GM is good for the country."

Third, there is a conceptual divide between manual and mental labor. The activities associated with manual labor are execution, production, and delivery, while mental labor activities include conception, planning, oversight, and administration. Some classical economists went so far as to label these latter activities as "unproductive" because they did not add value to the final product. Another crude description of these two different areas is denoted by the terms "base" and "superstructure."

The irony of this last juxtaposition is that while manual labor is presented as more important to the economy, it is mental labor that has always been much more highly compensated. The reason for this is that mental labor activities are more closely associated with the roles of ownership—decision-making and control. Thus, from a different perspective, it is mental labor that sets economic activities in motion and determines the key parameters of where and how much to produce. In other words, one decision may be more important to the fate of an enterprise than thousands of hours of labor on the line. Or, in terms of finance, a process that reduces borrowing costs by 25 percent can be the equivalent of a savings of 5 percent of earnings of your production workers.

Understanding the office economy also explains why it is futile to look for the "key driver" that will lead us out of the recovery. The focus in past recessions has always been on auto or housing or some other manufacturing sector. Yet, as the data presented here show, more and more economic activity is based on managing production than producing physical goods. The combination of office activities, health care, education, and other high-skill services is responsible for over 70 percent of earnings. Because these sectors are not directly affected by inventory cycles (overproducing items that lead to production cutbacks), the economic business cycles over the last forty years have been quite tame. It has taken a massive financial crisis to cause the severity of the current downturn, but once the effects of the financial paralysis are overcome, the positive cycle of increasing demand leading to more demand can occur based on the strength of the office and high-skilled service sectors.

CHAPTER 6

The Offshoring Myth: Jobs Are Disappearing Because of International Trade

MANY ARE CONVINCED that the emergence of China and India will lead to America's decline. Newspapers regularly report of companies closing plants in the United States to relocate to low-cost facilities in China, India, Mexico, and other less-developed countries. While this movement was previously limited to manufacturing jobs, there are now stories of many service jobs like call centers, accounting services, and IT jobs being outsourced as well.[76]

Ted Fishman, in his 2005 *China, Inc.: How the Rise in the Next Superpower Challenges America and the World,* sees an unprecedented leap in production in the world's most populous country and foresees China dominating in all economic areas in the next several decades. If this prediction is accurate, we clearly will not be living better after we rebound from our current economic downturn.

In an unusual twist, both liberal and conservative commentators alike are critical of the negative effects of trade on American workers. One is just as likely to hear how foreigners are taking away our jobs

[76] There have been many prognosticators in the past saying that either trade or automation would lead to workers being unable to find employment. See the Luddites, books by Stanley Aronowitz and William DiFazio, *The Jobless Future*: Sci-Tech and the Dogma of Work (Minneapolis: University of Minnesota Press, 1994) and Jeremy Rifkin's, *The End of Work: The Decline of the Global Labor Force and the Dawn of the Post-Market Era* (New York: Little Brown, 1995).

from conservative talk-show hosts as from union leaders. And who can forget Ross Perot's colorful imagery in the 1992 presidential election of the "great sucking sound" arising from the massive outflow of jobs to Mexico if the North American Free Trade Act (NAFTA) were to be enacted.

Running against the negative consequences of free trade is very popular within the Democratic Party. While President Clinton twisted arms to get the NAFTA passed in 1993, both his wife and Obama ran as opponents of NAFTA in the 2008 Democratic primaries. The fifteen Democratic house members who voted for the Central American Free Trade Act 2005 deal are derisively called the "CAFTA 15," and Senators Byron Dorgan of North Dakota and Sherrod Brown of Ohio each have books cataloging the purported costs of free trade to American workers, including lost jobs and lowered incomes.

Support for globalization and trade has been declining: Congress has failed to extend the President's trade promotion authority for many years: the DOHA round of trade talks (named for the capital of Qatar) were the first world trade initiative to fail; and the responses of many governments to the global economic crisis have been to restrict trade and provide government support to their domestic companies. Beyond blocking new agreements, some in Congress would go further and would renegotiate NAFTA and America's participation in the World Trade Organization (WTO).

While economists have traditionally been strong supporters of open trade, there have been a number of major defections who now argue that the old orthodoxy no longer applies. For example, Nobel Prize winner Paul Samuelson has criticized economists' "oversimple complacencies about globalization," and former Federal Reserve vice chairman Alan Blinder wrote that up to 40 million American jobs are at risk of being outsourced to equally productive, but cheaper, foreign labor.[77]

When people hear that 40 million jobs could be going overseas, many jump to the conclusion that an equal number will be thrown out of work in this country and unemployment will skyrocket. A group of distinguished economists (including Nobel Prize winner Kenneth Arrow) said that a realistic economic future for America would be one in

---

[77] Gregory Clark says that "With the march of technology, the size of the future American underclass dependent on public support [could be] 100 million" ("Tax and Spend or Face the Consequences," *Washington Post,* August 9, 2009).

which "future generations will be sorted into three groups of roughly equal size—a privileged professional and technical elite, a blue-collar working class, and the warehoused population of those unable to find jobs or even capable of productive employment."[78]

In this chapter, I will evaluate three distinct claims about the negative effects of trade: (a) the decline of the absolute number of jobs available—the imagery of Perot's "great sucking sound" as jobs leave the country; (b) the declining compensation in this country for less-skilled workers; and (c) the future pressures on America due to an increase in our foreign indebtedness as a result of trade deficits.[79]

Why Economists Favor Free International Trade

On its surface, trade seems to be a rather benign exchange of things of equal value that expands the division of labor and increases overall output. What is the alternative to trade—self-sufficiency? Specialization and the division of labor are the underpinning of trade in goods, services, and work for wages. We don't think twice about trade between different states. Indeed, federal law prohibits anything that creates barriers to interstate trade. Should we think twice about trade between countries?

For lots of people, the answer to this question is "yes." In fact, some of the earliest economic writings from 1500 to 1750 took the position that countries should sell more abroad than they purchased from abroad (this school of thought was called "mercantilism," and people today who believe in the negative effects of running a trade deficit are sometimes called "neo-mercantilists"). The logic was that the difference would be made up by payments of gold bullion and the country would be richer as a result of this surplus.

---

[78] Kenneth Arrow, Samuel Bowles, and Steven Durlauf, eds, *Meritocracy and Economic Inequality* (Princeton: Princeton University Press, 2000) p. xi.

[79] The arguments in this chapter were originally presented in William Dickens and Stephen Rose, "Blinder Baloney: Today's scare talk of job outsourcing is grossly exaggerated," *The International Economy,* October 2007.

To accomplish the goal of having more exports than imports, Mercantilists favored tariffs on foreign goods. One of the fallacies of this approach is that a surplus in one or several countries must be offset by deficits in other countries. Consequently, if all countries raise tariffs to try to run surpluses, trade will contract while most countries will end up with balanced trade accounts. Many economic historians have concluded that the Great Depression persisted much longer than it might have because of the presence of high tariffs protecting each country's domestic industry (e.g., the Smoot-Hawley Tariff Act of 1930 in the United States).

The evolution of "classical economics" as represented by Adam Smith's *The Wealth of Nations* (published in 1776) was a direct refutation of Mercantilism and focused on how specialization and the division of labor maximized production and consumption. In 1817, British economist David Ricardo introduced the concept of "comparative advantage" to show that countries that traded freely and specialized in what they were relatively best at producing would lead to higher consumption levels for all trading countries.[80]

The problem with international trade is that people can conceive of the jobs that might be available locally if the trade had not occurred. For example, in the 2009 stimulus bill, there was a provision that all of the steel used on new infrastructure projects had to be produced by American mills. Since American steel companies were only at 50 percent of their capacity, it seemed reasonable to provide them with extra work. Superficially the logic of this position makes a lot of sense until one realizes that other countries can retaliate against American protectionism of steel by making it harder for American firms like Caterpillar to sell their construction equipment abroad. So, we might end up trading a steel job for equipment-maker job, and face the possibility of increasing tit-for-tat trade restrictions.

---

[80] About twenty-five years ago, a series of young economists (including *New York Times* columnist and Nobel Prize winner Paul Krugman) showed that in a dynamic world in which first-movers could have a lasting advantage, it was possible that government encouragement of specific industries and protective tariffs could have a lasting positive effect. However, a decade later, most of the proponents backed away from this conclusion because there were no clear examples of successful interventions and there were mainly attempts to use the theory as a way of encouraging protectionism.

Another problem is that people really don't understand what is traded. Shoppers see that iPods and various other items in the store are "assembled in China" and assume that this means that the Chinese made these products. This is a false notion because a high proportion of the value of these products comes from the efforts and activities of American workers or workers from other advanced industrialized countries.

A group of researchers at the University of California at Irvine did a thorough breakdown of the costs of Apple iPods and found that the largest share of the value of this hi-tech product went to Apple in the form of royalties (used to fund new research and products) and that the retail outlets in America took in the second largest share.[81] Apple licensed some technology from Japan, leaving relatively little of the work to be done by Chinese workers. So in this case "assembled in China" means that less than 2 percent of the final price goes to China.

In essence, economists view trade like productivity growth since both lead to greater efficiencies that, in turn, lead to higher standards of living. It may be counterintuitive, but as will be argued below, the economy can absorb productivity rises and trade deficits without leading to higher unemployment.

The paradox of trade is that a few people are hurt very badly as they lose their jobs and significant amounts of income. Offsetting this loss is the larger overall gain of a lot of people having cheaper products and effectively higher incomes. The plight of the losers is very evident. Since these are deserving victims who have played by the rules and been hurt through no fault of their own, public opinion is sympathetic and willing to help these people.

In fact, their supporters have only focused on the negatives and have called the benefits of trade into question. For example, on a Madison, Wisconsin, radio talk show in 2006, the host pressed me on the decline in Milwaukee and other cities throughout the state as a result of increased job loss due to trade. Of course, he neglected to talk about the economy of his home city, which had seen fast growth and rising home values (because it was the home of the state government and a major university).

---

[81] Greg Linden, Kenneth L. Kraemer, and Jason Dedrick, "Who Captures Value in a Global Innovation System? The Case of Apple's iPod," Personal Computing Industry Center, University of California at Irvine, June 2007.

Without knowing the data, I guesstimated that total employment and income per person in Wisconsin had grown by at least 10 percent since the passage of NAFTA. My logic was that regions are more dynamic and capable of adaptation than individual workers. The common misperception is that whole states are in economic distress because of the loss of manufacturing jobs. This simply is not true: As Appendix 5 shows, all of the midwestern states that have been in the news because of lost manufacturing jobs experienced growth in employment in the post–NAFTA period (1993–2005) of at least 14 percent and economic growth (as measured by state product per person) of at least 15 percent.

The Economic Pie Keeps Growing

There are many people who doubt that the free market economy can continue to expand and absorb new workers. This is not surprising because capitalism is chaotic as it relies on millions of individual decisions to lead to stability and prosperity. The basic capitalist act—starting a business to make a profit—is based on a leap of faith that putting up money today will lead to more money in the future. The possibility that large numbers of people would no longer have the trust to make this gamble concerned early writers. In fact, many of the original classical economists predicted that economic "stagnation" was a constant danger.

Other writers were even more pessimistic and focused on the difference between owners and workers. Since workers only got a fraction of the value of what they produced, the question is, "Where is the effective consumer demand?" to purchase all of the output. An implicit assumption is that the owners are so rich that they do not consume enough because they already have so much. Or as former Secretary of Labor Robert Reich wrote in April 2008: "American consumers don't have the buying power they need to absorb the goods and services that the U.S. is capable of producing."[82]

In the 1950s, a variant of the stagnation argument focused on automation as something that would displace many jobs and lead to a high "structural" unemployment rate. These fears have not been realized because economies expand by producing new goods and services. In

[82] "Is the Game About To Stop?" In *The American Prospect,* April 2008, p. 44.

fact, economic growth is based on productivity advances that lead to fewer workers being able to produce the same amount of output. This is the key to understanding the huge historical transformation of the United States from an agricultural to an industrial economy. And today it still holds true—e.g., our total steel production is about at the same level that it was in 1965 but only one-fourth as many production workers are needed. Growth means that resources are freed up to produce other consumer goods.

The introduction of new products—cars, air travel, cell phones, computers, etc.—occurs because it takes fewer workers to produce what we consumed in the past. The trade pessimists focus on the jobs lost and do not understand that more new jobs are created as our population grows. At each stage, some commentators have claimed that we have hit a level of affluence that has satisfied all of our wants. Therefore, since our consumption level is assumed to be fixed, any productivity gains or increases in foreign trade should lead to rising unemployment.

The logic of an ever-expanding market is called Say's Law—supply creates its own demand.[83] Put another way, as more workers enter the economy, output and demand rise in tandem. This theory presents free markets as continuing to incorporate productivity gains to produce our former consumption basket for less, thus permitting the expansion of the market into new goods and of having old luxuries become available to more and more people. Before 1945, large surges up and down were common even though the long-run trend was one of substantial real growth over time. After 1945, the swings were much smaller; even the huge decline associated with the financial meltdown of 2008 would be considered a moderate decline by historic standards (assuming that there is not another big drop in 2010 or beyond).

In fact, the number of employed is always rising with population growth at the same time that increasing productivity makes it easier to produce what we formerly produced. Further, there have been a number of cases of large labor force surges that have not led to rising unemployment. For example:

---

[83] This "law" was presented by French economist Jean-Baptiste Say in 1803. This work was part of the development of classical economics, which argued for the viability of a market economy. Say's Law is meant to reflect long-term trends and does not rule out short-run disequilibria.

- In Western Europe, the initial incorporation of Spain and Portugal into the European Economic Union and then the incorporation of some of the former Eastern bloc countries did not lead to any identifiable employment losses or GDP contractions in any country;
- In the United States, the entrance of the baby boomers and women into the labor force added millions of new workers with no real negative effect on unemployment; and
- In France, migration into the country after the Algerian War did not increase France's unemployment rate.

The theory that "our needs have been totally met" has been proven wrong over and over again. Robert Frank in *Luxury Fever* shows the many consumer options for the very rich—from having built-in outdoor gas grills to ski vacations in Colorado, to guided tours around the world. Furthermore, in *The Harried Leisure Class*, Staffan Burenstam Linder argued that as people made more money they would tend to work longer because they would not pass up the extra earnings. Conversely, when not working, they would take expensive, experience-rich vacations with their added income. And indeed the highest-paid workers tend to work the longest hours.

The problem with economic growth and trade is that they are disruptive. As production techniques become more efficient it takes fewer workers to produce the same, and eventually greater, output. This means that workers are displaced from the old jobs and have to find new sources of employment. For older workers, this transition is very difficult because their skills may not be easily transferable to new occupations.

The clearest example of this is agriculture: as discussed previously, in 1800, 80 percent of workers were connected to the land; by 1900, this figure had fallen to 40 percent; and today it stands at 1 percent. When the majority of the work force is in agriculture, there is no time or money for TVs, no travel, no automobiles, etc. Economic growth means that labor is "freed up" to produce other things. At each moment, the transition is painful for those caught in the middle. Clearly, their old way of life is disappearing and their children will move on to other activities and other parts of the country. But unless we are economically satisfied now where we are, there are going to be more displacements in the future. Individually, it can be a painful process, but collectively, society has managed to adjust and prosper without generating higher levels of unemployment.

If employment is flexible then the worry that cheap producers will lead to unemployment is lessened. As a consequence, people flock to Walmart and other discount stores because the low prices are based on low-wage foreign workers producing standardized products. These products could be produced here but they would cost more. One careful study on the purchasing practices of low-income families shows that the standard of living of these low-income families is effectively higher because they disproportionally purchase low-cost, foreign-made items.[84] Another study by a key Obama economics adviser found that Walmart paid the prevailing wages in the areas in which its stores were located and tended to benefit low-income families with their low prices.[85]

Recent History on the Relationship Between Trade and the Size of the Labor Force

One thing that disturbs critics of current and past trade policies is that the United States is now running a large negative balance of trade in goods produced. As Figure 6.1 demonstrates, America ran annual trade deficits from the end of World War II through 1982. Since then, our trade deficit grew massively, especially since 1993.

Yet, the unemployment rate did not respond to the run-up of these huge deficits. During the years when imports were growing fastest, the unemployment rate declined (see Figure 6.2). In fact, comparing changes in trade deficits or imports with either changes in total employment or changes in the unemployment rate over the last forty years do not show that trade has had any negative employment effect. Rather, increasing imports are associated with employment gains and with declines in the

---

[84] Christian Broder and John Romalis, "Inequality and Prices: Does China Benefit the Poor in America," March 2008.
[85] Jason Furman, "Wal-Mart: A Progressive Success Story?" Center for American Progress, November 2005.

Figure 6.1: Trade Balance 1947–2008, Billions of Dollars

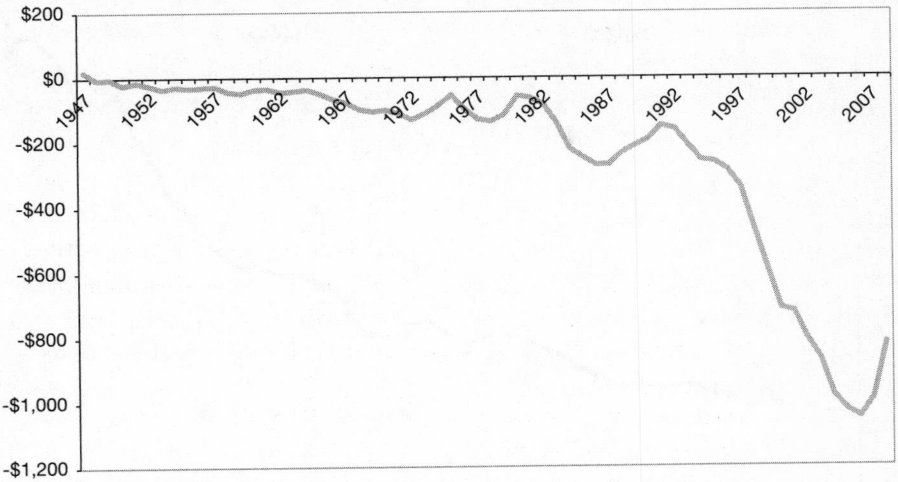

National Income and Product Accounts

unemployment rate (as they were in the late 1990s). A strong economy leads to both growing employment and increasing imports.

There are various measures to reflect the positive effects of trade on employment: imports and exports represent one-quarter of our GDP; one in twenty workers is employed by a foreign-owned firm; close to one in three workers is employed by a firm engaged in international trade; and the flow of money into the United States from foreigners buying U.S. Treasuries (see discussion below) adds liquidity to our financial system, which helps keep interest rates down and investments up.

What many people fail to appreciate is how dynamic our economy is. In any given month in 2003 through 2005, about 5 million workers severed an employment relationship (most voluntarily) with their employers. At the same time, there were approximately 5.1 million new hires. Thus, over the course of a typical year, there were about 60 million people leaving jobs and approximately 60 million people starting new ones. In the current recession, the number of workers leaving jobs is down to 3.5 million workers a month while the number of new hires in 2009 was 3.2 million workers.

This number is inflated by the multiple moves in and out of the labor force by teens and other marginal workers—it is estimated that

Figure 6.2: Share of Imports Versus Unemployment Rate, 1947–2008

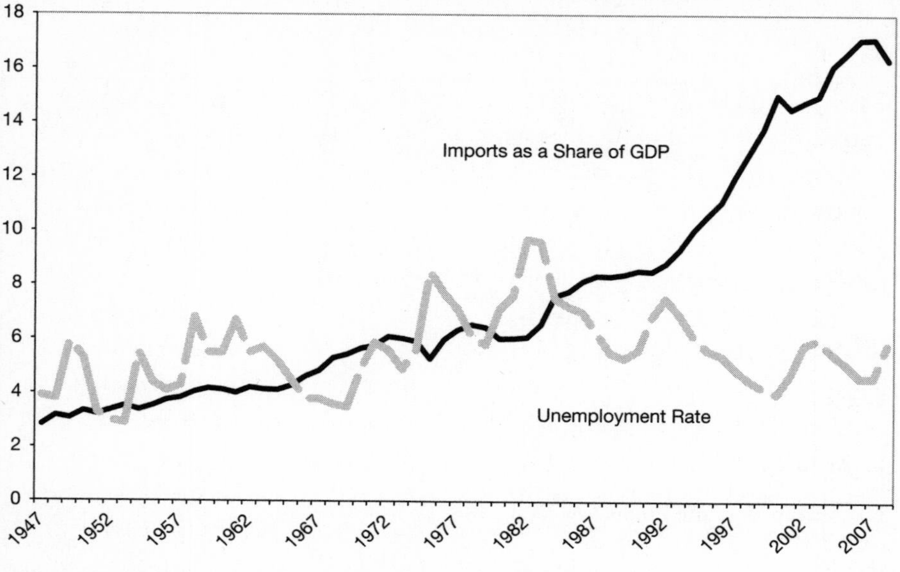

Bureau of Economic Analysis and Bureau of Labor Statistics

there is an 100 percent employee turnover at most fast-food outlets over the course of a year even though the total number of employed at each store remains constant month in and month out. If we focus just on positions, about 30 million jobs are created and eliminated each year. Another relevant observation is that about 70 percent of workers who have a specific job at the beginning of the year will still be employed by the same company at the end of the year.

Ultimately, the size of our national economy is determined by the skills of our workforce, the technology that firms use, and our open product and capital markets. While history has shown that tight monetary policy can destabilize an economy, central banks have learned this lesson and provide enough liquidity to ensure high levels of employment. There are no data for any country in the world for any period of time in the last sixty years that show total employment falling because of increased trade. The notion that trade can lead to job loss is based on a narrow focus on those individuals who lost their jobs and not on an analysis of the economy as a whole.

International Competitiveness and the Fallacy of the "Race to the Bottom"

The argument that low-wage countries can outcompete high-wage countries is remarkably persistent considering that there is no evidence to support it. This is another example of how people can become fixated on one economic fact and not take in the whole picture. In this case, the argument is based on the simple logical progression—low wages lead to low prices, which in turn leads to bigger market share.[86]

Missing from this argument are the factors of productivity and the quality of the output. It is axiomatic that poor countries are poor because they have low productivity. In isolated cases, we can find factories with state-of-the-art production facilities. These are the exceptions as most factories in poor countries rely on relatively simple machinery and low-intensive production processes (often in plants using older technologies purchased from more advanced economies as their factories upgraded to newer technologies).

There are a number of hurdles that low-income countries must overcome to move up the development ladder. First, a large percentage of their workforce has no or low literacy skills; this limits their ability to read instructions and work complicated machines. Second, these countries have poor infrastructure, which increases costs and decreases the reliability of receiving inputs or getting final goods to market. Third, these countries have poorly functioning legal systems. Bribes are usually common and quality controls will often be ignored—for example, the

---

[86] Even in the United States, the race-to-the-bottom argument is not a good explanation for the relative growth in states over the last several decades. On the one hand, businesses have learned to pit states against each other by arguing that local taxes are too high. Rather than lose local employers, states have given businesses incentives (e.g., lower taxes or state-provided infrastructure enhancements) to either relocate or stay put. On the other hand, however, if we look at the economic record over the past decades, there is only a little convergence between high-income and low-income states. The low-tax Southern states continue to have the lowest incomes per person while the high-tax states of the Northeast continue to have the highest incomes per person. The growth of the Sunbelt states is not so much a result of lower taxes but is a movement of people to places with warmer climates made more livable by advances in air-conditioning.

2008 Chinese scandals of lead paint in children's toys and the harmful contaminants found in milk and milk products. Fourth, whistleblowers who expose their companies (especially those from the United States and Europe) to the charges of running sweatshops and treating their workers (often young women) like slaves in violations of laws and norms of the destination markets are often treated badly.

In response to these problems, some First-World activists have demanded that free trade pacts adopt "labor standards" that include a minimum wage. While certainly motivated by good intentions, one cannot just mandate that countries jump up the development ladder. Not surprisingly, labor organizations in many developing countries have opposed labor standards because they feel that this would lead to massive job losses. Jagdish Bhagwati, in his 2004 book *In Defense of Globalization,* highlights this paradox but then grudging admits that that First-World lobbying groups help to minimize the worst labor abuses occurring in underdeveloped countries.

The race-to-the-bottom argument is another version of the claim that Americans cannot compete in today's globalized world and this is evident because we have a huge trade deficit. As will be discussed below, the trade deficit is driven by the balance of capital movements, which affects the exchange rate of the dollar. In terms of international competitiveness, the World Economic Forum in Switzerland since 1979 has published a biennial *Global Competitiveness Report.* A team of over 100 researchers in dozens of countries collaborates in rating each country on twelve pillars of competitiveness (which they define as "the set of institutions, policies, and factors that determine the level of productivity of a country)." The twelve pillars are organized into three grand areas: factor-driven economies, efficiency-driven economies, and innovation-driven economies.

A score for each of the twelve factors is created (the Global Competitive Index or GCI) for each country and these scores are added in a single competitiveness rating. Although individual researchers would disagree on many of weighting factors, this endeavor represents the most elaborate and the most continuing analysis of any source. In its 2008–2009 report, the United States had the highest GCI, as it has had for the most of the years that the index has been computed. The reason for America's continued strength in this rating revolves around its large lead in innovation-driven factors. Here is the 2008–2009 report's summary of America's top position:

Notwithstanding the present financial crisis, the United States continues to be the most competitive economy in the world, a position it has held for several years. This is because the country is endowed with many structural features that make its economy extremely productive and that place it on a strong footing to ride out business cycle shifts and economic shocks. Thus, despite rising concerns about the soundness of the banking sector and macroeconomic weaknesses, the country's many other strengths continue to make it a very productive environment (p. 8).

A year later in its Global Competitiveness Report, 2009–2010, more weight was given to the financial crisis and Switzerland edged out the U.S. for the top spot.[87]

Another global measure of economic strength has been created by the Organization for Economic Cooperation and Development (OECD), a Paris-based body consisting of the thirty most industrialized countries in the world. Since exchange rates vary so widely from year to year, researchers have developed a "purchasing power parity" index to compare average incomes across countries. Once again, the United States has led the way for a number of years. In 2006 (the last year that data were available), our major competitors were significantly behind the U.S. level: Britain (−24%), Japan (−25%) Germany (−27%), France (−29%), and Italy (−35%).

Finally, there is the issue of whether American leadership in science and technology (S&T) is slipping. In 2006, the Committee on Prospering in the Global Economy of the 21st Century of the National Academy of Sciences published a 500-page treatise calling for urgent action to avoid "the scientific and technological building blocks critical to our economic leadership [from] eroding at a time when many other nations are gathering strength."[88] Concerns about this issue prompted the Office of the Secretary of Defense to commission a study from the Rand Corporation to evaluate the state of the United States's technical prowess

---

[87] IMD, another Swiss-based group, publishes a *World Competitiveness Yearbook*. In its 2009 report, America was also rated first by a substantial margin over its European competitors; in 2010, the United States dropped to third behind Sweden and Denmark.

[88] *Rising Above the Gathering Storm: Energizing and Employing America for a Brighter Economic Future,* Washington, D.C.: National Academies Press, p. 3.

now and in the future. Their 2008 report, "U.S. Competitiveness in Science and Technology," was based on a comprehensive review of the literature and a 2007 conference with dozens of expert presentations. The report concludes that, "In short, our assessment of the measures we have examined indicates that the U.S. S&T enterprise is performing well. We find that the United States leads the world in S&T and has kept pace or grown faster than the rest of the world in many measures of S&T" (p. xxiii).

To say that we are ahead of other countries does not mean that we shouldn't do more in this area—it just means that the alarmist claims are overblown.

Can China and India Really Provide Everything That We Consume?

While all of these data are fine in explaining the past, others say the rules of the global economy have changed with the emergence of China and India. These countries are so large that they can produce enough for the whole world. This argument fails for two important reasons.

First, despite their huge populations, China and India do not have a supply of adequate labor. There have been so many tall tales of how much they can do that one forgets that these are underdeveloped countries with huge pockets of rural poverty. In 2006, there were stories of how skilled services were next in line to be outsourced: Given the ease with which X-rays and MRIs could be sent over the net, the outsourcing of the diagnostic services of radiologists to India was supposedly on the rise.[89] Shortly after these stories appeared I was at parties where people cited this new "fact" by saying that one-half of all radiological readings were now being done outside the United States.

This story is indicative of how false information leads to fantastic prognoses of the future. In response to the original news stories, two researchers at MIT did a careful analysis of this specific case and found that fifteen radiologists in India had been engaged in reading X-rays or MRIs for American patients.[90] They investigated further as to whether

[89] See Robert Stein, "Hospital Services Performed Overseas," *Washington Post,* April 24, 2005.
[90] Frank Levy and Kyoung-Hee Yu, "Offshoring Radiology Services to India,"

this was just the beginning of a movement and concluded that there was little chance that Indian radiologists would perform more than a tiny fraction of U.S. radiological readings. The reasons involved several factors: there were just too few highly trained specialists in India; there was a huge demand for their services within their own country; and there were constant upgrades in how radiological scans were evaluated so the technique was constantly changing and it was very important for radiologists to interact with their colleagues.

Another repeated story is that 300,000 engineers graduate each year from Chinese universities. The impression is that soon they will be at the leading edge of every industry. Of course, this 300,000 figure includes graduates from what we would consider to be junior-college technical programs. These are not the kind of workers that are going to make China a juggernaut in the auto industry, as some proclaim. Instead, at the 2007 Shanghai auto show, it was noted that there were virtually no new auto designs from Chinese companies. In addition, the target date for when China will be able to export cars in bulk to the American market has been pushed back to 2020 at the earliest.

India offers a similar story. That country has a handful of world-class universities, but the quality declines dramatically after that. A lot of workers at the call centers have bachelor's degrees and there are now reports that the employers who cater to the American market are having difficulty recruiting enough "skilled" workers.

Also missing in this discussion of producing for export is the requirement for China and India to produce for themselves. If these countries are going to be as successful as many people project, then they first must move up the developmental ladder and create their own middle-income classes. Because these countries have such large populations, even the relatively small percent of the population that has moved into the middle class represents many millions of people. As the fruits of their success become evident, there is every reason to believe that wages for many other workers will edge up as well.

This is a good thing. But these increasing incomes will translate into higher earnings and will force China and India to refocus their development model to one more geared to satisfying the needs of their own domestic markets.

Industrial Performance Center, Massachusetts Institute of Technology, September 2006.

The American International
Capital Position

The second problem with the scenario that two billion low-wage highly productive workers will lead to massive job losses in the United States is the failure to understand that trade is an exchange of equals and that the flow of money in and out of the country must be in balance. While we have run negative trade balances over the last twenty-five years, *we have run a neutral balance of payments.*

The movement of payments for goods and services across international boundaries is just one of three flows of money. The other two flows involve capital transactions. On the one hand, profits and bond payments flow to the holders of assets held outside one's country. On the other hand, there are purchases of stock, government and corporate bonds, and direct investment for plants, equipment, and purchases of foreign countries (the balance between the capital inflows and outflows is called the "current account").

The flipside of the United States running consistent trade deficits is that it has had a capital account surplus. As Figure 6.3 shows, from 1976 to 1986, Americans had more investments abroad than foreigners had investments here. This is consistent with the position of the United States having the world's strongest economy and being in a position to expand its production activities to other countries. Beginning from a position of parity in 1986, by 2006, foreigners owned nearly $2.5 trillion more in U.S. assets than Americans owned of foreign assets.

The biggest difference was driven by the $4 trillion of American public securities (e.g., U.S. Treasury bonds, bills, and currency, and securities issued by other public agencies including state and local bonds) held by foreign investors. By contrast, Americans held very few government securities from other countries. The other two components of our net capital position are foreign direct investment (the value of company plants and facilities in other countries) and portfolio investment (stock and bonds of another country—e.g., when you invest in a mutual fund that invests abroad). While direct investments of American companies overseas are slightly larger than direct investment by foreigners in the United States ($3.3 trillion versus $2.4 trillion), portfolio investment was very much tilted to the United States: Americans had $5.2 trillion

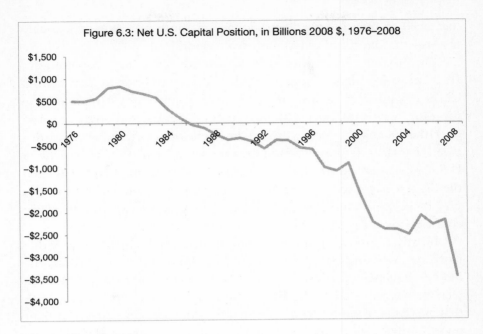

Figure 6.3: Net U.S. Capital Position, in Billions 2008 $, 1976–2008

U. S. Treasury Department

of foreign corporate stocks and bonds versus just $2.8 trillion of foreign holdings of American stock.

Another way to describe the accumulated American capital deficit is to say that we have become the world's largest "debtor nation." Since some of this money comes from China and other less-developed country, there has been a net flow of capital from the poor countries to the richest one. While this "reverse flow" seems odd, no one is putting a gun to the heads of foreign investors, so they must have good reasons for investing here.

On the one hand, there are lots of good business reasons for foreigners to invest here. For example, firms that sell a lot in the United States—e.g., Japanese automakers—find that there are advantages to being close to one's market as well as the positive political considerations to counter the claim that good jobs are being exported overseas when you buy a foreign product. "Buy American" can be interpreted to mean buy a Japanese car made in the United States by American workers. Further, there are the normal diversifications in which investors buy stocks and bonds of other countries. This is particularly true of oil-exporting countries that need to recycle their "petrodollars" because of a lack of adequate investment opportunities in their own economies.

On the other hand, there is a distinct advantage for a foreign government to hold large amounts of U.S. Treasury bonds in their central banks as a bulwark against an attack on their currency. After watching successive crises in Russia, Mexico, Latin America, and Southeast Asia over the last twenty-five years, many developing countries have decided that the only sure way to avoid the same fate is to have a cache of U.S.-based assets on hand. In a variation on this theme, China has been the biggest buyer of U.S. Treasuries and many people interpret this as a way of keeping their currency value artificially low so that they can continue to be a mass supplier of low-cost goods.

Finally, China has followed an export-led development strategy that worked so well for Japan, South Korea, Singapore, and Taiwan. A surprising consequence of this strategy is that they have had to buy American securities with some of the profits from these sales. One might think that this money would be better used for domestic investment in their own countries and to increase the wages of their workers. Having made this choice to sacrifice internal consumption, they have enjoyed a very rapid growth of their economies.

Is the U.S. Debt Position a Ticking Time Bomb?

Some feel that these foreign claims on U.S. assets will burden us in the future with a "day of reckoning" when foreigners no longer have confidence in the dollar. Harvard economist Benjamin Friedman predicted just this in a 1988 book of the same title. In the second chapter entitled "America in Economic Decline," he argued that America would need four years of zero growth with productivity rising to rectify the debt that we ran up during the early 1980s. He thought it very likely that a lower standard of living "for ourselves and our children in the not too distant future" (p. 30) would follow.

Fortunately, this prediction turned out to be way off the mark, disproving the old theory that no country (even the one with the world's global reserve currency) could stay out of long-term capital balance for years on end. No one had conceived that poor countries would have capital surpluses while the richest country would be the largest net debtor. This failure was based on the inability to foresee the benefits of holding U.S. Treasury bonds as an insurance policy against future sudden currency declines.

But it is possible that the situation today is different because we have been running deficits for a long time, and because the deficits between 2003 and 2008 were particularly large (they have fallen in 2009). Yet, with the world's financial institutions on their brink of collapse in 2008, the U.S. dollar strengthened rather than declined because more people bought Treasury bonds. This "flight to quality" was remarkable and totally unexpected because the crisis as well as the highest concentration of bad assets were in America (This is the reason for the sharp falling line on Figure 6.3 between 2006 and 2008).

Even though this underscores the importance of the American economy, our debt position cannot just keep increasing. One of the checks on this is the downward pressure on the value of the dollar as countries cease building up ever more stockpiles of U.S. Treasuries. A cheaper dollar in turn causes exports to rise, imports to fall, and the current account deficit to shrink.

Another possible and more dire scenario—the "hard landing"—has been predicted by those who see a point where the holders of U.S. assets start to dump these assets and refuse to buy any more. The spark that may send off this run on the dollar is concern that a continuing decline in its value is effectively a partial default (you're getting less in your own currency than you invested). So, to avoid this fate, you will try to be the first to cash in your assets before the depreciation continues dramatically downward. This "first to the exit approach" is precisely how a bank run begins: once a run starts, the herd tends to follow.

The hard-landing school, however, has been around for a long time and there are several reasons we won't have a hard landing this time either. First, borrowers and lenders are inextricably linked, and lenders will be significantly hurt if the financial condition of the borrower is severely impaired. For example, if China were to try to sell its U.S. Treasuries quickly, the price would fall and the value of their dollar-based assets would go down dramatically. This might make sense if there were a chance that the United States would completely default on its obligations, but no one believes that this is possible.

The second reason why a hard landing is unlikely has to do with America's position as "buyer of last resort." The big exporting countries

(China, Germany, and Japan) rely on being able to sell lots of their output to the United States. If America is thrown into crisis for any reason, these countries suffer greatly. One sees this very clearly in the 2009 downturn. So it is very much in the interest of these exporting countries to nip any hard landing in the bud because a hard landing would lead to a rise in unemployment in their own countries.

Finally, the huge number of capital assets in the United States (estimated at $50 trillion) is another back stop against a hard landing. With a hard landing, the U.S. dollar declines and inflation rises. While this hits U.S. Treasuries particularly hard, foreigners could sell Treasuries and buy U.S. companies and stock. If there were a run on U.S. bonds, the trillions of dollars of assets that U.S. companies own overseas could be a stabilizing factor. During such a run, the value of the dollar would plummet and foreigners could rid themselves of their excess dollars (which they might be worried would lose yet more value) by offering very high prices for these American assets held abroad.

While the experience of the last couple of years has taught analysts to never say that a financial run can't happen, these safety valves make the hard landing scenario less likely. In addition, as the 2008 crisis has shown, when America declines, the rest of the world tends to decline more—like the old saying goes, "When the United States sneezes, other countries catch a cold." Consequently, any run on the dollar would raise the specter of a devastating worldwide economic collapse with no winners.

Trade and the Quality of Jobs

A simple methodology is chosen to see how the pay of jobs has changed during the years in which the trade deficit was rising: first, the labor market performance of prime-age (25–62) men and women are tracked separately; second, jobs are divided into four categories: low-pay (under $25,000 in 2007 dollars), low moderate pay (between $25,000 and $50,000), high moderate pay ($50,000 to $75,000), and high-pay (over $75,000); third, the distribution of jobs in the first period (1979) is compared with the distribution of the net new jobs created (the difference within each gender pay group between 2007 and 1979).

As Table 6.1 shows, the distribution of pay for prime-age men in 1979 differs greatly from the distribution of pay for the net new jobs with most of the new jobs being either low-pay (under $25,000) or high-pay (over $75,000). The growth among high-pay jobs is particularly large: only 10 percent of 1979 male workers earned more than $75,000 while the comparable figure among the net new jobs was 34 percent. At the bottom end of the labor force, 23 percent of the jobs were in the lowest pay category versus 36 percent among the new jobs. By contrast, moderate-paying jobs (between $25,000 and $75,000) represented 67 percent of male employment in 1979, but only 30 percent of the new jobs created.

TABLE 6.1
CHANGE IN JOBS BY EARNINGS CLASS, PRIME-AGE MALES, 2005 $

	Low (<$25,000)	Low Moderate ($25,000– $50,000)	High Moderate ($50,000– $75,000)	High (>$75,000)
1979	22.8	43.8	23.0	10.4
2005	26.7	37.8	18.0	17.5
New Jobs 1979 to 2005	35.9	23.4	6.2	34.4

1980 and 2006 March Supplements of the Current Population Survey

Table 6.2 presents parallel data for women workers. It is striking that less than 1 percent of female workers in 1979 earned more $75,000 in 2005 dollars (which would have been $30,000 in 1979 dollars); and only another 3 percent earned between $50,000 and $75,000. Thus, the highest paying jobs in 1979 were almost completely male: over 33 percent of men and only 3 percent of women workers were in the top two categories. By contrast, among the net new female jobs created since 1979, over a third (36 percent) were in the top two earnings categories. At the other end of spectrum, fully 61 percent of prime-age women workers in 1979 earned less than $25,000 while only 17 percent were in this earnings range among the net job gainers.

Even though female workers moved to higher paid jobs and new men's jobs were concentrated at the high and low end, the 2005 distribution of earnings still shows that men had much higher-paying jobs. In the lowest-paid category, there were more than 46 percent of women and fewer than 27 percent of men. By contrast, at the high jobs that paid more than $75,000, there were nearly three times as many men (17.5 percent to 6 percent).

TABLE 6.2
CHANGE IN JOBS BY EARNINGS CLASS,
PRIME-AGE FEMALES, 2005 $

	Low (<$25,000)	Low Moderate ($25,000–$50,000)	High Moderate ($50,000–$75,000)	High (>$75,000)
1979	60.7	27.6	2.8	0.5
2005	46.4	36.5	11.1	6.0
New Jobs				
1979 to 2005	17.2	46.4	22.6	13.8

1980 and 2006 March Supplements of the Current Population Survey

It is important to understand how labor markets operate. Over time, the distribution of pay changes because of two factors: the creation and loss of different job slots on the one hand and because of the change of pay within established jobs. Further, because of inflation, the real pay of workers can decline while the actual pay (or "nominal pay" as economists call it) can increase. So, very few declines in pay are due to actual pay cuts.

For women, their increased participation meant that they were gaining more seniority and, hence, higher real pay. Also, as they increasingly moved into job titles that had previously been denied to them, their employment distribution was much more weighted toward high-paying positions. Their increased job options put pressure on employers of traditional female jobs to raise wages as well. Consequently, a combination of factors led to women getting higher pay across the board.

For men, a less beneficial combination of factors affected their job prospects. While there was an expansion at the top end, there was great pressure on blue-collar jobs. From 1945 through 1965, American-based manufacturing companies were in a unique position because their major international competitors had been devastated in World War II. Profits were high despite the fact that unions were able to extract generous pay and benefits packages. Over time, increased competition from Japan, Western Europe, and from newly industrializing countries that developed low-wage platforms to produce standardized products, combined with productivity growth (in steel production, for example, the same production requires one-quarter the number of workers), caused employment in manufacturing to decline precipitously as a share of total employment in the economy.

Consequently, for men, the rise in low-paying jobs was not due to an increase in jobs that were very low-pay but to a decline in pay of jobs that were once more highly compensated. Table 6.3 gives the major job titles

TABLE 6.3
MAJOR OCCUPATIONS OF NET NEW JOBS, 1979 THROUGH 2005

Job Description	Male Jobs		Female Jobs	
	No. of New Jobs (in millions)	Share of All New Jobs %	No. of New Jobs (in millions)	Share of All New Jobs %
Business professionals	6.1	32	7.6	34
Self-employed, supervisors, and managers in sales and retail	3.9	21	2.8	13
Other Professionals and technicians	2.4	12	6.8	31
Blue-collar crafts, supervisors, police and fire	3.8	21	1.3	6
Low-skilled sales-clerks and service workers	2.7	14	3.5	16
Total	18.9	100	22.0	100

1980 and 2006 March Supplements of the Current Population Survey

for the employment increases that occurred from 1979 to 2005 (18.9 million for men and 22.3 million for women as the labor force went from 42.9 percent female in 1980 to 46.2 percent female in 2005). For both men and women, about one-third of the new jobs were in high-level business jobs—managers, sales representatives, stockbrokers, insurance agents, accountants, etc. Many of these slots were responsible for the sharp rise in employment in the highest earnings category.

Table 6.4 presents the same data from a slightly different approach. Because job titles had different numbers of incumbents in 1979, it was possible to have a large number of slots created even though the growth rate was low. Therefore, there are four categories in this exhibit based

TABLE 6.4
JOB GROWTH BY OCCUPATION TITLE

	Male Occupations	Female Occupations
Declining Share—absolute decline	Farmers and farm laborers	Factory workers, laborers, and farm workers
Declining Share—slower than average growth	Skilled blue collar, factory workers, laborers, clerical, and teachers	Clerical workers and salesclerks
Steady Share—grew at average rate	MDs, lawyers, blue-collar supervisors	Low-skilled service workers, skilled blue-collar workers
Increasing Share—faster than average growth	Business professionals, nonprofessional self-employed, sales and retail managers, police/fire, non-MD health professionals and technicians, and low-skilled salesclerks and service workers	All managerial and professional occupations, health technicians, sales and retail managers, and fire/police

1980 and 2006 March Supplements of the Current Population Survey

on the rate of job creation. With few exceptions, there was job growth in every occupational title, so the real difference was whether the growth rate was average or below or above average.

This table shows clearly that the highly paid managerial and professional jobs were big gainers relatively as well as absolutely. Therefore, there is no anomaly that the workforce had higher educational attainment because indeed there were expanding opportunities for these newly minted college graduates.

TABLE 6.5
CHANGE IN JOBS BY EARNINGS CLASS,
PRIME-AGE MALE HIGH-SCHOOL GRADS

	Low (<$25,000)	Low Moderate ($25,000–$50,000)	High Moderate ($50,000–$75,000)	High (>$75,000)
1979	21.5	48.9	24.3	5.4
New Jobs 1979 to 2005	87.0	29.0	−28.2	12.2
Difference	65.5	−19.9	−52.5	6.8

1980 and 2006 March Supplements of the Current Population Survey

In order to show the difficulties of workers who did not have any postsecondary education, Table 6.5 tracks the job growth by earnings class of male workers with just a high school diploma or GED. Remarkably, seven out of eight of the new jobs were in the low-pay category. This methodology results in negative net new jobs if the number of jobs in a category in the last year is less than it was in the first year. In this case, there are negative new jobs in both the moderate-pay categories, clearing reflecting the decline in reasonable-paying, often unionized, manufacturing jobs for men without postsecondary education. Finally, the growing number of high earners even affected those with low education (they were probably business owners), as the share of high-paying jobs increased a bit for this group.

There was a significant shift in the race and ethnic composition of the workforce. Since the concern is about the poor performance of male workers, Table 6.6 presents the median incomes by race/ethnicity of prime-age males. Overall, median male earnings fell by 1 percent (as opposed to a 54-percent increase of the female median). But this fall hides the facts that earnings went up for most of the race/ethnic groups: For Whites the gain was 4 percent; for Blacks it was 6.5 percent; and for Asians, it was nearly 15 percent. The fall in the earnings of Hispanic male workers was due to the large influx of low-earnings immigrants.

The reason that the earnings of the separate groups could mainly go up while the whole group declined is because there was a large demographic shift leading to the declining share of non-Hispanic Whites from 83 percent of workers in 1979, to 65 percent in 2005. Since the earnings of non-Whites are significantly below the earnings of Whites, the increasing shares of these groups tended to bring the median down.

Table 6.6
Median Earnings by Race/Ethnicity, Male Prime-Age Workers

	1979	2005	Change	1979	2005
			Composition of Work Force		
All	$40,370	$40,000	−0.9	100	100
Non-Hispanic White	$42,773	$44,388	3.8	83.3	65.4
Non-Hispanic Black	$28,160	$30,000	6.5	9.9	12.3
Hispanic	$29,156	$26,000	−10.8	5.0	15.1
Asian/Other	$34,888	$40,000	14.7	1.8	7.2

1980 and 2006 March Supplements of the Current Population Survey

Conclusion

In the late 1990s, Europeans were taken aback by the rise of computer applications and the success of the Internet and asked themselves: "Could Microsoft have been a European firm?" At the 1998 World Economic Forum in Davos, Switzerland, the consensus answer was "no" because Europeans liked to deal with old contacts and would have been loath to provide the funding and initial market for a new product like the personal computer.

This is one of the many indicators that explain why America is consistently rated as the world's most competitive economy and why it has the highest income per person. Consider, for example, what happened when the financial crisis exploded. Given that the problems originated in America and were most severe here, it would have been reasonable to assume that the dollar would fall in value and the economic downturn would have been greatest here as well.

Instead, the dollar rose in value as investors sought the safest place to park their money. The demand for short-term U.S. Treasury bonds was so great that the price was bid up to a point where the rate of return on this investment was virtually zero.[91] By contrast, foreign money exited such places as Eastern Europe, Russia, Southeast Asia, and other formerly high-growth economies, causing their currencies to lose over 25 percent of their value. Other high-fliers such as Ireland and Spain (which use the Euro) saw their economies decline dramatically.

When the global recession ends, economies throughout the world will rebound and first reach, and then surpass, their former output levels. In the 1980s, economist William Baumol talked about a "convergence club" in which the world's advanced economies tended to converge to a similar high standard of living. He also postulated that the United States was the leader of this club and would likely remain in that position for the foreseeable future.

This prediction was made at a time when many people thought that U.S. predominance was on the decline. The Japanese model, in particular, was highly praised as more efficient (witness the rising market

---

[91] Bonds are in effect loans made (in this case to the federal government) at a fixed maturity and rate of return. However, they also are bought and sold, so that higher demand results in a higher price paid, effectively lowering the rate of return (interest paid) as this is a fixed amount.

share of Japanese companies in the United States and the world auto market) and property in downtown Tokyo was selling for more than the combined value of all the property in California. Europe, too, was considered to be on the rise, and economist Lester Thurow predicted that the strengths of the new European Union would lead them to become economically stronger than America by the first decade of the twenty-first century.

From today's vantage point, Baumol's convergence club approach with America in the lead has been a much better predictor of events than the alternative scenarios. In fact, over time, more countries have moved up the development ladder to middle-income status.

Overall, the globalized economy has increased our and the world's standard of living. A trio of studies have estimated that the gains from international trade have increased our GDP by $1 trillion. This is due to direct effects (cheap products from less developed countries) and indirect effects (high quality products from advanced countries that have spurred on Americans to improve their own production techniques). The bottom line is that capitalism is a very dynamic system in which old industries decline in importance and new industries arise. For those caught in the whirlwinds of "creative destruction," the costs can be fatal, but overall the gains are much greater, and America has a series of unique capacities to ensure that it will thrive in the coming era.

In the midst of the global downturn, many countries, including the United States, have passed laws to help domestic industries, e.g., the requirement that stimulus money be used to purchase goods from U.S. firms. Certainly, the experiences of the Smoot-Hawley Tariff Act of 1930 show that protection begets protection and everyone is left worse off. Although domestic losers turn to their local governments for support, protective actions so far have been limited and met with warnings of the need to avoid a global trade war. This is a good thing, as lots of trade between countries is an integral part of the modern world and an integral part of a strong global recovery.

CHAPTER 7

Health, Wealth, and Retirement: The Myth that Employee Benefits Are Disappearing

FOR MANY, the financial crisis has deepened the fraying of the social safety net, a process that supposedly has been afoot since 1979 under both Republican and Democratic presidents. When America emerges from the financial crisis, some analysts claim that few people will be prepared for retirement, many people will not receive their full Social Security benefits, many families will have crushing levels of debt, fewer people will have access to adequate medical care, and many young people will be unable to pursue a college education. The only thing that can prevent this bleak future, according to these analysts, is the establishment of a "new social contract" to improve many Americans' standards of living.[92] So the strength of the recovery is based on implementing new policies that don't currently exist. Since few of these policies are likely to be implemented, then the recovery is projected to be weak.

Once again, a careful analysis of the trends reveals that the negativists have overstated their case. This chapter shows that health care spending has risen dramatically while new retirees will have slightly more income than previous retirees. But, because the population has aged, the amount spent on income transfers to the elderly is rising and will continue to rise as the huge age cohort of the baby boomers moves

[92] One book that brings these arguments together is Jacob Hacker's *The Great Risk Shift*.

into retirement. Consequently, the total societal amount of money spent on health care and retirement has been on a steep upward path. In turn, these added expenditures have put strains on private businesses and the economy to support these programs.

Given the complexities of the developments in the health care and retirement sectors, I'll discuss each area separately. Furthermore, since retirement involves savings and net worth, I'll talk about debt in the retirement section. Both the provision of health insurance and financing to support the elderly are provided jointly by public and company plans. All industrialized countries have a mix of public-private funding, but the U.S. system is more heavily weighted to plans connected to private employers. To better understand the evolution of the U.S. system, I'll present the history of how these health and retirement plans evolved.

Health Care

Health care is the 800-pound gorilla in the room because of its explosive growth, with total spending in 2007 reaching $2.2 trillion ($7,421 per person). The rising economic importance of health care has been very dramatic: Total spending on medical care was just 5 percent of the economy in 1960; by 1982, this figure had risen to 10 percent, and in 2007, it was 16.2 percent of GDP. While it seems clear that medical spending is going to rise to 20 percent of the economy, it is probable (because of the aging of baby boomers and the introduction of new technologies) that it will continue to rise to 25 percent of the economy by 2025.[93] There is nothing necessarily wrong with a highly productive economy spending this much on health care, but it does seem odd that health care would grow so large that it crowds out other forms of consumer expenditures.

Everyone agrees that something must be done to reform our health care system, but exactly what "that something is" is hotly debated. Part of the confusion is that there are two major issues in health care reform:

---

[93] The Congressional Budget Office ("Growth in Health Care Costs," testimony of Peter Orszag before the Committee on the Budget, U.S. Senate, January 31, 2008) projects that health spending will be 25 percent of GDP in 2025 and 49 percent in 2082 (the seventy-five-year projection that has to be made in conjunction with evaluating the fiscal health of Medicare).

cost and access, and each requires a different solution. In fact, these two goals are slightly at odds as more access is likely to lead to higher costs.

Let's start with a bit of history to determine how we got to where we are. Private business began providing health insurance in the 1920s and 1930s. The science of medicine was progressing and leading to greater confidence in the ability of practitioners to make people healthier. The system was growing with people mostly paying for their own health care, while charity hospitals run by religious orders served the indigent for critical-care issues. Life expectancy was also relatively low so the problem of long-term care for the elderly was mainly addressed at the family level.

When the creation of Social Security was being debated in the 1930s, many advocates wanted to include a health insurance component. President Franklin D. Roosevelt decided that opposition to this program (especially from the American Medical Association) might undermine support for cash payments to the elderly so he did not include a health insurance component in the final bill. Instead, private companies were encouraged to provide health insurance to their workers, and an early decision was made to treat company contributions as a nontaxable form of compensation.[94]

During World War II, wage controls prohibited companies from recruiting and retaining workers on the basis of rising pay. A loophole, however, was that benefits were not capped and large firms expanded their health insurance programs to reward their workers. This precedent was followed after the war as unions (38 percent of private sector workers were in unions in 1950) bargained for more generous benefits packages to accompany wage gains. Consequently, in 1949, when President Truman tried to pass a public program guaranteeing health insurance for all, the unions were weak supporters because they thought they could get a better plan through their private employers. Without the political clout of organized labor supporting universal health care, the opponents of

---

[94] This tax preference is quite costly, and many commentators have long called for its elimination or at least its reduction. Candidate Obama criticized candidate McCain for proposing to fund his health care reform package by taxing workers' health insurance benefits. As president, Obama has warmed to this idea and is considering some form of taxation on benefits. By contrast, many congressional leaders have strongly supported maintaining the current approach (see Robert Pear, "Rangel Bars Any Taxes on Worker's Health Care," *New York Times,* May 6, 2009, A18). At the time of this writing (early December, 2009), the Senate health care bill is supported in part by taxes on health insurance premiums above a fixed level (the so-called "Cadillac plans").

universal health insurance—small businesses, ideologues who felt that the market should be left alone, and the American Medical Association—effectively stopped this early attempt at health care expansion.

By contrast, the defeated countries in World War II had very weak economies and private companies could not afford the extra expense of insurance benefits for their workers. Further, government provision of social benefits had begun in Germany in the 1880s, and the new governments wanted to show that they were doing something for their people, given the public distrust of political leaders following the destruction caused by the war.

The lack of widespread health insurance in the 1950s had a relatively small effect because there were relatively few effective medical treatments. Even as late as 1960, health insurance premiums of American corporations represented only 1 percent of payroll expenses. The coverage, though, was quite sparse and mainly limited to hospital care; visits to the family doctor for preventive and routine care were not covered and neither were dental expenses or eye care. Community hospitals were still the major source of care for low-income people, and they practiced cross-subsidization: insurance companies paid more than the direct costs of hospitalization, and this excess offset the costs of uncompensated care for the poor and elderly.

Over the next twenty years, the relative size of health care in the economy would double as many things changed. First, despite the opposition of the same players that stopped Truman in 1949, Medicare for seniors and Medicaid for low-income people were passed under President Lyndon Johnson's administration. Much to the surprise of the medical establishment, it soon found out that the government was a generous payer and its revenues rose dramatically under the new programs.

Second, private companies provided more generous health care plans with increasing coverage for many more procedures and expanded coverage to include dental and eye care. Union contracts led the way as companies seemed more willing to add to benefits than monetary wages. Companies also began to give retirees health benefits as another "low cost" way to settle labor disputes. Little did they know how much this provision would cost in future decades. As figure 7.1 shows, companies now pay 8 percent of compensation for health insurance premiums for their workers.

Third, insurance companies eventually started to bargain more ef-

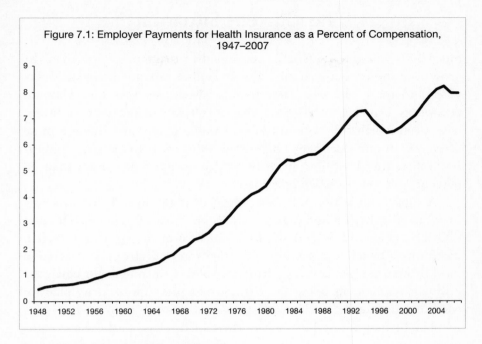

Figure 7.1: Employer Payments for Health Insurance as a Percent of Compensation, 1947–2007

National Income and Product Accounts

fectively with health care providers. As costs rose higher and higher, companies pressured insurance companies for better rates, and insurance companies in turn learned that they could use their market clout to slightly check rising costs. Of course, the unintended consequence of this cost containment was the reduction of cross-subsidization for uncompensated care (which hospitals were required to provide if they received federal funds and had an emergency room).

All of these factors were in place in President Bill Clinton's second year, when comprehensive health care reform was tried. In an attempt to satisfy all players, including the insurance industry, a detailed 1,400-page plan was introduced to mostly positive reviews. When Congress went on recess, a series of effective commercials featuring a middle-aged couple (Harry and Louise) sitting around a table discussing all of the potential downsides of the plan was repeatedly broadcast. The insurance industry, which had pledged to stay neutral, changed course and funded the commercials that changed the minds of many people who were unsure of what was in the new program.

The Current Situation

Since 1993, medical costs have continued to rise much faster than the growth of the economy. This is due to higher inflation in medical services and more effective care. In *Your Money or Your Life,* Harvard economist David Cutler argues that increasing medical expenditures have been worth the costs in terms of living longer and living a more active life in our older age. The big success story involves our number-one killer: the death rate from heart disease has fallen more than 50 percent over the last several decades.

A significant reason for these advances is the introduction of new drugs to treat high blood pressure and high cholesterol levels. The case of AIDs "cocktails" is a dramatic example of changing a near-certain death into a treatable condition. The importance of drugs is reflected in most insurance plans covering drug costs and in the one major new government entitlement being the passage of a prescription drug plan for Medicare recipients.[95]

The biggest failure has been a slowly rising share of those age eighteen to sixty-four without medical insurance—going from 16 percent in 1987 to over 19 percent in 2007. As opposed to food or housing, which can be denied to people, medical care is available even for those without insurance in emergency rooms and some government clinics, but the lack of insurance affects people's lives in many direct ways.[96]

All other attempts at cost containment—HMOs (Health Maintenance Organization, Preferred Provider lists, high deductible medical insurance plans, and Health Savings accounts)—provided limited savings and did not halt the relentless increases in health care expenditures. Remarkably, we have a system that spends close to twice what other

[95] Once again, new public health care services were provided to seniors because they were "deserving" of access to drugs, which were now an essential part of medical treatments. The Republicans who were in control of Congress in 2005, when this bill passed, put their unique stamp on the structure of the benefit: It would be provided by competing private plans with the government prohibited from negotiating price.

[96] In a perverse pricing mechanism, hospitals and doctors charge much lower fees for their services to insured patients (whose insurance companies bargain for a preferential rate) as compared with those charged to those who are not insured. This means that low-income people without insurance face very high costs when they get care.

countries spend for health care (adjusted for population size) yet delivers mediocre results. While it is difficult to measure the effectiveness of medical care across countries, the life expectancy of Americans is lower than that of inhabitants of other developed countries, and our infant mortality rate is at the level of developing countries like Costa Rica.

In other countries, the share of health care expenditures is rising at about the same rate as the United States, but the share of medical expenditures in the economy is only at two-thirds the level of American level (e.g., in 2006, when U.S. medical spending was 15 percent of GDP, the comparable figures for Canada, France, and Germany was between 10 and 11 percent).

In terms of the American delivery of medical care, there are a number of misaligned incentives that have led to such high costs here. The health care cost juggernaut is obvious fueled by the industries that gain from its expansion. But this is not different from any other consumer good. What separates out the cost of health care are several unique features that make it easy to keep on expanding.

Consider the following seven characteristics that have driven up health care costs:

First, health care represents an "expertise driven" commodity—we go to doctors and trust that they will provide the appropriate level of service. The last thing on our minds when we are sick or bringing in a sick child is cost.

Second, in most cases, it is insurance or government that is paying the bulk of the cost. Therefore, we are looking for the best care and as many tests as are needed to determine what is wrong.

Third, doctors are paid by the number of procedures that they do, so they have a financial incentive to do many tests and procedures.

Fourth, specialists get paid more than general practitioners (GP, or family doctors) so, not surprisingly, more doctors have become specialists.

Fifth, mistakes are made and can be punished by malpractice (lawyers have an interest in building up this area). But, sometimes negative outcomes aren't caused by mistakes but by low-probability events. Nonetheless, juries will often be open to deciding that any negative outcome is due to negligence. As a consequence, doctors pay high premiums for medical malpractice, especially for those who deliver babies (where unforeseen complications are common). In order to minimize their risks of being sued, doctors practice "defensive medicine," and order all possible relevant tests.[97] The medical establishment is partially to blame for this system because they have been so hesitant to investigate and discipline doctors who make mistakes even in cases of repeated egregious errors.

Sixth, innovation is rewarded handsomely. Compared with thirty years ago, medical practice has expanded greatly—e.g., new drugs, advances in medical imaging (MRI, CAT and PET scans), and microsurgery requiring small incisions. Various studies have estimated that about 50 percent of the increase in medical costs is due to this factor.[98] In difficult cases, patients scour the internet and find stories of unusual treatments that were successful. Patients demand the latest, and often very expensive, treatment options. For them, the issue of whether there is proof of success is of secondary importance.

Seventh, in the last ten years, drug companies have advertised prescription drugs directly to consumers. Everything is a syndrome rather than just growing old, being tired, having trouble sleeping, not being as sexually active, etc. Consequently, patients come in asking for specific drugs even before they have received any medical diagnosis.

The continuing rise in medical expenditures has produced a number of reactions. Insurance companies are at the center of cost-containment strategies as they pressure doctors and patients on costs. For consumers, it is common experience to get a letter from the insurance company denying payments for a bill that was expected to be covered. In my last colonoscopy, for example, the insurance company paid the doctor but not the facility in which the procedure took place. It took eight months and four rounds of resubmitting documentation before the final reimbursements were made. This was a significant additional hassle for me and the billing department of the facility.

Another way insurance companies try to manage costs is to limit

[97] In October 2009, the Congressional Budget Office estimated that proposals that limit the cost related to medical malpractice ("tort reform") would save the federal government $54 billion over the next ten years.

[98] See Table 1 of previously cited CBO testimony of Peter Orszag.

"high cost" people from coverage. While they can't do this for large firms (their risk is minimized because of the large numbers involved), small firms, the self-employed, and people seeking individual coverage are very much affected by the issue of preexisting conditions. If a small enterprise of twenty employees has one person or dependent with a serious illness generating high costs, it can either expect to lose their coverage or see a steep rise in premiums.

It is important to emphasize that as health care expenditures have grown, everyone has had to pay more. In many early company-provided insurance plans, the company paid the entire premium and there were no co-pays for covered medical treatments. Starting in 1980, more companies required workers to contribute to their health insurance payments and co-pays became more common. Since this shift occurred, the share that companies pay for insurance has remained relatively constant at 86 percent for individual coverage and 74 percent for family coverage.

Although workers are paying more in absolute terms, their share of total medical costs has actually declined from 42 percent in 1987, to 34 percent in 2004.[99] The reason for this is that more expenditures are covered by insurance—e.g., more plans cover dental and eye care and prescription drugs. In addition, the costs of reimbursable medical expenses (e.g., hospitalization and doctors' fees) have gone up more than over-the-counter drugs and other medical items bought directly by consumers—leaving a progressively smaller share of total medical expenditures to be paid directly out of pocket. Here are the numbers: in 1987, workers paid $2,044 a year (2007 dollars) for out-of-pocket expenses and health insurance out of a total value of $4,880 for medical insurance and out-of-pocket expenses; the comparable figures in 2004 were $2,853 out of $8,301.

Workers see the rise in their insurance contribution and co-pays as proof that they are paying more for their medical care. But they fail to appreciate how many additional medical services they are consuming—this is what a rising share of medical expenditures out of GDP means.

[99] According to the Office of the Actuary of the Centers for Medicare and Medicaid Services, the fraction of health care costs paid as out-of-pocket payments and insurance premiums by households fell by approximately one-third between 1960 and 2007.

Some companies have stopped providing health insurance or have capped maximum payouts. But to date, these have been smaller companies as over 99 percent of companies with over 500 workers continue to provide health insurance to their workers. Surveys also show that companies expect to be providing medical insurance for their workforce for the foreseeable future.

Will Rising Health Care Costs Bankrupt Our Economy?

As a society, we have decided that minimal medical care will be provided to everyone. This is accomplished by requiring every hospital that has an emergency room to treat anyone who comes in.[100] Obviously, there is the hassle of waiting a long time, and there may be difficulty getting all of the drugs that may be prescribed. But utilization studies do show that poor people have close to the average number of doctor visits per year as other people in the country. Since they tend to be sicker, this certainly does not mean that they get the same level of care.

By taking into account uncompensated care, public clinics, Medicare, and Medicaid, a lot of health care spending is for low-income people (perhaps 50 to 70 percent of what is spent on health care for middle-income Americans). By contrast, wealthy people certainly have more options, get better care, have access to all the drugs that they need, and have more than their share of cosmetic surgery. Nonetheless, spending on health care is more equally divided than income or wealth. This has important implications in understanding whether we can "afford" rising health expenditures.

As long as medical spending rises faster than the overall economy, its share of the economy will continue to rise. A simple extrapolation shows that medical activities will be *one-half of all economic activity* somewhere around 2085. Using the same projections, spending on Medicare and Medicaid will equal 20 percent of GDP.

Is this doable?

---

[100] We actually provide quite good medical care for prison inmates, and there are cases of death-row convicts getting very expensive heart treatments while they wait for their execution date.

The short answer is yes; but we are not likely to take this decision. As long as we don't change our commitment that everyone is entitled to basic care and the elderly to good care, the costs of funding these commitments will continue to rise, which will mean an increase in taxes on the middle class and wealthy to support the medical consumption of the elderly and the poor.

Health care is central to our lives, and all societies are committed to spending a large amount of money to ensure its availability. As will be discussed below, there is reason to believe that a lot of health care spending does not lead to better outcomes. Consequently, there is a sound foundation to argue that we can find a way to rein in costs.

How Big Is the Access Problem?

While public coverage has been extended to the elderly and the young, prime-age working people have been left to fend for themselves. Because of expansions in eligibility, virtually all seniors (over 99 percent) are covered when they turn sixty-five. At the opposite end of the age spectrum, 91 percent of children under eighteen years old are covered because they have access to S-CHIP and other public programs if they are not covered under their parents' policies.

By contrast, 19 percent of those eighteen- to sixty-four-years-olds are without coverage in a typical month.[101] The lack of coverage, however, varies across demographic groups. For example, 10 percent of our population are not U.S. citizens (most are legal residents but many are not). Since they have more difficulty getting and keeping a job, noncitizens are much less likely than citizens to have health insurance and represent one-quarter of the uninsured. Among prime-age people, fully 47 percent of noncitizens are without insurance versus 11 percent for citizens; among children, the difference in noncoverage is 37 percent for noncitizens to 8 percent of citizens; and even among the

---

[101] In terms of access, there are problems with some of the measures: The most widely quoted number for those without health insurance in 2007 is 47 million, cited in the Current Population Survey. Most researchers find that the questions used to derive this estimate to be confusing and prefer to use other surveys to determine how many people in a given month are without insurance. The 2007 National Health interview survey, for example, reports that 43 million people did not have insurance at the time of the survey.

elderly, 11 percent of noncitizens have no coverage versus 0.5 percent of citizens.

Another crucial difference is age. Among citizens, nearly one-quarter of eighteen- to twenty-nine year-olds do not have coverage in a typical month. This is a very healthy group, and many times these young people will turn down coverage even when the costs are relatively low. As people get older, the importance of coverage becomes clearer and fewer citizens do without insurance: among citizens, 15 percent of thirty- to forty-nine-year-olds do not have coverage while just 11 percent of fifty- to sixty-four-year-olds are without coverage.

But being without health insurance is not a permanent condition; most of those without health insurance will obtain insurance within a year. This is both a good and bad thing. On the one hand, very few people lack health insurance for years at a time. On the other hand, a greater number of people will have a "spell" of not being covered over a multiyear period. Fortunately, there is a recent longitudinal data source that asked monthly questions on insurance coverage from 2003 to 2007.[102]

To track health insurance continuity over this four-year period, the question is not one of coverage or non-coverage but how many months out of the forty-eight months did a person have coverage. To simplify the presentation, three groups were defined: stable (coverage in all forty-eight months), never covered (no coverage in any of the 48 months), and "gappers" (those with some coverage be it for 1 to 47 months). Because people are followed for four years, the group "18–64" consists of those who started at 18 to 60 and ended at 22 to 64; this is the only way to ensure that no one was ever younger than 18 or older than 64.

Among this adult group, 71 percent had stable coverage, 23 percent were gappers, and 6 percent (10 million people) had no coverage at all. Once again, noncitizens had much less coverage: just 35 percent had stable coverage, 42 percent were gappers, and 22 percent never had cov-

---

[102] The Survey of Income and Program Participation (SIPP), conducted by the Census Bureau, asked 25,000 families a battery of questions about their monthly status (they were asked these questions every four months so recall was limited to providing information on each of the previous four months) including health insurance coverage from 2003 to 2007.

erage. By contrast, if we focus on citizens, excluding the youngest group of 18- 21-year-olds (a group with a low level of stable coverage), then 77 percent had stable coverage, 19 percent were gappers, and just 4 percent never had insurance. Put in slightly different terms, 32 million out of 140 million prime-age citizens had at least some break in their insurance coverage over these four years.[103]

An important part of coverage is whether it is from private sources (mostly through work) or public sources (mostly based on disability or low income). Of prime-age citizens, 64 percent had stable coverage through private sources, and 6 percent had stable coverage through public sources each month. As Figure 7.2 shows, family incomes are closely related to type of insurance coverage. Not surprisingly, those with public coverage had the lowest median income (just $23,058). This was even higher than those with no coverage at all ($27,739). The median income of the gappers was $36,760 versus $56,886 for those with stable coverage from both public and private sources. Finally, the incomes of the nearly two-thirds of prime-age citizens with stable coverage from private sources were much higher than any other group with a median of $78,764.

Table 7.1 (pp. 194–95) presents the distributions among these five continuity categories on the basis of various demographic or family characteristics. There are two ways to look at the relative percentages in this table. On the one hand, since health insurance is predominantly received through employment, those with better jobs are much more likely to have stable insurance through their employer. On the other hand, even among the wealthiest and most successful Americans, a sizeable number

---

[103] See Anne Kim, Stephen Rose, and David Kendall, "Checking Up on Harry and Louise: The Health Care Coverage of the Middle Class." (Washington, DC: Third Way, 2009). The data are organized in four-month chunks. In moving from one chunk to another, about 1.5 percent of those with coverage lose their coverage and about 15 percent of those without coverage gain coverage. This means that about 4 percent over four months change their insurance coverage while the other 96 percent maintain their insurance status. Of those that lose their insurance coverage, 42 percent will regain it within one year and keep coverage for at least the next two years; another 14 percent will regain coverage within a year but lose it again within two years; another 15 percent will regain their coverage within one to three years of losing it (the limitations of the study don't allow us to know how long they keep their regained coverage); and 29 percent will never regain coverage in the ensuing two to three years. These numbers provide a sense of how successful people are in regaining coverage.

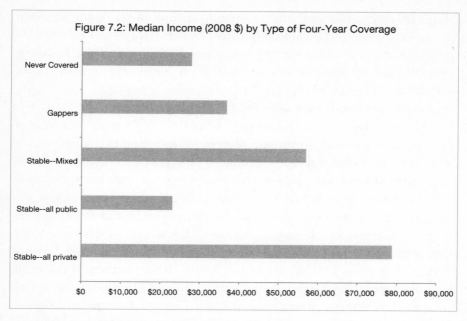

Figure 7.2: Median Income (2008 $) by Type of Four-Year Coverage

2004 Survey of Income and Program Participation

of people still rotate through coverage. Consequently, the most revealing numbers in this table are found in the first column (stable private insurance) and the sum of the last two columns (gappers and never covered).

With the exception of gender, the status variables in this table reveal large differences between the most successful and least successful Americans:

- In terms of education, 50 percent of those without a high school diploma have spells without insurance and only 21 percent have stable private insurance; those with a high school diploma and no postsecondary education do much better: only 30 percent have periods of time without insurance, and 54 percent have stable private insurance. However, only 9 percent of those with bachelor's and graduate degrees have periods without insurance, and 85 percent have stable private insurance.
- In terms of age, once one passes thirty years of age, employment and family situations tend to stabilize and insurance continuity does not vary much. For the age group that starts at twenty-two- to

thirty-year-olds and ends at twenty-six to thirty-four, there are much more likely to be interruptions (38 percent) than those that end at thirty-five to forty-nine (21 percent), or those that end at fifty to sixty-four (18 percent).

- In terms of race/ethnicity, non–Hispanic Whites have the strongest insurance continuity with 71 percent having stable private insurance versus 19 percent with at least some period without insurance. By contrast, only 44 percent of Hispanics, even those who are citizens, have stable private insurance and 42 percent have periods without insurance. African-Americans have 45 percent with stable private insurance and fewer people with interruptions (33 percent). Finally, those of other races (primarily Asians) have a slightly stronger profile of insurance continuity than either Blacks or Hispanics.

- Not surprisingly, those who are married throughout the forty-eight-month period have the advantage of two people who can obtain insurance through their workplace and have a much higher share than those who are unmarried or married for some period with stable insurance (84 percent versus 64 percent). At the same time, only 16 percent of the always-married group and about 36 percent of the never or sometimes married group have periods without insurance.

- The relationship between family income and insurance continuity is strong. Among low-income families (less than $35,000), only 25 percent have stable private insurance and 50 percent have periods without insurance. By contrasts, families with incomes of $105,000 and higher are very likely to have stable private insurance (89 percent) and very unlikely to have a gap in their coverage (6 percent). But, while 6 percent is a low number, this shows that even among the affluent some people have gaps in their coverage over four years. So, it is not unreasonable for everyone to have at least some worries about losing their coverage even without large drops in income.

- There are three employment categories in Table 7.1: share of time with at least one family member working full-time, the number of months working full-time for the individual, and annual individual earnings. In all cases, those with greater labor force attachment and higher earnings have fewer periods without insurance

TABLE 7.1
CONTINUITY OF INSURANCE BY DEMOGRAPHIC CHARACTERISTICS

	Stable—all private	Stable—all public	Stable—mixed	Gappers	Never Covered
Gender					
Male	64.3	6.3	5.2	19.4	4.9
Female	64.4	7.5	6.5	17.8	3.7
Education					
1. High school noncompleter	21.1	22.9	5.8	33.9	16.5
2. at most HS/GED	54.5	9.4	6.6	24.1	5.4
3. some college/AA	64.3	5.6	6.8	19.8	3.5
4. BA/Grad	84.7	1.8	4.4	8.3	0.8
Age					
26–34	51.6	5.4	5.6	32.6	4.9
35–49	67.7	6.3	4.9	16.9	4.3
50–64	66.7	8.3	7.1	13.9	4.0
Race/Ethnicity					
1. Non-Hispanic White	70.5	5.3	5.3	15.3	3.7
2. Non-Hispanic Black	44.6	13.8	8.5	27.6	5.5
3. Hispanic	43.6	9.3	5.6	33.8	7.7
4. Other	57.1	10.6	8.9	19.6	3.9
Marital Status					
Always Married	74.4	4.2	6.1	12.4	3.1
Never Married	47.9	13.0	5.4	26.9	6.8
Mixed (married/single)	50.9	5.9	6.2	32.8	4.2

Months with Full-Time Work					
0–36 months	31.8	11.9	9.2	38.5	8.8
37–47 months	56.9	4.0	7.8	25.5	5.9
48 months	80.0	2.0	4.2	11.4	2.4
Average Family Income					
0–$35,000	24.7	20.2	5.7	37.9	11.6
$35,000–$70,000	64.7	4.5	6.9	20.2	3.7
$70,000–$105,000	81.5	2.2	6.1	8.9	1.4
$105,000 and higher	89.1	1.1	4.4	5.2	0.3
Personal months worked full-time					
0–36 months	36.1	19.7	9.3	28.8	6.1
37–47 months	63.7	2.0	6.4	23.7	4.2
48 months	84.2	1.0	3.2	8.5	3.1
Average personal earnings					
0–$25,000	40.6	14.5	8.2	29.2	7.6
$25,000–$50,000	77.9	0.9	4.7	14.0	2.5
$50,000–$75,000	90.8	0.3	3.2	5.3	0.4
$75,000 and higher	92.7	0.2	3.1	3.7	0.2

2004 Survey of Income and Program Participation

and are more likely to have stable private insurance than those with weaker labor force characteristics.

Possible Solutions

Some believe that there is a "magic bullet" that will reduce medical costs and increase access. Barack Obama, for example, ran in 2008 on a platform of reforms that would supposedly decrease medical spending for a family of four by $2,500. This sort of "eating your cake and having it, too" rarely occurs. The savings supposedly come from the adoption of electronic medical records and from avoiding the high costs of serious diseases by more extensive screening. Both of these are worthy activities that will increase health outcomes by reducing medical errors and spotting diseases early enough to make a difference in the effectiveness of treatment, but in the short run, they are investments that are likely to add costs. The bottom line is that covering more people is going to be more expensive in the short run and that cost savings will potentially appear many years later.

Conservatives believe that we can increase access and control costs by adopting "market-oriented" strategies that make consumers face the real costs of their choices. There are two problems with this argument. First, many people will delay treatments in order to save money and will only go to doctors when they are quite sick. Studies show that we are not intelligent consumers when we are paying the full cost of the care, and it is very beneficial that our marginal cost for a visit is so low. The second problem is that, as was stated above, the consumption of health care is not like the consumption of other consumer goods because it is very difficult for consumers to know how to judge costs and outcomes. Consequently, most experts feel that the gains from market-driven reforms are limited.

The biggest increase in medical spending has been the expansion of government expenditures. In 1965, the public share of all medical spending was 25 percent; today it is just under 50 percent. This increase has been almost entirely driven by the rise in the federal share from 11 percent to 34 percent over this period.

Medical spending is very unevenly distributed with most of the costs concentrated among the sick: the bottom 50 percent of the medical care consumers account for just 3.1 percent of all spending. By contrast, the 15 percent who consume the most medical services are responsible for three-quarters of all spending, while the top 1 percent accounts for 23 percent. So, the big savings are to be found in the treatment of chronic conditions and people who are on the verge of dying. Not surprisingly, the elderly who represent 11 percent of the population account for over 35 percent of all medical spending.

The McKinsey Global Institute has performed a series of careful studies to allocate the extra health care expenses in the United States versus other comparable industrialized countries.[104] They begin by noting the strong positive relationship between what health care spending per person and wealth level (GDP per person). Since the United States has the highest GDP per capita (see below for a discussion of purchasing power parity), it can be expected to spend more than any other country. However, when they extrapolate the line of "expected spending according to wealth (ESAW)," the United States still spent $650 billion (out of $2.1 trillion) more than expected.

While some people think that the United States is bloated with massive paperwork, this report finds that the only $91 billion is expended on insurance and administration over its ESAW level.[105] The biggest contributor to the difference is outpatient care (emergency care, same-day treatments in hospitals, and visits to doctors and dentists' offices) which is $436 billion over ESAW; the two other big contributors are drugs ($98 billion over ESAW), and new medical technologies ($50 billion over ESAW).

A very interesting set of comparative studies (the Dartmouth Medical School's Atlas project) finds large cost differences in treatments for the same disease across counties within a state and across states. Even adjusting for the severity of the condition, these studies show wide variation in costs without any difference in terms of the outcomes.[106] When apprised of these results, doctors in high cost areas are incredulous that the less

---

[104] "Accounting for the cost of U.S. health care: a new look at why Americans spend more." December 2008.

[105] They may underestimate the administrative costs that are embedded in hospitals and doctors' offices.

[106] In the June 1, 2009 issue of *The New Yorker* magazine, Atul Gawande reported on the differences between two Texas counties with similar demographics but vastly different health care expenditures ("The Cost Conundrum"). This article attracted the attention of the president and put the issue of standardized care in a much more prominent place in the national debate.

intrusive medical regimes produce similar outcomes and continue to support their approach as the necessary standard of care.

Shannon Brownlee in her book *Overtreated* reviews all of the related studies and argues that "too much medicine is making us sicker and poorer" (the subtitle of the book). If this is true, then the road to cost savings is through standardizing care in each specialty at the levels of the low-cost areas. Brownlee proposes forming a national board to review procedures to come up with the relevant standards of treatment for each disease.[107]

This promising idea, however, is likely to be met with protests from doctors and patients about limiting care to the lowest common denominator. The Obama administration has budgeted $1.1 billion for studies comparing the effectiveness and costs of various treatment alternatives; these plans led to immediate opposition from medical device makers, coalitions of doctors, and Rush Limbaugh who labeled it as a move to socialized medicine.[108] In England, they do set the total budget to be spent on health care, and accordingly have kept medical costs down to a relatively low level of all spending (8 percent of GDP). While there is some grumbling about waits, there is widespread public support and wealthy people often pay for many treatments at home or abroad. At some point, America may find the political will to face the problem of skyrocketing costs. This will be a political *battle royale* and may require the business establishment to side with the reformers. Without some controls on spending, the upward trend of the size of medical spending in the economy will only continue to increase.

Retirement

With the baby boomers approaching retirement and the fall in home and stock prices, there is widespread concern that retirement as we have known it over the past twenty years will no longer continue to exist.

---

[107] UpToDate, the most widely used medical information service used by MDs, provides an encouraging sign of the ability of evidence-based medicine to save money: A study showed that the more doctors referred to UpToDate, the lower the hospital costs were.

[108] Barry Meier, "New Effort Reopens a Medical Minefield," *New York Times,* B1, May 7, 2009.

According to David Smith and Heather McGee, "it is becoming increasingly apparent that Americans' future retirement years—if they have them—are poised to mirror the anxiety, insecurity, and inequality of their working lives."[109] This pessimistic sentiment is expressed in the following list of headlines that have appeared over the last five years:

SOCIAL SECURITY WON'T BE THERE FOR YOU (and polls show a lot of people believe this);

THE SAVINGS RATE IS VERY LOW, WAS EVEN ZERO FOR A COUPLE OF YEARS, SO PEOPLE WON'T HAVE ENOUGH MONEY AND WILL HAVE TO WORK IN THEIR OLD AGE;

COMPANIES HAVE ABANDONED TRADITIONAL PENSIONS AND WALKED AWAY FROM THEIR RESPONSIBILITIES TO THEIR WORKERS; and

THE GOVERNMENT PROGRAM THAT INSURES BENEFITS TO WORKERS FOR COMPANIES THAT GO BANKRUPT IS OVERBURDENED AND WILL SOON RUN OUT OF MONEY.

Reflecting this negativism, AARP found that most of the 3 million Google hits on baby-boomer savings that they reviewed were negative.[110]

Yet, most current retirees are not complaining even though they have much lower monetary incomes than the nonelderly. For the bottom quarter, media stories document the low living standards, especially when pressed by high prescription-drug costs. Most of these people, however, had relatively low incomes when they were younger.

There have been a number of surveys asking current retirees about their attitudes as regards to their current living standards, and their answers are mostly positive. In 2003, the Survey of Income and Program Participation (SIPP) found that most retirees considered that their current living standards stood up quite well to their living standards in their early fifties: 15 percent said much better, 20 percent answered somewhat better, 39 percent the same, 18 percent somewhat worse, and 8 percent much worse. In the Health Retirement Survey (HRS) of 2002, sixty-one- to seventy-one-year-olds were asked two questions about their attitudes toward retirement. In response to the general question, "All in

---

[109] In "Shredding the Retirement Contract," in *Inequality Matters*. 2006. James Lardner and David Smith, eds. New York: The New Press, p 79.
[110] Available at: http://assets.aarp.org/rgcenter/econ/dd143_wealth.pdf

all, would you say that your retirement has turned out to be very satisfying, moderately satisfying, or not at all satisfying?" about 60 percent of retirees responded that they are very satisfied with their retirement, with another third responding that their retirement is moderately satisfying. Other surveys also show that somewhere between 65 and 80 percent of retirees are at least moderately happy with their current situation.

So one of the things you don't see is "scared-straight" documentaries of elderly people telling people not to make the mistakes that they made. To be sure, financial companies fill the airwaves with advertisements for investment products that will make retirement more fulfilling. But these are upbeat (they are shooting for people with a fair amount of resources) and not couched as "get busy now or else."

Ultimately, to understand the problem of future retirees, we need to return to the two basic principles of economics: the size, and the distribution of economic output. Some commentators focus on the declining number of workers per retiree. While this is certainly relevant, the more important ratio is that of nonworkers (retirees and children) to workers. For example, in the 1950s, the share of nonworkers grew very quickly (baby boomers) and we still had strong economic growth. There is every reason to believe that the size of the economic pie as expressed in GDP per person will continue to grow at a reasonable rate for the foreseeable future. So we will have a bigger pie to deal with when we reach a larger retirement population.

The retirement issue then revolves around the distribution of the pie, and there is nothing to stop us from changing the rules to ensure that a certain class of nonworkers can enjoy an adequate standard of living. As Steven Landsburg notes: "People in 2050 will essentially face four questions: how much young and old people should work and how much young and old people consume."[111]

The Evolution of Retirement

Before the middle of the twentieth century, few people retired. In 1900, 86 percent of men who were still alive at sixty-five were working. On

---

[111] Steven Landsburg, *More Sex is Safer Sex: The Unconventional Wisdom of Economics.* (New York: Free Press, 2007): 241.

top of this, only about 2 percent of people born in the middle of the nineteenth century reached their seventieth birthday. So, as people aged, they continued to work as long as they were able and then relied on their adult children to support them, if the seniors were unable. Very few people had incomes high enough to put money aside to support themselves independently without working or relying on their families.

As modernization and medical advances increased longevity, the issue of a rising number of old people had to be faced by all industrializing countries. While various U.S. states took the initiative in developing programs to help the elderly, the passage of Social Security in 1936 was the major turning point in U.S. policy. Although it had several coverage holes when first passed, it validated the premise that the federal government would guarantee minimum incomes, without work, for the elderly. Certainly, private firms were not filling the gap because less than 20 percent of workers were eligible for a private pension at the time Social Security was passed.

After the enactment of the Social Security system and retirement began to be a possibility for more people, it was still slow in affecting new retirees who had contributed very little into the system. By 1950, the average male did not retire until seventy and could expect to live another eight years. As Table 7.2 shows, since 1950, the average male worker has gone from working 70 percent of his life to just over 50 percent. Over the last ten years, the median male retirement age dropped to sixty-three, and this person can expect nineteen years of retirement. In addition to these eleven more years of retirement, the modern retiree spent fewer years in the labor force because of the added years of schooling. The 1950 retiree probably left school between the ages of fourteen and sixteen, and spent fifty-five years—or 70 percent of his life—in the labor force. Today the average retiree did not finish schooling until the age of twenty, which means that he spent forty-three years in the labor force (discounting the years he may have worked part-time while still in school), or 52 percent of his life working. For those with graduate degrees who retire at sixty-three, they will have only spent 46 percent of their lives in the labor force.

At the same time that people are working less, their incomes have been rising. In 1959, the elderly poverty rate was 35 percent (versus a national level of 25 percent) while 40 percent of men over sixty-five worked. The elderly poverty rate did not fall to a level very close to the poverty rate of nonelderly adults until the beginning of the 1980.

TABLE 7.2
WORKING AND RETIREMENT YEARS, 1950 TO 2010

	Average Retirement Age	Life Expectancy	No. of Retirement Years	Age Leaving School	No. of Years Working	Share of Life Working
1950	70	78.1	8.1	15	55	70.4
1960	66	78.2	12.2	18	48	61.4
1970	65	78.8	13.8	20	45	57.1
1980	63	79.7	16.7	20	43	54.0
1990	63	80.7	17.7	20	43	53.3
2000	63	81.7	18.7	20	43	52.6
2010*	63	82.4	19.4	20	43	52.2

*Estimate

Bureau of Labor Statistics

1993 to 2001, the two were basically equal. Starting in 2001, the elderly poverty rate dipped below that of rate for other adults, and in 2006, the elderly poverty rate was 9.4 percent while the nonelderly adult rate was 10.8 percent.

This improvement is noteworthy, but it should also be emphasized that the cash incomes of the elderly are much lower than the cash incomes of the nonelderly adults (see Figure 4.1). However, Burtless and Svaton find that the difference in incomes between the elderly and nonelderly is much less if a more comprehensive income analysis is used. By including the value of medical services consumed but not paid for out of pocket, and a broader definition of capital income, most of the elderly shortfall of "income" disappears: the incomes of the nonelderly would increase about 8.2 percent while the incomes of the elderly would shoot up by 37 percent.[112] This shift to more income, less work, fewer ailments, and access to more health care is a tremendous sign of progress and is the basis for understanding why the elderly rate their current situations so highly.

Pension Coverage

The dynamics of workers participating in an employee-sponsored pension plan revolve around several issues: The employer must offer a plan, the employee must choose to participate, and the employee must be "vested" (usually requiring from five or more years of employment until the employee is entitled to receive the benefit of the employer contribution). Not surprisingly, the most important determinant of a company having a plan is its size: For firms of ten employees or fewer, only one in seven offers a company pension plan as opposed to six out of seven companies with 500 or more workers having a plan.

The combination of not all employers offering a plan, the limitations of plan participation to full-time workers, and the decision of workers to participate in a plan leads to only half of workers being plan participants.

[112] Similar results using the Survey of Consumer Finances are reported by Edward N. Wolff, and Ajit Zacharias, "Household Wealth and the Measurement of Economic Well-Being in the United States." Levy Economics Institute Working Paper No. 447. (Annandale-on-Hudson, NY: Levy Economics Institute, Bard College, 2006).

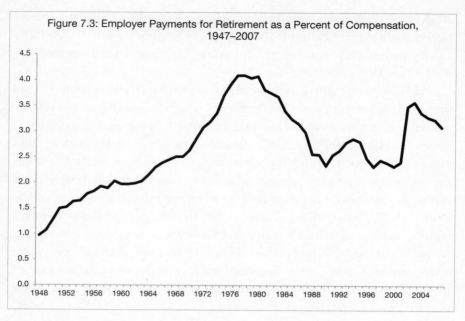

Figure 7.3: Employer Payments for Retirement as a Percent of Compensation, 1947–2007

National Income and Product Accounts

Historically, only 17 percent of workers were in an employer-sponsored retirement plan in 1940, and this figure rose steadily through the 1970s when it reached 52 percent. Since then, it has stayed mostly stable within a range of 48–52 percent. Over the course of a career, however, it is projected that approximately 70 percent of future retirees will receive at least some money from an employer pension fund.

Company commitment to providing for workers in their old age was originally greater than their contributions for health insurance premiums: through 1960, companies were contributing twice as much to pensions as they were paying for health insurance plans. As Figure 7.3 shows, contributions as a percent of compensation continued to rise through the 1980s before declining significantly through the 2000s. With the stock market crash of 2001, private companies had to add a significant amount of money to what they had set aside for their workers in order to keep their plans financially sound. Paradoxically, the movements of stock prices strongly affected the yearly contributions of companies. New regulations in the 1970s required that these plans be financially sound and the bear market of the 1970s required high company contributions. The bull market of 1980s and '90s had the opposite effect and allowed company contributions to decline. And lastly, the crash of 2000 required a quick infusion of cash.

As with health insurance premiums, companies feel that their retirement plans are key components in recruiting and retaining their workers. Historically, this meant providing their workers a "company pension"—a monthly payment based on previous pay and years of service. This "gold standard" benefit encouraged employees to stay with the same company because benefits were based on a formula related to highest pay. As a consequence, a worker who stayed with one company for thirty years got significantly more than a worker who moved between two similar companies that he stayed with for fifteen years each (the first company pension would be based on the highest pay of the fifteen years during the first half of the person's career when earnings were much lower).[113]

Because these "defined benefit" (DB) plans are skewed in favor of long-term employees, most workers did not qualify for generous benefits. In a study by the Massachusetts Institute of Technology wealth researcher James Poterba, 80 percent of DB plan payouts went to just 20 percent of workers. Starting in the 1980s, companies began changing their retirement benefit 401(k) programs (named after the provision in the tax code that regulates these plans). Instead of getting a defined benefit, the employee agrees to take a "defined contribution" (DC) into an account in his or her name. In virtually all cases, the companies match employee contributions with the most typical plan being a 50 percent matchup to 6 percent of a worker's salary (which makes the company contribution 3 percent).[114]

There are advantages and disadvantages to DC plans in comparison to traditional DB plans. From the worker's point of view, under the DC plan they get credit for all the years of work. In the old system, changing jobs could lead to the complete loss of pension benefits. Even if the worker was vested in the former company's plans, the future benefits could be lower than a DC plan would have provided.

Which plan benefits a particular worker depends on the specific payout

[113] The expected present value of a defined benefit pension typically increased very slowly in the early years of a career and then more rapidly after roughly ten to twenty years, a pattern that encouraged younger workers to stay in a job; but after around twenty to thirty years of tenure or at ages fifty-five to sixty-five, pension accruals then dropped or became negative, encouraging retirement.

[114] One of the consequences of the financial crisis is that 15 percent of companies have temporarily discontinued their matching payments.

details of the available DB or DC plan. For employees who end their career with twenty or more years with the same employer, DB plans will usually provide higher retirement income than DC plans. However, for other types of workers, the payouts may be quite similar, and for workers without long-term tenure with any company, DC plans will provide more income than DB plans. Since most workers change jobs often, another study by Poterba and associates found that 80 percent of workers would have higher benefits at retirement under a DC plan than a traditional company pension.

Other downsides of DC plans for the worker have to do with the freedom to make mistakes. First, enrollment in DB plans is automatic while workers don't have to participate in a DC plan. A 2007 law allowed companies to make the "default option" participation in a DC plan, meaning that workers are required to opt out of the plan or else they will be covered. Second, workers have the choice of how much to contribute. At a minimum, workers should always contribute up to the maximum rate because this represents added money from the company to their compensation since the company is required to match their contribution at an agreed-upon rate. Yet, research shows that a lot of workers fail to do this and often invest just a couple of percent of their earnings for retirement. Third, when workers change jobs, they can choose to take their retirement contributions as a lump-sum payment or roll them over into another retirement account. All too frequently, workers, especially young ones, cash out and set back their retirement savings. Fourth, workers can take loans from their 401(k) accounts, which may reduce their long-term savings.

A hidden downside in DB plans in the current economy is that the employer may go bankrupt. While the employer is supposed to have a dedicated fund to support its commitments to its retirees, these are often underfunded, especially during periods in which stock prices decline. In addition, as companies start having problems, they skimp on their contributions to their retirement accounts. There is a backup to company pension plans in the form of the Pension Benefit Guaranty Corporation (PBGC). Established in 1974, the PBGC is funded by a tax on the sponsors of DB pension plans. For plans that close with inadequate resources, the PBGC insures 100 percent of the first $11 monthly payment per year of service and 75 percent of the next $33 monthly payment per year of service with a maximum of $4,500 a month. In the current economic downturn, the PBGC is expected to not have enough resources to meet its expanding commitments in the next few years.[115] At present, the federal government has committed to loaning the PBGC money in order to avoid reducing payments.

From the company's point of view, the switch from defined benefit plans to defined contribution plans is mostly positive. First, they no longer have to actively manage the investments for their workers and no longer have to worry about market declines. Second, depending on the funding formulas, most companies save money when they switch from DB to DC plans. Often, companies will use the savings to establish "profit-sharing" plans in addition to their 401(k) plan. This makes them appear generous to their workers and they only have to make distributions when the company is doing well. The one downside to the employer in switching from a DB to a DC plan is that it may alienate its senior workers who benefited so generously from DB funding formulas.

Given the relative advantages and disadvantages of workers and companies, there has been an overwhelming switch from DB to DC pensions. In 1980, 60 percent of covered workers were in DB plans only (an extra 20 percent were in both DB and DC plans); by 2007, this number had fallen to 11 percent. The only industry that has continued to use DB plans widely is the government sector. This makes more sense because these workers tend to stay with the same employer for long periods of time and are enticed to work for the relatively low wages of government employees because of the promises of job security and good long-term benefits.

Social Security: A Crucial Component in Most People's Retirement Plans

This is a remarkably successful and popular program. In 2007, 84 percent of the population agreed with the statement, "Even though I might be able to do better on my own, I think it is important to contribute to Social Security for the common good." The problem on the horizon, however, is whether it will be there in the future. Although it has the appearance of being an insurance system (you contribute when you are

---

[115] The PBGC had invested its surplus in stocks and lost a lot of capital with the 2008 market downturn.

young and then collect what you put in when you are old), it is far from that as the current system operates under unique funding and benefit formulas.

On the funding side, both employers and employees contribute 6.2 percent of earnings up to $102,000 in earnings (2009 maximum level). The payout schedule is based on the highest thirty-five years of earnings adjusted for inflation and wage growth—the so-called average indexed monthly earnings (AIME). Once the AIME is computed, monthly checks are determined by the following formula:

90 percent of the first $711 of AIME;
32 percent of the AIME between $711 and $4,288; and
15 percent for the AIME above $3,955.

The steep progressivity of this formula means that low earners get a much higher return on their contributions than high earners. Ultimately, the people who make over $60,000 while working are subsidizing those who made $25,000 or less. Many people only talk about the flat tax rates with an earnings cap as being proportional taxation for most and regressive (pay less than their proportional share) for the very wealthy without looking at the benefit side. However, as a Congressional Budget Office reports notes, once the benefits and contributions are both included, the system as a whole is progressive.[116]

This progressivity is very important for low earners in the bottom 20 percent, with the lowest incomes going to the elderly who receive 79 percent of their income from Social Security and another 8 percent from other government programs for low-income people in 2006.[117] The next 20 percent of the elderly receive 80 percent of their incomes from Social Security (and just 2 percent from other government sources). In terms of other benefits from work-related retirement accounts, the

[116] Despite calls to increase the top earning level that is subject to taxation, congressional leaders have not implemented this proposal because they think that the political compromise that supports this system would be weaker if more high earners felt that the system was such a bad deal for them. The leaders remember that Bush's privatization plan was not politically attractive but worry that it might become more palatable if the levels of the taxes were changed.

[117] Data are from: Table 8.A5, U.S. Social Security Administration, Office of Retirement and Disability Policy, *Income of the Population 55 or Older, 2006,* available at: http://www.socialsecurity.gov/policy/docs/statcomps/income_pop55/2006/

bottom two quintiles received 4 percent and 9 percent, respectively, of their income from these sources.

Even the middle income quintile of the elderly received 65 percent of their income from Social Security, 9 percent from their current earnings, and 24 percent from savings and company pensions. It is only in the fourth quintile that the share of income from Social Security dips to 46 percent versus 34 percent from pensions and returns on saving. And, it is only in the fifth income quintile when Social Security payments represent a small share (22 percent) of their annual cash payments as compared with 41 percent from pensions and savings.

These ratios are based on shares of family income from various sources. The levels of income for those over sixty-five are remarkably low: the incomes at the 20th percentile in 2006 were: $11,519; at the 40th percentile, it was $18,622; at the 60th percentile, $28,911; and at the 80th percentile, $50,069. Even though these are the official census numbers, they are too low. For example, compared to data from IRS and bank data, reported interest income on this census survey are 'underreported' by 14 percent while dividend income is underreported by 39 percent. More troubling for the analysis of the incomes of the elderly people, pension income is underreported by 25 percent. Another problem is that withdrawals from 401(k) plans would not be treated as income according to the census approach.

Because of these problems, the census data on the distribution of elderly incomes must be used with great care and might be 25 percent higher than reported. Even with this adjustment, the dollar amounts are low yet a high proportion of the elderly evaluates their retirement favorably. So the reduced expenditures, lower taxes, free health care, and no or low mortgage payments (81 percent of the elderly are home owners and 67 percent of this group has no mortgage debt) mean that their money goes further while they have more time to pursue their interests.

In terms of the dollar amounts of pensions, only 41 percent of all retirees received any payments. Of this group, 31 percent received less than $6,000 per year; another 22 percent received between $6,000 and $12,000; 28 percent received between $12,000 and $25,000; leaving just 19 percent receiving more than $25,000. Even if these figures were increased by a third (incomes that are underreported by 25 percent have to be increased by a third), the share of people covered and the amount of money received shows that the good old days when company pensions were the norm, did not adequately serve most of the population.

The Other Side of Wealth—The Myth of Drowning in Debt

The signs of trouble seem everywhere with the number of bankruptcies and home foreclosures at very high levels. Various commentators talk about credit card debt being out of control with the average debt being $10,200 for each household. The problem has gotten so bad that a credit counseling industry has been created to help people get out from under a crushing mountain of debt. Finally, some say that our prosperity over the last fifteen years has been based on a borrowing spree that can't continue. Consequently, these doomsayers are predicting a day of reckoning when the debts will have to be repaid causing consumer demand to shrink and the economy to implode.

The evidence that Americans are drowning in debt revolves around too many people with high credit card debt, late payments, declaring bankruptcy, rising debt to income ratio, and share-of-income dedicated to debt repayment. Each claim purports to find that the number of persons with debt overload is rising fast, leading many to the breaking point. As will be shown, approximately 20 percent of the population has debt problems and this number has just risen a bit over time. The alarmists bank on people's nervousness about being late on their payments to generate a state of panic.

Public feelings about debt mirror other opinion-poll findings that people worry about the problem, in general, but don't think that these problems affect them personally. For example, in response to a question about "the issue of household debt on things like credit cards, car loans, home mortgages, and payday loans in this country," 47 percent think it is a very serious problem and another 35 percent think it is somewhat serious.

In the same poll, 48 percent are worried about not having enough to pay all their bills. Yet, the share drops to 23 percent when they are questioned about specific kinds of debt such as whether they are going deep into credit card debt or do not have enough money to pay their monthly mortgage. In terms of practices, a majority, 51 percent, say that they almost always pay their credit card debts on time each month.

When asked about the causes of high personal debt, the most frequent answer was individual consumption (35 percent), followed by the economy (24 percent), and even the government (23 percent found a way to blame the government for high personal debt). Surprisingly, only 10 percent said that it was lending institutions that cause the high debt. The fact that so many people can blame government for a problem that has so little relationship to their personal finances shows how much the public sector is blamed for any problem in the country.

A number of researchers (Weller, EPI, New America Foundation) have tracked the growth of debt in relation to disposable income: this figure stood at 74 percent of income in 1979 and rose to 132 percent in 2005. It is argued that this growth shows that consumers are awash in debt and that this level of debt has reached an unsustainable level.

Even though it is superficially logical to think that debt should not be greater than income, this argument fails for three reasons. First, when comparing debt to incomes, averages are used. But wealth and debt is very unequally distributed and the differences between average and median are very large in this area. Of those with debt, the average level was $103,000 but the median was half that amount at $55,000.

Not everyone had debt however: 23 percent of households in 2007 had no debt of any kind. When this group is included, the average debt of all households was $97,070 and the median was $27,700. That's right, the median level of debt of all households including mortgages, student debt, credit card debt, and auto debt was just $27,070, which puts the ratio of median debt to median income at about 60 percent, and not the 130 percent cited.

Second, the increase of debt over the decade was due to the rising amount of mortgage payments which rose from 46 to 96 percent of income. This meant that 83 percent of all consumer debt was tied up in residential property (72 percent for the primary residence and 11 percent for other residences). In the past, mortgage debt was not considered as frightening as other forms of debt because it was backed with an asset of greater value and because the alternative to not having a mortgage was paying rent.

There is no doubt that the current crisis has changed the relationship between home values and mortgages. Given that prices have gone down 20 to 30 percent from their 2006 peak and more than that in selected markets, the value of many people's mortgages is now greater than the price that they can sell their house for. Too many people took out home equity loans or refinanced their homes with larger mortgages to use the extra money for home improvements or other reasons.

So at this particular moment, more people have trouble with their debts than ever before, but this is not a trend; it is the result of the unique circumstances of the run-up in housing prices from 1996 to 2006. It should be noted, however, that many of the people that are underwater have other assets (e.g., businesses and retirement saving accounts) that still keep their net worth in positive territory.

Other key findings about credit card debt in 2007 are:

- 54 percent of households had no credit card debt after paying their monthly bill; this means that the median credit card debt of Americans is zero.
- Of those with outstanding credit card debt at the time of the survey, the median debt was $3,000.
- Among young people under thirty-five, 54 percent had no credit card debt, and the median debt for those with debt was only $1,900.

This is a far cry from stories about the average American family having $8,000 to $12,000 of credit card debt.[118] There are several reasons why these popularly cited numbers are so different from the median figures cited above. First, they use averages rather than medians; a few wealthy and not so wealthy people with large credit card debts can drive up the average (5 percent of households had credit card debt of at least $22,000. Second, the numbers that they cite refer to households with credit cards, which excludes the 25 percent of households with no credit cards. Third, the high average credit card debt figure is based on the daily average credit card balance as reported in bank monthly reports. One might think that this is a very credible number until one looks more closely. When looking at credit card debt, the issue is how much is left over after paying the monthly bill. The bank reports, by contrast, only track daily balances without adjusting for people who pay their balances on time. Furthermore, the bank reports include the monthly charges of self-employed professionals who use their credit cards for business purposes.

The other indicators of the debt crisis have increased only slightly over time. First, according to various findings by the Survey of Consumer

---

[118] In all of *Payback,* Margaret Atwood has one short discussion about current debt levels (a case of a pastor who counsels a family with $75,000 in credit card debt while earning $50,000). According to the Survey of Consumer Finances, there were only three-tenths of 1 percent of households in this income range with this level of credit card debt.

Finances (SCF), the median debt payments out of income for debtors increased from 15.3 percent in 1989, to 18.6 percent in 2007. Second, the share of households that devote 40 percent of their income to debt (remember this includes the home mortgage) rose from 10.0 percent to 14.7 percent over the same years. Third, the share of debtors with payments at least 60 days late was relatively low, in 2007, at 7.1 percent of households, but has probably risen significantly because of the economic crisis. Finally, fourth, the number of personal bankruptcies rose substantially from 1980 to 2006 when a new tougher bankruptcy law was passed; nonetheless, even at its peak of nearly 2 million filings for bankruptcy protection in 2006, this represented less than 1 percent of all adults. A rough precrisis estimate of those with substantial credit problems would be 19 percent—having a bill sixty days late, paying over 40 percent of one's income to debt service, or having a credit card balance of over 20 percent of income.

The Financial Health of Those Approaching Retirement: Have People Saved Enough?

Many commentators have focused on the low overall savings rate to argue that Americans nearing retirement age are totally unprepared for retirement. Their focus on the near zero savings rate in the mid-2000s is evocative but inappropriate. Because much of retirement spending is counted as "negative savings," the saving rate of all consumers is not indicative of what is happening with nonretirees. A paper from the Center for Retirement Research carefully disaggregates the numbers and finds that the savings rate for those under sixty-five was never near zero. Instead, the saving rate (including personal savings embodied in businesses) was 10 percent in 1980 and 8 percent in 2003 (the first and last years of their analysis).[119] Another indication that people are indeed saving for retirement is the rising net worth of people as they age.

But even if people were saving, was it enough? First, it should be noted that it is not clear what standard should be used to judge how

[119] Alicia Munnell, Francesca Golub-Sass, and Andrew Varani, "How Much Are Workers Savings?" (Center for Retirement Research at Boston College, 2005): Issue Brief #34.

much money retirees need. At the low end, the expected state of future retirees could be judged against the conditions of today's retirees to determine if their absolute standards of living are higher or lower. Some people would use a higher standard and judge future living standards against how near retirees live today. This "replacement ratio" approach requires more income because many of the future retirees have had higher incomes than the generation before them at the same age.

The replacement ratio approach, however, can lead to the odd result that retirees with a $25,000 yearly income may be considered to have met their goal while other retirees with an income of $75,000 may be considered to have failed to meet their goal. The reason for this is because replacement ratios are driven by normal income before retirement. If the retiree with low income had low income for retirement (say, $30,000 to $35,000), then the retiree would have met his or her replacement ratio. By contrast, if the retiree with a high income had an average family income of $150,000 a year before retirement, then he or she would have too low a replacement ratio to be considered as having enough income in retirement.

Replacement ratios are also very dependent on the definition of what income has to be replaced. Alicia Munnell and other researchers at the Center for Retirement Research at Boston University have developed a "retirement risk index" based on comparing expected retirement income as a share of people's incomes in their early fifties. John Karl Scholz from the University of Wisconsin, on the hand, has published a series of studies based on maintaining one's consumption levels over the course of a lifetime. The Munnell approach leads to a high share of mid- and late–baby boomers not having enough savings to maintain their living standards in retirement. On the other hand, the Scholz approach finds that 81 percent of upcoming retirees have enough money to maintain their living standards (based on their lifetime and not just high point consumption level) while the other 19 percent are not that far off.[120]

---

[120] In John Karl Scholz's approach, the presence of children has a big effect. Because he is interested in consumer goods available throughout one's lifetime, incomes for families with children are shared among more people. This makes the standards of living of adults when they have children effectively lower than the number of dollars would indicate. By contrast, when the subjects are in their early fifties, the children are no longer living at home and the effective living standards are higher.

The effect of the massive declines in home and stock prices obviously has had a big effect on people's retirement. Those under fifty probably have enough time to adjust their savings and hopefully see a rebound in stock and home prices. But for those between fifty and sixty-four, this change in asset values has been very distressing. For example, an April 2009 Pew poll found that people in this age group were most likely to have lost money on their investments (66 percent versus 44 percent for people of other ages) and most likely to say that the "current economic problems will make it harder to take care of their financial needs in retirement (75 percent for fifty- to sixty-four-year-olds versus 67 percent for eighteen- to forty-nine year-olds and 56 percent for those sixty-five and older)."

Since the most recent data on the financial status of near-retirees is from the 2007 SCF, the reported wealth is not a good indicator of people's financial status in 2009 and 2010. For 2007, median net worth increased by 20 percent from 2004 (in inflation adjusted dollars) to $120,000 for all households. Since wealth is very much related to age, householders who were fifty-five to sixty-four years old were found to have a net worth of $253,000.[121] The authors of the study estimated the effects of the decline in housing and financial assets as of late 2008, and concluded that median net worth as of that date was slightly lower than the level in 2004.

There were many studies using the 2004 SCF and related surveys, and they can be used as proxies for current conditions, especially if the dollars are reported in 2004 rather than 2009 dollars (in effect, this builds in another 15 percent decline). In most studies, people approaching retirement are presented as having more financial resources than their predecessors (who, we presume, had more resources than the retirees that preceded them). In a typical study from three Federal Reserve economists ("Do Households Have Enough Wealth to Retire?"),[122] elaborate statistical procedures are used to simulate total wealth holdings by using SCF 2004 data supplemented by capitalized estimates of

---

[121] Alicia Munnell, Francesca Golub-Sass, and Dan Muldoon find that the total net worth of the typical 55- 64-year-old was $676,500. This figure includes nearly $300,000 as the value of their expected Social Security payments. Center for Retirement Research, March 2009.

[122] David Love, Paul Smith, and Lucy McNair, staff working papers in the Finance and Economics Discussion Series. (2007–17).

the value of expected Social Security and defined benefit payments. They find that the average household of those with at least one member fifty-one or older has a present net worth of $536,000 with an expected annuity value of $32,000 a year.

Because of the inequality of earnings and incomes, the average hides the fact that 21 percent of future retirees will have low incomes when they retire: 12 percent of households are expected to have incomes below the poverty line and another 9 percent are expected to be between 100 and 150 percent of poverty. This number is quite comparable to the current share of retirees with low incomes.

Even though retirement incomes are projected to still be slightly higher than those of previous retirees, preretirement incomes of upcoming retirees were much higher than current retirees. So, the financial hit from the current crisis has undercut the retirement plans of many people. One of the strategies to deal with a shortfall is to work longer, and elderly labor force participation rates have been trending up after decades of decline.

In order to reduce Social Security costs, "normal retirement age" (the point at which one earns full benefits) has been pushed back by two years. These changes reflect the fact that our retirement system was created when people were working 60–70 percent of their life span. As was shown in Table 7.2, people are now only working 52 percent of their life spans and are healthier in their sixties and seventies.

This is a classic political choice of how generous we want to be to elderly nonworkers. Some see these changes as "takeaways" from the time when the system was more generous. Another way to look at this is changing the rules in light of changing conditions.

Possible Solutions

Economists can be very cold and analytical. For them, living well in retirement is a problem of trading current consumption when you are young for future consumption when you are old. This "consumption smoothing" depends solely on individual time preferences, and in an ideal world, people should be left to make their own choices.

In reality, people are not as careful as economists believe they should be, and too many seem not to save enough for retirement. For this reason, the federal government stepped in and set up Social Security systems to guarantee a minimum level of income for the elderly. Because we weren't going to let old people live in near starvation, public policy preempted people from making bad decisions that government was going to have to pay for anyway.

A secondary system of company contributions or pensions for retired workers developed in parallel to Social Security. Again, this is somewhat a validation that people left on their own will make bad decisions. Companies offered pensions because they could attract and keep the best workers on the basis of this added benefit. Once one large firm started this practice, it spread to other firms as a defensive mechanism to not lose workers.

Some people have proposed making traditional company pensions portable. This seemingly provides the benefits of DB payouts with universal coverage. Like many things, the problem with this proposal is its cost. First, many firms don't contribute to a retirement plan for their employees and 20 percent of workers choose not to participate even when one is offered. In order to make the system work, both firms and workers would be required to participate and to contribute. Second, the payout under traditional pensions could be generous because only 20 percent received the maximum rate of return on the highest salary level. So, this proposal is really an expansion of Social Security with very generous payouts to middle- and high-earning workers. To be financially self-sufficient, it would require quite high premiums from both workers and employers. Given the reluctance to raise Social Security taxes, it seems hard to believe that people would support the massive increase in taxes and company contributions necessary to support this system.

Conclusion

Most people use the terms "social contract" and "safety net" interchangeably; to the degree that there is a difference, the social contract has more to do with benefits that employers provide their employees while the safety net is more concerned with government benefits provided to nonworkers. In any case, both terms refer to providing people with incomes and services, especially for the poor, infirm, elderly, and unemployed.

With the exception of health care and Social Security, the other elements of the government safety net are rather sparse when compared with other industrialized countries: our minimum wage has often lagged behind inflation; we have cut back on welfare payments and limited eligibility to five years; we don't provide for child care; and unemployment benefits have strict eligibility requirements, are limited to six months (except during times of recession), don't replace a high proportion of earnings, and are capped at a fairly low level. In terms of retraining displaced workers, other countries have much more extensive "active labor market policies."

By contrast, we spend considerably more money on health care services and on providing adequate incomes in retirement. Over the last twenty years, the costs of these commitments have expanded a lot, and they are going to expand even more in the next twenty years. Surprisingly, these added costs have sometimes been presented as cutbacks. The critics note that in the 1970s, a majority of companies paid all of the premiums; now, workers are forced to pay part of ever-rising insurance payments through co-pays and deductibles. They also note that company pensions used to be the norm; now, private firms rely mainly on 401(k) and profit-sharing plans. These shifts are the basis for claims that corporations are unilaterally breaking the old social contract.

But these claims have been shown to be false. When health insurance costs were smaller, companies were often paying the total amount. As insurance premiums rose, companies had a choice—to continue to pay the entire premium and give lower pay raises or to charge employees for a small portion of the insurance payments and give larger pay raises.

From the employer's view, it is the total compensation package that matters and the division between pay and benefits is based solely on how they think employees will best react. To think otherwise is to view health insurance as a free good that has no consequences on company costs. In fact, companies know that workers care about both wages and benefits, and try to balance the mix given the rising costs of health insurance.

With respect to retirement, companies are still contributing the same share of payrolls but have shifted from traditional pensions to 401(k)s. This transition from defined benefits to defined contributions does somewhat shift the retirement risk onto workers. But the old system was only really generous to workers with more than twenty years of service with the same company. This was never a large share of the work force, and it is a much smaller share today.

In the end, our growing health care and retirement commitments have been mostly immune from cyclical contraction and provide a source of economic strength. While unemployment has been rising, one of the major sources of new jobs has been in our health care sector. The incomes of workers in this sector and the spending by retirees will be key elements in our rebounding from the crisis.

CHAPTER 8

Conclusion: Why We Will Rebound

IN RETROSPECT, the decisions of the mid-2000s on things like financial regulation, mortgage lending, CDOs and the like seem ridiculous. What were they thinking (or smoking)? Yet, behavioral psychologists have shown repeatedly that a collective closed-mindedness can develop as people don't see contradictory evidence (inattention bias) and only see evidence that supports their position (confirmation bias).[123] In Chapter 1, investors, home buyers, evaluators, and financiers made the same mistaken judgment about the future of housing prices. Other people who were responsible for providing oversight against excessive evaluations and risk-taking—e.g., home appraisers, rating agencies, reappraisers, compliance officers, and federal regulators did not see the high level of risk either.[124]

From 1945 through 2007, one could have confidently asserted that a mixed economy with large government safety nets and reasonable regulations created a "self-correcting" system that kept growth going with minor interruptions. The movement to offices and high-skill services

[123] Professor Anne Sibert provides a number of references that show that men are more prone than women to take high risks. "Why did the bankers behave so badly?" is available at: http://www.voxeu.org/index.php?q=node/3572.
[124] As Robert Shiller notes in *The Subprime Solution*, "[U]ltimately an important reason why all these factors fed the bubble has to be that the very people responsible for oversight were caught up in the same high expectations of future home-price increases that the general public had" (p. 53).

added extra stability as firms no longer needed big inventories. Further, innovations like just-in-time production created efficiencies in managing product flow from conception to sale. Finally, the added competition from overseas firms and potential hostile takeovers ensured that management was aggressive in pushing the company to being its most productive.

So, we seemed to have the best of all worlds—overall macrostability and pressures on individual firms to innovate and cut costs. But the success of the system encouraged a certain smugness and laziness about downside risks. The financial industry took advantage of these attitudes and pursued a multidecade strategy to undo the limitations imposed on them by Glass-Steagall and related laws. They argued that the steady growth and greater importance of investing in the general population led to more financial reporting in the media, chat rooms, specialized Web sites, and day traders. Consequently, financial markets needed less government regulation because these new institutions would be effective in exposing fraud and bad company performance.

By 2000, two new laws greatly reduced the regulation of financial corporations, and the banks responded with a tidal wave of financial consolidation. The new superbanks and the old investment banks became much more aggressive in developing profit-making strategies based on new financial instruments. At the same time, the rise of generous stock options as compensation encouraged the taking of large risks because yearly bonuses in the millions were determined by single-year results. The manic search for profits first led to the accounting frauds at Enron and other companies, and then to the crazy combination of subprime mortgages, CDOs, CDSs, and SIVs.

The theory that the market could correct the bad behavior of financial institutions turned out to be a mirage, and we careened from a bursting stock bubble, to corporate scandals, to a growing housing bubble, and finally to financial collapse. This should not be a surprise because investors are not positioned by temperament or ability to police financial institutions. Also, the financial media found that strong optimism made for more compelling reporting than balanced or negative reporting. Finally, by consolidating retail stockbrokers with investment houses, stock analysts were unlikely to be critical of companies that might do business with another branch of their organization. This meant that stock analysts became strong proponents of recommending company stocks as two-thirds of all stock analysts' recommendations were either for buy or strong buy: In February 2000, on the eve of the one of the worse stock market crashes ever, just seven out of 1,000 analyst recommendations were for selling a stock.

The self-correcting mechanisms that worked so well for decades were overwhelmed by a financial implosion that stopped the normal flow of loans to companies and consumers. The economy had become so wedded to the free flow of credit that the disruption of this flow immediately caused the economy to contract, and each successive layoff led to falling demand and additional layoffs. A negative feedback loop developed as the implosion of the financial sector undermined the real economy, and the decline in the real economy made the financial problems that much worse.

But one should remember that the crisis caused no buildings to fall down, no highways to disappear, and no knowledge to be erased. In fact, the crisis and fall in stock and home values has a "cleansing" effect. Because home prices are lower now, it is easier for first-time buyers (especially young people) to purchase a home at a reasonable price. Companies that laid off workers because of slack demand can reorganize to become more efficient. Finally, although it may not seem so, the financial industry has learned the limits of certain strategies as few investors will purchase CDOs, CDO-squareds, and other exotic instruments in the future.

Because of the lessons learned from the Great Depression, the government intervened quickly with massive infusions of money in the forms of a stimulus package to increase consumer demand and bailout money for the financial institutions to stabilize lending. Further, we are not the Japanese with their ten-year stagnation (the "lost decade"), following their simultaneous crash of stock and housing prices. Americans are a much more "can-do" optimistic bunch. With the slightest opening, they will go out and form new ventures and they will return to shopping as if there were a robust ahead. To the degree that "animal spirits" matter,[125] we have them in spades.

The fact that all of the minifinancial crises through 2002 caused so little lasting economic damage gave us a false sense of confidence as to what could happen if risk-taking were pushed ever higher. We have learned this lesson and can develop a sensible regulatory framework to restore our economy to a stable footing. Unfortunately, the financial

---

[125] The title of a book by George Akerlof and Robert Shiller.

industry acted as many adolescents do—they kept testing the limits until they found danger. In the end, this learning process is beneficial for adolescents. While one would have thought that a mature financial sector did not need to be taught new lessons, apparently it did, and it will be reconstructed on a sounder basis.

The kind of society that will emerge after the crisis passes will be very much like the one that existed before the crisis. As were shown in chapters 3 through 6, economic growth over the last several decades has rewarded those with high educational attainment who have succeeded in the office and high-skilled service sectors. These trends are likely to continue and young people should be encouraged not to leave high school but to attend at least one or more years at a two- or four-year college. Young women seem to have gotten the message and are now attending postsecondary schools at a considerably higher rate than their young male counterparts.

We are a very rich society with the capability of producing vast amounts of goods and services. We need to unravel the financial mess and start the positive feedback loop in which more production leads to more demand, which leads to more production. This will occur, the only question is when.

Many people expected quick results when they saw the vast amounts of money expended in the stimulus and bailout packages. In promoting these policies in its first month in office, the Obama administration made the mistake of overpromising when they talked about the unemployment rate reaching a maximum of 8.5 percent if the stimulus package passed. While this may have affected a few votes on a crucial piece of legislation, it turned out to be off the mark because it was based on macro models that have consistently underestimated the negative impact of the financial crisis.

In late 2009, the unemployment rate went over 10 percent and will likely remain over 8 percent throughout 2010. It takes time to initiate production, earn profits, and start the positive feedback loop of more production, more demand, and more hiring. Just as the unraveling took many months (the first signs of the crisis appeared in February 2007), the rebound will take a while as well. Another negative is that the European recovery is expected to take longer because their businesses are slower to fire and hire workers. In an integrated world, their slow recovery will be a drag on ours.

It is hard to forecast the exact timing of how the world will recover.

But the positive forces are progressively becoming stronger than the negative ones, and the engine of our economy is starting to pick up steam. Staying with same metaphor, the financial crisis can be thought of as having thrown sand in our economic engine. Normally, our economy is so diversified that one sector cannot have a very large negative effect. But finance, because it is so intertwined with all industries, is the exception. The fact that we can isolate the cause of the current recession shows that there are no structural constraints impeding the recovery.

However, the negative downward spiral has had a big effect, and to speed up the recovery, the federal government needs to continue to "prime the pump." The huge losses of so many financial institutions mean that many firms are effectively insolvent and reluctant to take on added debt. Attempts to rid these companies of these assets have proven to be more difficult than expected. The numbers of potential assets involved are truly massive and the government does not have the capacity to purchase them all at their face value. Other attempts to form entities to purchase these assets have not developed as quickly as some had hoped because the holders of the assets have held out for a high price.

While the Federal Reserve has driven interest rates to very low levels, the main tool available to the government is an expansionary fiscal policy. The original stimulus package has been slow to take full effect. While this means that there will be added stimulus throughout 2010, it still makes sense to pass another stimulus package or to use some of the returned money from the federal budget for a job creation program.

Some fear that too much stimulus could lead to high inflation in the future. The downside risk of inflation, however, must be weighed against the risk of weak or no economic growth (much like what happened in Japan in their lost decade). The risk of inflation is very low because it is hard to see how a wage-price spiral could develop in the midst of an economy with this much unemployment. In addition, the weak economies in the rest of the world provide checks on inflationary pressures. Finally, the Fed is watching carefully for signs of inflation and is ready to change policies to counter any inflationary pressures.

Additional stimulus can take the form of extending unemployment insurance and helping state and local governments that don't have the luxury of deficit spending. Giving money to people in need will ensure that the money is spent quickly and can avoid untold numbers of human tragedies. In our past and in other countries, public service employment has been used to keep morale high, to provide incomes, and to maintain a person's working habits. While this approach has strong political opposition, it is still important to find ways to provide income to people in need.

Finally, on the mortgage front, restructuring of distressed mortgages has proceeded slowly. Despite the high costs of foreclosures for the holders of the mortgage debt, banks have been surprisingly reluctant to set up the needed procedures to make restructuring easy. They have announced grand proposals but have not followed through. The FDIC has been in the forefront of calling attention to this problem and should be encouraged to continue to prod the banks to do more restructuring.

Future Fiscal Problems

There is a lot of discussion about the coming entitlement explosion: the Peterson Foundation has a $1 billion endowment to educate the public about the pernicious effects of the size of our federal deficits. There are several other organizations like the Concord Alliance that assert that we are creating a future nightmare with the accumulation of so much debt. Certainly, many members of Congress and newspaper editorial boards have been convinced, and demand that we begin to reverse the sea of red ink once the crisis ends.

There are three key issues that have received a lot of attention: Can we afford the run-up in Medicare and Medicaid spending? Will Social Security be there for me? What are the impacts of high federal deficits? These are somewhat related issues because Social Security spending affects spending and deficits. However, the real driver of federal deficits is the explosive growth of health care spending in the Medicare, Medicaid, and health insurance contributions for government workers and retirees.

Although you've probably heard the question, "Can we afford the current growth in medical spending?" on many nightly news and public affairs shows, you have not heard on the same shows the questions, "Can we afford the number of people living in suburbs?" or "Can we afford the number of people having McMansions?" or "Can we afford the number of people taking ski vacations or who are members of country clubs or who go on guided adventure tours in Africa, Asia, and Latin America?"

Since you have not heard these questions, does this mean that people living in suburbs or in big houses or who take nice vacations are doing more important economic activities than consuming medical care? The answer to this question is obviously "no," but the juxtaposition of these questions does show that some decisions are political choices, and others are left to individual consumers based on a very unequal distribution of assets and incomes.

If we go back to the fundamental economic questions of size and distribution of the economic pie, we can better understand the relevant issues. Given our high level of productivity, we *can afford* to consume lots of different combinations of consumer baskets.

Medical spending is different from most other spending because we provide it to the whole population. The majority of the population is insured indirectly through the workplace or by purchasing insurance directly. The employer connection creates a bit of confusion because we don't see the money that is spent. In essence, employer contributions for their workers' health insurance policies should be considered a form of personal income. As was noted in chapter 7, we chose this approach somewhat by accident, but conceptually, individuals are "paying" for their own insurance because they are passing up higher cash wages in place of insurance benefits.

The elderly, many children, and the poor are neither insured through an employer nor can they afford private insurance. As a society, we have decided to provide care for these people through different public programs and through hospital emergency rooms that provide services for which they do not receive full payment. Medicare is the largest and most generous of these programs because we think the elderly have significant needs and have earned the right to the best medical care.

Nonetheless, the bottom line is that providing medical care at low or no cost represents a transfer of resources to these people; it's no different from giving these people money to buy insurance on their own. The source of this money is other people's taxes.

Although there are trust funds for Medicare and Social Security, it is important to understand how they really work; let's just follow Social Security, although the same analysis with a few different specifics applies to Medicare. Since 1983, more taxes have been collected in each of the trust funds than are needed in that year to pay for the benefits. This surplus is presented as a "prefunding" of the money needed to finance the benefits for the huge baby-boomer cohort, which has already begun to retire (retirees can get reduced social security benefits starting at age sixty-two).

This prefunding mechanism is somewhat of a charade because the surplus is held as government bonds: in essence taxes are collected from one source (Social Security and Medicare taxes are 6.2 percent of workers' wages—up to $102,000—paid both by the worker and the employer), used to buy government debt, and then spent on current government programs. In essence, this is simply a tax increase with the Social Security system being left with claims on future government revenues.[126]

Some have mistakenly argued that this sleight of hand means that Social Security will not be able to meet its future obligations. This is not true because the opposite sleight of hand will begin in 2016 when Social Security revenues will be less than Social Security payments. For the following twenty-one years (2016 to 2037), taxes from FICA and other sources will be paid to the government, and then the money will be distributed to Social Security and other government programs as promised.

So, in the years ahead, the accounting surplus of FICA taxes over benefits paid will decline through 2016. As this is happening, expenditures for Social Security benefits will be rising (more retirees), which will put a strain on the federal budget. But the Social Security component of that strain is no different than any other federal commitment. In essence, the budgetary position will have benefited from the unusual surplus in the Social Security accounts from 1983 through 2016.

In 2037, (the exact year changes with each successive forecast) the surplus is projected to disappear. At that time, the Social Security system is not "bankrupt"; it just will not have any surplus in the trust fund to draw on, and yearly FICA collections will support 74 percent of promised benefits. To get to 100 percent of payments, there are several options: first pay the remainder out of general funds; second, increase FICA taxes now

---

[126] Since the trust fund holds government bonds, it is credited each year with the interest that is due on that bond. Again, this is not a cash transaction but an accounting procedure—the "value" of the trust fund is increased by the amount of interest on the bonds.

to further "prefund" expected benefits (this could be done through an across-the-board rate hike or by increasing the maximum earnings level subject to FICA taxation); and third, reduce benefits.

It is important to emphasize that there is no such thing as "prefunding" or "intergenerational transfers." Each year, the number of people working determines the amount of output subject to the technology and fixed capital in place. Total output, in turn, is divided among workers, profits, and nonworkers. Prefunding is simply an exchange of revenue flows—workers from 1983 through 2015 agreed to put extra money into the general fund in return for a promise to take money out of the general fund from 2016 to 2037. This is considered "fair" because those who paid into the general fund in the earlier period will be the ones taking money out of the general fund in the latter years.[127]

So the key questions for 2037 are: Do we want to make another prefunding exchange? Do we want to give retirees fewer benefits? Do we expect elderly people to work longer? All of these are political questions; the economy, we trust, will be much more productive in 2037, and will be very capable of supporting a large share of nonworkers at a reasonable to comfortable standard of living.

Of course, all this discussion assumes that our overall government finances are in order. For virtually every year since 1950, the federal government has run a yearly budget deficit. On the surface, this seems illogical and dangerous. Yet, after so many years of deficits, the public has become a bit blasé about hearing about more deficits. Many politicians have reacted to this lack of concern by saying that "deficits don't matter."

The reason for this odd development is that the federal budget is subject to a different accounting approach than other bodies. At a personal level, when you purchase your first home, you don't subtract the cost of the house from your income and report a big loss in that year. Instead, this is treated as part of your "capital" account, and the mortgage represents a loan against the value of the house. Similarly, businesses don't report loans for major expansions or purchases of machinery

---

[127] One of the little-known secrets of the Social Security Program is that the first beneficiaries through the 1960 beneficiary did not "prefund" their benefits. The money for their benefits was taken from general tax revenues. If this money was credited to the Social Security trust fund, there would be no Social Security shortfall in the future.

on the income statement but rather on their balance sheet—the new asset on one side and the debt on the other side. In terms of their yearly income statements, they deduct as cost the "depreciation" of their assets.

As opposed to state and local governments, the federal government does not have a separate capital budget. Instead, the federal government treat the purchase of long-term assets (a building, a road, a piece of equipment, armaments, etc.) the same way it treats the purchases of pencils, pens, and the wages and benefits of public employees—in accounting terms they are "expensed" in the year in which the asset was bought. State governments can't run deficits in any year but they have capital budgets in which bonds are placed to pay for infrastructure projects. Often, these state budgets limit the share of interest payments as a way to limit capital spending.

While there are many experts who think that a federal capital budget would be a clearer way to present federal spending, old ways die hard and this change is unlikely to happen. Instead, we need to accept that the federal government can run a yearly deficit of two to three percent of GDP without creating financial problems.

Total public debt as a share of GDP is the best indicator of our fiscal position, and this ratio has varied widely over the last seventy-five years and varies widely across countries. A lot depends on what the debt has been used for. For example, exiting World War II, the ratio of our federal debt to national income level was very high, but this did not prevent us from growing quickly in the twenty years after the war. Over time, our economy grew faster than the debt, so this ratio declined steadily even as we were running small yearly deficits.

At the end of the Clinton years, the debt level was very low and government surpluses were projected for several coming years. Federal Reserve Board Chairman Alan Greenspan and others actually worried about the effect of the disappearing national debt. The recession, the Iraq war, and Bush's multiple tax cuts brought back large deficits. In the last few years, the government's response to the crisis has been to open the federal money taps in the form of a nearly $800 billion stimulus package and a $700 billion "troubled asset" program. Consequently, deficits have skyrocketed and are projected to remain high for years to come. Even when the recession ends, revenues will not keep up with expenditures because of Obama's middle-class tax cuts and his commitment to increase health care access (and because the Social Security surplus is dwindling).

The size of these deficits is somewhat troubling but there may be some mitigating factors. First, the government bailout of the financial industry was based on loans and partial ownership. If the experiences of the S&L and LTCM bailouts are a guide for the future, it is possible that a lot of money will be flowing back into federal coffers in the next several years. Second, economic growth may reduce the size of the deficits relative to the size of the economy as a whole.

Third, the deficit does not fundamentally change the basic economic act of producing and distributing output. The only intergenerational transfers that occur involve the stock of machinery, buildings, and knowledge that is the product of previous investment. The primary means by which the federal deficit negatively impacts future generations is through the indirect effect of driving up interest rates and decreasing long-term capital investments. By and large, this is a small effect, and each recent American generation has done an adequate job in providing a strong knowledge and physical base to ensure strong future production cycles.

A secondary means by which the government deficit can impact future generations is through our international debt. Although many people think that all federal debt is bad (their prejudice against debt), debt held by Americans does not directly impact national income in any given year. From the point of view of the economy as a whole, government debt held by Americans represents a transfer of money from taxpayers to bondholders. Instead of one person having the money to spend on consumer goods, a different person now has the money.

Debt held by foreigners potentially affects consumption patterns because the flow of interest payments out of the country represents a drain on current incomes in the country (from taxpayers to foreigners). However, there are three reasons why this is not a big problem. First, it is hard to make the direct connection between the federal government running a deficit and capital flowing out of the country. As was discussed in chapter 6, our capital imbalance is connected to the value of our currency and the desire of other countries to run trade surpluses. Second, to date, our outflows of interest payments, dividends, and reinvested earnings to foreign countries have been in balance despite the fact that we have a net deficit of $3.5 trillion. Finally, even if this capital-payments flow turns negative, it is not likely to be a large figure relative to the size of the whole economy.

The bottom line of the entitlement crisis is that it is primarily a distributional issue and the real issue is taxes: Deficits and entitlements can always be resolved by increasing taxes. People unfortunately want a "free lunch"—generous medical payments and incomes for the elderly and low taxes. Economics does not work this way, and this is the basis of our "crisis." At this moment, the tax-cutting passion of the Republicans has affected the Democrats (who are tired of being beaten over the head as the party of high taxes). Further, the recent experiences in California don't inspire confidence that an engaged public will treat deficits seriously.

Health care expenditures are almost certain to rise in the next decade, and we are almost certain to continue to provide top-quality care to seniors and modest care to the indigent. Unless we turn our backs on these commitments, we will have to contribute more in taxes. But one should remember that this process occurs slowly and as the economy continues to grow. So although we will have to pay higher taxes, the standard of living of future taxpayers will be considerably higher than ever before.

"We can't afford higher taxes" is the claim of some, but this is nonsense. European countries have had higher tax rates for decades and have kept pace with our economic growth. If you have ever gone to Europe, you know that Europeans don't live at Third World levels. The myth of "Euro-sclerosis" often pops its head whenever there is a short period when growth in Europe is below that of American growth. But over long stretches of time, their standard of living has improved in tandem with ours despite tax rates as high as 50 percent in many countries. The argument that taxes discourage work or that taxes undermine our international competitiveness is belied by the European experience.

An interesting take in Europe comes from Russell Shorto recounting his experiences of moving to Holland for several years. First, he was appalled by the 52 percent tax rate; then he was enthralled by the many services and subsidies he received; and then he was ambivalent, missing the many services that were readily available in America (e.g., stores open longer hours) but not in Holland, and a bit taken aback by the power of conformity and the lack of the drive for excellence.[128]

[128] "Going Dutch: How I Learned to Love the European Welfare State," *New York Times Magazine,* May 3, 2009, p. 42.

Four Other Issues to Consider

To say that the economic glass is three-quarters full means that there is much that needs to be done. The alarmists think that they can scare the majority into supporting a massive expansion of public programs.

Instead of large changes, here are four areas, which will be at the center of public policy debate in the next few years.

1. Education

Reforming our educational system is both an investment—a more educated workforce will produce better—and a transfer of resources to low income people (because it is their low level of educational attainment that is the problem). It is generally agreed that our elementary and high schools are mediocre, and this is reflected in many international exams in which American youngsters score poorly on math, science, and reading exams. On the other hand, our graduate-level programs are considered the best in the world by a wide margin, and draw the best and the brightest from many countries. Since graduate programs are tied to undergraduate programs, our colleges are also very highly rated.

So, the key problem is how to improve our elementary and high schools so that more people can be fed into our superior postsecondary educational system. Harvard economists Claudia Goldin and Lawrence Katz in their 2008 book, *The Race Between Education and Technology,* underline the importance of succeeding at this task. They argue that one of the main engines of our economic growth over the last 150 years has been our commitment to the expansion of educational opportunities to our children—first, public education at the primary level, then high schools at the secondary level, and finally college at the tertiary level. Since about 1970, the share of each cohort having a four-year degree has remained constant at approximately 30 percent. In 1970, this was ahead of the rest of world; now there are many countries with similar and even slightly higher college graduation rates.

Much of the attention about access to college has focused on affirmative action for African-Americans and Hispanics at highly select universities. The reason for these programs is that these two groups would be severely underrepresented if a purely merit-based approach were used for admission criteria in accepting students to the top 10 percent of colleges: Blacks and Hispanics each represent close to 20 percent of each age cohort in high school yet would each constitute approximately 2 percent of each new entering class admitted to elite colleges if the decisions were based exclusively on grades and SAT scores.[129] As social policy, we think that this disparity undermines social cohesion and does not adequately prepare a diverse next generation of business and political leaders.

It should also be noted that the student bodies of these 146 elite colleges are very skewed with respect to social class: If the family socioeconomic (SES) backgrounds of students are divided into four ordered "quartiles," then 74 percent of students in top schools come from the top quartile, just 3 percent come from the bottom quartile, and another 6 percent come from the second quartile. This means that less than 10 percent of the students in elite colleges come from the bottom half of the social ladder.

This occurs because of a series of cascading advantages. Children from affluent class backgrounds are more likely to have parents who read to them, to enter primary school with a bigger vocabulary, to get early remediation for any educational problems, to go to better high schools, to take rigorous academic courses, and to engage in music, art, or other cultural activities at an early age. These students anticipate attending college and undertake the many necessary activities it takes to be fully prepared to apply. Of those in the lowest SES quartile, three-quarters do not take a college entrance exam, and most of those who take the test score below 1,000. In the second-lowest SES quartile, fully 81 percent either do not take the test or score below 1,000. Even in the third SES quartile, nearly 70 percent are in the no-test and below-1,000 groups. It is only in the top SES quartile that most students take the college entrance exam.

Social class also affects the extent to which equally talented students take a college entrance exam and whether they go to a four-year college. Even among students who score the same, those in a higher SES category are more likely to take the SAT or ACT, and are more likely to go to four-year schools. As part of this survey, participants were given an assessment prepared by the Educational Testing Service, referred to

---

[129] See Anthony Carnevale and Stephen Rose. "Socioeconomic Status, Race/Ethnicity, and Selective College Admissions," in *America's Untapped Resource: Low Income Students in Higher Education*. (New York: The Century Foundation Press, 2004).

here as the NELS test. Among those in the top NELS test quartile but the lowest SES quartile, fully 43 percent took neither the SAT nor the ACT, whereas only 13 percent of the high scorers in the top SES quartile did not take either test.

In terms of the intersection of class, ability and access to college, 81 percent of those in both the top NELS test quartile and the top SES quartile enrolled in a four-year college within two years after completion of high school. By contrast, only 44 percent of those from the lowest SES quartile, who had high NELS test scores, went directly to colleges granting bachelor's degrees. In fact, fully 31 percent did not attend any postsecondary institution. In an odd equivalence, the lowest-scoring young people from the top SES quartile went to college at the same rate as the highest-scoring young people from the lowest SES quartile.

Some people focus on the high costs of attending college as the reason why low SES children don't go to college. While it is certainly true that college tuitions and fees have been rising rapidly, the majority of the evidence shows that only few college students forgo postsecondary education because of high costs. For example, the share of each age group attending a post-secondary institution has risen slightly at the same time that costs were rising. Even with the recession, the share of new high school graduates enrolling in four-year colleges has remained constant. To the degree that costs affect decisions, students are more likely to select public colleges and schools closer to home.

The "sticker prices" of universities is actually very different from the prices that most people pay because only about one third of students in four-year schools pay the posted rate. Higher prices mean that those who do pay the full rate provide institutions with more money for grants for students who cannot afford to. Consequently, although federal educational grants have not kept up with rising costs (Obama plans a big increase in these programs), the share that moderate and low-income families have paid out of their incomes for sending their children to school has not increased over time.

But this is not good enough as many people think that a higher proportion of young people need postsecondary education, especially given the relatively poor quality of K–12 education in America. Since our elementary and secondary schools are run locally, the federal government has decided to put pressure on them to improve performance through testing-based evaluations of their students (e.g., Bush's No Child Left Behind initiative).

The bottom line is that education is a huge part of our economy and a huge factor affecting our future. Nearly a quarter of the population is enrolled in school (73.7 million in 2007), total education spending was $972 billion or 7.4 percent of our GDP, and there were 5 million teachers and another several million administrative and support personnel. And managing this system are thousands of local school districts operating under a variety of state rules.

Finally, it is still the parent that plays a key role. Within every income layer of society, there is a wide variation in parental involvement. Consider President Obama's mother who gave him English lessons at 4 A.M. each morning while he was an eight-year-old in Indonesia. Studies show that early education is very important and that we need to provide universal prekindergarten schooling. In the years ahead, it is going to be less a question of pouring additional money into our educational system that makes a difference but a commitment to improving quality instruction and parental involvement in for our elementary and secondary education.

2. Green and infrastructure development

Although not part of the central theme of this book, global warming and our profligate use of fossil fuels require a series of economic responses. Economies change dramatically over time, and "green development" represents a new series of products and industries that will play a greater role in the future. In the short run, new technologies tend to be too expensive to be commercially viable. In past transitions, the government has played a key role in providing funding and early markets for new innovations, such as railroads, airplanes, and computers, and we can expect this to happen again in this area.

In the coming decades, the movement to energy efficiency will proceed along several tracks. First, in terms of power generation, solar, wind, and even ocean and tidal waves provide a huge pool of sustainable resources. Second, there will be new automobile mileage standards that will lead to the greater use of hybrids and electric engines. At some point, hydrogen-powered cars will start to become commercially viable. Third, in the short run, energy efficiencies will be achieved in our current power plants by the judicial use of a cap and trade system that encourages the most cost-efficient systems to be adopted first.

In a parallel manner, infrastructure spending represents a similar initiative that requires public leadership and investment. This is an example of a "natural monopoly" because one water supply system for a town is all that is needed; it would be very difficult to create a market for water systems with companies competing for business and with customers changing companies over time.

As publicly funded activities, infrastructure expenditures go through waves of expansion and periods of underinvestment. Over the last several decades, we have not been spending enough on the maintenance and new investment in roads, bridges, sewer systems, water mains, and related activities. As the falling bridge in Minnesota demonstrated, some of these deficiencies are past the critical point (another example is the main water delivery line into New York City).

Apparently, the antitax fever has impeded political leaders from raising more funds. But this is a bit surprising because infrastructure is something many people have a daily connection with: they drive on the roads and go over the bridges. The money lost to increased wear-and-tear of vehicles and lost time in traffic jams is substantial. So, in many ways, these investments are very visible and have a high rate of return.

The government needs to take a more proactive approach to economic development. While some people think that "industrial policy" often fails because it is impossible to pick winners, the experiences of the development of most technologically advanced products such as airplanes and computers show that big advances often occur in concert with public action.[130] Although our history of providing subsidies to energy-efficient technologies (e.g., solar panels, wind farms, and alternative fuel automobiles) have not yet led to dramatic results, the future demands more action and we must be very aggressive in ensuring that American companies are part of this industrial wave.

3. Family-friendly work policies

One of the major social and economic changes in our lifetimes has been the entry of women into the labor force. While this is mostly a positive trend, there is no doubt that this has made it more difficult for

---

[130] The Information Technology and Innovation Foundation, a small Washington-based organization, has been at the forefront in proposing "pro-growth" strategies based on policies to assist the development of human capital and technology.

families to do routine chores, especially child care and caring for elderly parents. Historically, these tasks have been the wife's responsibility, and there are lots of pressures for this pattern to be maintained. For families that need to free up time for one of the parents to spend more time on family needs, the decision is weighted toward the wife taking the time off because she generally has lower earnings than the husband.

While the yearly census report shows that the "gender earnings gap" has fallen to 23 cents on the dollar, this is a misleading number because this comparison only applies to full-time, full-year workers in a single year. Because women are much more likely to move in and out of the labor force, their combined earnings over fifteen years is much different from men than the limited one-year census snapshot finds. For example, I found that the earnings of women workers were 43 percent lower than comparable male workers when their entire work experiences from 1983 through 1998 are compared.[131] There is a self-reinforcing system that keeps women's earnings low. In order to meet family responsibilities, a married couple loses less money when the woman forgoes working. Since career interruptions reduce long-term earnings, women's jobs are built to accommodate women moving in and out of the labor market and thus pay less.

As women have stayed in the labor force more persistently, pressure has called for the adoption of family leave programs. By making these programs open to men as well, families are better able to balance work and child and elder care. In addition, four states (New York, New Jersey, California, and Hawaii) permit pregnant women to receive payments for the working time that they miss. These payments make it easier for women to make the transition in and out of the labor force during the months before and after their delivery.

We need to expand on the rights established by the Family and Medical Leave Act by ensuring that that all adults can take time off for family responsibilities without facing job loss or lack of career advancement. In addition, approximately half of all working parents with young children have no access to child-care programs and are forced to juggle work schedules and informal care arrangements.

---

131 Stephen J. Rose and Heidi Hartmann. "Still a Man's Labor Market: The Long-Term Earnings Gap." (Washington, D.C.: Institute for Women's Policy Research, 2004). It should be noted that the gaps in incomes are much less because women spend the major part of their lives in husband-wife couples.

4. Helping the needy

There is a long history of public provision for low-income people, and the debate on "best policies" continues today. On the one hand, we are very generous to the elderly because we believe that they are "deserving" of society's assistance. Our views toward assisting young adults are more ambivalent and President Clinton ended "welfare as we know it." Fifteen years later, the results are mixed—there has not been an explosion of homelessness and dire poverty as some on the left predicted but there also has not been a radical decrease in poverty as people purportedly become more responsible for their own well-being.

But the issue of helping the needy is not simply one of dealing with the narrow layer of people who are permanently low-income. Even in good times, some companies contract and lay off workers. Older workers, in particular, may not have the updated skills to succeed in today's labor market. Other countries spend much more than the United States on "active labor market" policies that include money for retraining and support while workers are between jobs. The Obama administration is expected to unveil new plans in this area including "wage insurance," which would be an expansion in the approach of unemployment insurance such that working people could receive benefits if their new wages are considerably below their former level.

The lessons of the past, however, are mixed. In the midst of the downturn, unemployment benefits have been extended while programs serving low-income populations have been hit by budget cuts. Finding the correct balance between individual responsibility and a public safety net will continue to be a challenge: In the 1960s and 1970s, we swung too much to public support; since 1980, we have swung the other way and need to be more generous with public support for those who have not been able to succeed on their own. This is especially true given that the current crisis has negatively affected millions of people who "played by the rules," yet are now without jobs and/or have lost their homes to foreclosure.

State governments have many responsibilities for taking care of low-income people. Medicaid and TANF (Temporary Aid to Needy Families—the current official name for welfare programs today) are only partially funded with federal dollars and require state matches. State and local governments are the primary funders of educational expenses, and low-income people and areas are subsidized out of state revenues.

In the current downturn, state finances have been squeezed at both ends: Revenues are down and costs are up. As opposed to the federal government, states don't have the option of deficit spending and find it very difficult to raise taxes in this environment. Consequently, many states face fiscal crises, and there have been many battles in a variety of state legislatures over how to balance budgets. Many of the solutions are temporary fixes, and some reports project that ten or more states will be in budget crises for years to come. To date, some of the federal stimulus money have been targeted to states, and some call for an expansion of these intergovernment transfers.

Final Comments

Many scholars and commentators have earned their intellectual reputations on the basis of showing that American capitalism is in decline. In the 1950s and 1960s, the American economy was populated with "organizational men" and assembly-line workers who had uninteresting jobs that stripped them of their creativity and led to widespread alienation. The countercultural revolution was meant to change the priorities of a country that was obsessed with material possessions.

In the 1980s, Japan was widely predicted ready to become the world's number-one economic power on the basis of their superior economic model. Lester Thurow, a leading economist, predicted that a united Europe would surpass America by the beginning of the twenty-first century. Others saw rising government and international debt, and predicted a day of reckoning when America would face many years of declining standards of living to pay for our profligate ways.

Now, in 2010, many are claiming that the financial crisis has demonstrated that the American model has shown itself too vulnerable to large downturns and no longer a model that should be followed.

Since we have yet to exit this crisis, the critics have a certain standing of having predicted the crisis (you'll be proven right eventually if you predict a looming crisis for thirty-five straight years) and are calling for large structural changes.

The key economic debate that we are now facing concerns the nature of the recovery: Will it be V-shaped (sharp recovery), U-shaped (slow recovery), W-shaped (double-dip recession), or L-shaped (stagnation and very slow growth).

There are three broad schools of thought.

The "structural pessimists" feel that inequality is to blame and hope that a Democratic president and Congress will adopt sweeping changes (a new New Deal) to reverse decades of destructive economic policies under Democratic as well as Republican administrations that devastated the middle class.[132]

The "cyclical pessimists" argue from their reading of historical evidence that recoveries from large financial crises are weaker and take longer than normal recessions. They do not have the expansive social agenda of the structural pessimists but worry that the federal government will not have the capacity to maintain the right combination of stimulative monetary and fiscal policy. The tendency of the populace to want quick results and the rivalries between and within political parties make it very difficult for large and decisive actions once the threat of total collapse disappears.

By contrasts, the "optimists" base their views on the belief in Americans to bounce back from adversity. They see a strong resiliency in our entrepreneurial economy and trust the "animal spirits" of consumers and investors.

With a few prominent exceptions, most economists aren't structural pessimists and hence do believe that the economy will rebound over time. Based on America's economic track record from 1945 through 2007, they view this financial crisis as a deep recession and not as a fundamental end to our capacity to grow.

Some argue that the depth of the financial implosion will mean that it will take longer to recover, but this argument is based on the length of time to get to recovery, not on the ultimate prospects to return to robust economic growth.

Not surprisingly, the argument over the recovery is affected by partisan politics. Many Republicans think we are moving toward "socialism" by expanding government spending and regulation. Although they are in a bit of bind because it was their *laissez-faire* policies that permitted the financial institutions to create the mess that we are in (a few, though,

---

[132] To avoid stagnation or a double dip recession, prominent structural pessimists propose some combination of industrial policy (to restore the unionized manufacturing base), retrenchment on free trade (to avoid the rush to the bottom in terms of wages), expanded social spending (to reverse the abrogation of the old social contract), higher taxes (to pay for the new programs and reverse the effects of wage inequality), and new regulations (to stop the old patterns from repeating themselves).

make some far-fetched arguments that government made the financial mess), they focus attention on their two favorite themes of lower taxes and less regulation as the way out of our troubles. Since the Democrats control both Congress and the presidency, Republicans have mainly become critics, forecasting that Democratic policies will lead to slow economic growth.[133]

On the other side, liberal Democrats see great failings in our current economy and trace our problems back to the power of the rich and the corporations over the vast majority of population. They have produced a large body of research purporting to show that the conditions of the middle class are not that different from the conditions of the poor. By expanding the size of the problem, they think that they are building support for a much larger expansion of safety-net programs than those proposed by the Obama administration. Therefore, they are critical of the administration for not going far enough.

As has been noted, the negativists have gotten a lot of attention in the mass media. This has led to an "optimism gap" between what people think about their own well-being and what they think about the economic conditions of society as a whole. In poll after poll, worries are expressed about the state of the middle class at the same time that people report being satisfied with their own economic situation. For example, in a 2006 Pew survey, respondents were asked about how today's children will fare when they grow up, relative to how people are living today. The negative answer ("worse off") outpolled the positive answer ("better off") by 50 to 33 percent. Yet, this answer conflicts with that of the answer to the similar question comparing *your own* children to *your own* living standard. This question has been asked consistently since 1994 by the General Social Science survey (and in 2005 by *The New York Times* and in 2008 by Pew). In these surveys, the answers are more positive: 66 percent say that their children will live better, 18 percent the same, and 25 percent expect them to be worse off (5 percent did not answer). When the time frame is changed and the question is "How do your current living standards compare with those of your parents at a similar age," in a 2008 Pew poll, 67 percent said that they live better

---

[133] Of course, this reprises their comments on the 1993 Clinton budget and tax policies, which were passed without a single Republican vote and were predicated on the prediction that passing the bill would lead to no employment or economic growth for the next five years.

than their parents, 19 percent said about the same, and just 13 percent said that they are worse off than their parents.

The people are on to something. In the preceding chapters, I showed that neither the claims of the Right nor the ones of the Left represent what has been happening in the last several decades. America has had the most powerful economy in the world since about 1880. We have been blessed with many natural advantages, but we have also made many good choices: we have let lots of immigrants in and we have created an open economy for companies to grow and expand.

The freedom to succeed is also the freedom to fail and the freedom to connive and deceive. So, we have also come to realize that we need strong public programs to help those who don't succeed and regulations from stopping the strong from abusing their power and undermining the economy. A mixed system has worked well for us and other countries. Sometimes, the balance gets out of whack, and this time, the underpinnings of our economy was severely disrupted. This is a temporary problem, though, and we are in the process of getting back on our feet. Although there are challenges ahead and there will be disagreements over how to divide our economic bounty, our best days are still ahead of us.

Understanding the New-Fangled
Financial Instruments

THE INNOVATIONS on the securitization front involved the expanded use of CLOs (collateralized loan obligations), CDOs (collateralized debt obligations), and CDSs (credit default swaps). The key to selling mortgage-backed securities (MBSs) was having AAA-rated bonds. This was important because many buyers (e.g., pension funds, insurance companies, and municipal agencies) were limited by law to buying only AAA-rated bonds.

Consider the financial wizardry needed to make subprime mortgages the basis for AAA bonds.[134] First, you start by combining many mortgages (a few thousand) together. Let's say that the combined cash flow from all these mortgages is $103 million a month. The second important feature of MBSs is that the cash flow is prioritized into different streams (called "tranches" from the French word for slices).

The different kinds of bonds created from the pooled mortgages are based on their priority standing in getting their share of the combined mortgage payments. The typical MBS is "overcollaterized" in that only $100 million are pledged to the bonds; in other words, if 3 percent of the borrowers don't pay their bills, there will still be enough money to fully pay all of the bondholders.

A typical MBS with five tranches was structured as followed: The

---

[134] One uncharitable way that some on Wall Street described this process was "making chicken salad out of chicken shit."

trick to getting a AAA rating was to set up a senior tranche that received the first $80 million of payments from the combined pool; the second senior AA pool would get the next $11 million; the third would go to A-rated bonds for the next $4 million; the BBB-rated bond would get the next $3 million, and the unrated tranche would get the final $2 million.

The math is quite simple: If all the payments are made (no defaults), everyone gets their expected monthly check. If 4 percent of borrowers in this pool don't pay and the flow is only $99 million (the first three million just affects the originator of the bonds, which holds the excess collateral), then the top four tranches get their full monthly checks, and the holders of the bottom tranche gets $1 million instead of $2 million. If the default rate rises and only $94 million is available, then the lowest two tranches get nothing and the holders of the A tranche bonds get only three-quarters of their full payment.

The AAA tranche will only be affected if the monthly deficit is $23 million or higher. Since there was no history of default rates going this high, the rating agencies seemed on firm ground when they rated these senior tranches so highly. The attractiveness of the other tranches was that their prices were much lower to account for the added risk. If the housing market was strong enough that defaults were very low, then you would get a very high return on your investment.

But wait, there's more! If the financial manipulations had stopped here, the crisis would not have blown up with such fury. The next financial creation was a CDO based on the combination of the lower rated tranches of MBSs. In other words, the junior claims of various MBSs were combined, and their cash flows were prioritized.

Consequently, the senior tranches of these collateralized debt obligations (also called ABS—asset backed security) were based on the first claim to the cash flow of various junior claims. You need computers to keep these things straight and to figure out the probabilities of defaults of the various pieces to determine the probability that the holders of the senior tranches of the CDOs would get all their expected payments.

The problem of making CDOs is selling the junior tranches in which the risk is highest. In most cases, hedge funds with a high tolerance for risk were the main purchasers of these bonds. The sponsors of the CDOs often lent up to 80 percent of the purchase price to the funds to make this a more attractive investment for the hedge funds. This created a hidden risk to the sponsors: If the hedge funds defaulted on the loan, then the sponsor would be left with the worthless loans.

There are two variations of this dangerous approach to using secondary claims to create new structured bonds with senior AAA bonds. First, instead of using the lower tranches of mortgage-backed securities, the lower tranches of securities based on commercial loans or mortgages, student loans, or credit card debt were used to create "CDO-squareds." Second, instead of using first mortgages, a limited number of CDOs were based on second mortgages. In many ways, this cash flow was even more precarious than the flow of money based on the junior tranches of mortgage-backed securities because the second mortgages were the first not to be repaid.

There was some realization that even the senior tranches of bonds created in these ways were not as strong as the senior tranches of mortgage-backed securities. There were two ways to please the rating agencies or to protect the investors in these bonds. First, the companies that specialized in insuring corporate bonds (the "monoline" insurers—Ambac, Radian Group, ACA, and MBIA) expanded their business to insure CDOs. Second, another financial instrument, "the credit default swap (CDS)," provided the same service without regulatory oversight. The terms of a CDS meant that the seller of the swap would be paid an annual fee from the buyer in return for compensating the buyer whenever a defined negative "credit event" occurred.

The use of CDOs and CDSs exploded at the same time the worst of subprime mortgages was being created. In 2006, $224 billion of CDOs were sold (up 89 percent from the previous year), and the upper limit of CDS exposure (their "notional" value) was over $50 trillion. This is not a typo, the total value of the swaps was many times the value of CDOs because of the presence of speculators and hedgers (they were betting on or protecting themselves from certain market moves).

Not to miss an opportunity, the cash flows of the CDSs were then pooled into a "synthetic" CDO with the payments prioritized and turned into bonds. In fact, some CDOs were actually combinations of cash flows from mortgages, other CDOs, CDSs, and other debt instruments such as corporate bonds, credit card repayments, and commercial mortgages. The CDOs were very flexible because they could be "actively managed"—if a mortgage was repaid, the pool was replenished by buying the stream on income from a new debt instrument. Is it any wonder that once this system came under stress, no one knew how much each CDO and other related assets were worth? Another problem was that many of these contracts were very poorly written because of sloppy legal work.

Furthermore, all of the CDOs and CDSs were "over the counter trades" between consenting parties and not subject to any regulatory body. Up until 2000, a CDS would have been illegal because of the reforms initiated after the 1907 crash. One of the causes of that earlier collapse was the excessive speculation on future stock prices at "bucket shops." These were pure bets because one did not need to own the stock. After the panic of 1907, these street corner parlors were closed because it was felt that they caused wild swings in prices. In 2000, the Commodities Futures Modernization Act was passed that formalized the legality of derivatives and that limited states from regulating them with their anti-bucket shop laws.

Before we leave this financial maze, there is another institutional arrangement that needs to be explained. All of these instruments were created by large financial institutions that were charging fees to create them. In a remarkable sleight of hand, these institutions found a way to keep all of this activity off their books by setting up "conduits," "special purpose entities," and "structured investment vehicles (SIVs)." The advantages of this approach were that the investment was not subject to regulatory oversight and, because the money was in a different entity, the sponsoring institution did not have to increase its capital base (reserve levels) as a cushion against losses in this endeavor.

Here's an example of how it worked. First, a bank would set up a trust to pool the mortgages and create an MBS. Second, the bank would also set up an SIV (most often incorporated in the Cayman Islands) to purchase the cash flow from the MBS. Third, the SIV would borrow in the commercial paper market, up to 80 percent of the money needed to purchase the cash flow. Fourth, the SIV would sell bonds to investors for the remaining 20 percent.

The profitability of this scheme depended on the interest rate of the commercial paper (loans of three months or less) being less than the effective interest rate of the cash flow of the MBS that the SIV was buying. To get the lowest rates, these loans were often turned over every two to four weeks. But this "lending short to invest long" was obviously risky and the investors in SIVs demanded added protection. This was accomplished by the sponsoring institutions of the SIVs guaranteeing "back-up financing" if the commercial paper was not available at the appropriate interest rate. This liability of the financial institutions did not have to be disclosed on its regular reports to the public and financial regulators. This was no small omission given that SIVs in October 2007 held $1.4 trillion in various kinds of derivatives.

Financial Institutions

COMMERCIAL BANKS are intermediaries and their earnings are based in part on the interest rate spread between what they pay their depositors versus how much they charge their borrowers. Banks have to collect funds to be able to lend money. On the one hand, there are "demand deposits" in checking accounts. These are transactional balances that help individuals and companies pay for living expenses and other bills. Money flows into these accounts regularly from earnings or other sources of income, and flows out just as regularly. These funds are a source of capital because not everyone asks for all their money at the same time.

There is a second kind of account that provides banks with capital. Historically, saving accounts differed from checking accounts by paying interest on deposits. It appears that you can come into your bank and take out money at any time. While this is the usual practice, savings accounts are technically "time deposits" with restricted access and banks don't have to give you money when you request it.

Of course, today, banking is more complicated. Many checking accounts are money market accounts and pay a low interest rate for depositors who always keep a specified minimum balance. Certificates of deposits are a form of savings deposits in which depositors agree not to request their money for a specified time period (usually six months up to a few years). If an investor needs his/her money before the end of the contract, most, if not all, of the accrued interest is lost.

Based on long experience, banks know that they only need to keep a limited amount of money available ("fractional reserves" or more recently legislated reserve requirements) to meet the daily needs of their customers. They can lend the rest of their deposits and earn profits. Some of their assets are not loans but easily sold bonds so that they have an extra cushion should they need money to cover losses or depositor demands. Finally, banks have the ability to borrow from other banks if there are any daily problems with their meeting their reserve requirements.

In the past (and in other countries in the last ten years), there have been "runs" on the banks. This occurred when depositors feared that the bank was on the verge of collapse and they lined up to get their money out of what they thought was a failing institution. In many cases, the fears were based on large losses adversely affecting the banks' ability to meet their depositors' demands. Hence, whoever was at the front of the line was able to retrieve some of money while those at the end of the line were left with nothing.

At times, the runs were based on panic rather than real banking losses. Nonetheless, because banks keep relatively little cash on hand, even a bank with enough good assets could not meet all of its customers' demands for cash at the same time. In this situation, they are termed "illiquid" because they have assets but they don't have enough cash. In cases where banks actually lost money, they don't have enough assets to repay their depositors, they are "insolvent."

The Federal Deposit Insurance Corporation (FDIC) was created in the 1930s in the United States and (with similar entities in other countries) to assure depositors that their money was guaranteed (up to a certain limit) against bank failures if their bank was a member of the FDIC (some state banks have guarantees under different programs). This has successfully assured depositors that they would not lose their money to forestall a panic run on banks (the current limit on insurance was recently raised to $250,000).

Banks are not pure intermediaries and must have a certain amount of capital contributed by the owners of the institutions. This provides a cushion against loan losses. The level of capital required by a bank has varied over time and depends on the makeup of its depositors. Clearly, banks would have very low profit rates if their capital requirements equaled the total amount of the loans they made, and so banks are typically capitalized at a rate of between 5 and 10 percent of their assets.

This "fractional capital contribution" is more than enough of a cushion in strong economic times. While not all bank loans are repaid, the interest that borrowers pay (which varies according to their credit-worthiness) assumes a certain amount of nonpayment. When defaults rise, profits fall. If defaults rise to very high levels, there may be no profits, and when defaults rise to exceptionally high levels, losses will exceed all the bank's capital.

Since banks tend to have as little capital as possible, any losses that reduce ownership capital threaten the ability of the bank to maintain its capital requirements. If this fall is large, then banks can be declared insolvent and be shut down due to low capital reserves. If regulators are vigilant, banks with inadequate capitalization will have to sell assets, raise more capital, or arrange to be bought out by a stronger institution.

Sometimes, regulators will give "forbearance" to banks for their low capitalization for a period of time to allow them to get back on their feet. Many times this works. But other times, banks with low capitalization have little left to lose and "swing for the fences"—i.e., to regain capital they seek out risky, potentially highly profitable investments. In the worst cases where banks have no capital left, these "zombie banks" have invested very poorly and lost large sums of money that added to the costs of closing them down.

Finally, many other companies serve a role similar to banks by providing money to people who need it. *Investment banks* aren't depository institutions even though they have the term "bank" in their title. These entities (the major ones have all collapsed or been incorporated into other financial institutions during the current crisis) mainly advise businesses on mergers and acquisitions, and on trade. In addition, they create financial instruments, manage the funds of wealthy individuals, and are "prime brokers" for hedge funds and other financial institutions.

Insurance companies make their money by using the money paid for insurance policies. Their "underwriting" activities—i.e., collecting premiums and distributing money for claims—mostly break even. But like banks, they use the balances accrued by customers but not immediately needed for claims to invest in stocks, bonds, and other assets.

Pension funds are like insurance companies because they hold a lot of money and offer their clients a variety of investment options. In essence, these are long-term savings accounts that offer the option to invest in fixed-rate securities (bonds), stocks, or some combination of the two.

Hedge funds and *private equity firms* represent specialized investment companies. They get money from "experienced investors"—rich people and institutional investors—and pursue aggressive market strategies with lots of debt leverage.

Sovereign Wealth Funds are a relatively new form of investment. They started in oil-producing countries that collected huge royalties on the extracted oil. This money dwarfed the needs of public expenditures so was put into a separate investment vehicle controlled by the government. The Chinese and a few other countries copied this model when profits from state enterprises swelled up and needed a new outlet.

Refuting Three Studies

Using IRS Data

In 2005, Thomas Piketty and Emmanuel Saez published an academic paper tracking U.S. income distribution with data from the Internal Revenue Service. They also made their data available on Saez's Berkeley Web site in the form of fifty-one spreadsheets in a single Excel file. Piketty and Saez focused on the income of the richest 10 percent of Americans, and, more specifically, the richest 1 percent and one-tenth of 1 percent. Their published tables also showed that, from 1980 to 2005, those in the bottom 99 percent on the income scale had no income gains over the last twenty-five years, and average incomes actually declined for the bottom 90 percent.

The problem with IRS data is that they are based on tax filers and not families. To avoid higher tax rates, many older children living with their parents file separately. Consequently, there are almost 30 percent more filers than there are households. Furthermore, the IRS median income is 35 percent lower than the median incomes found in other government surveys, and the share of the IRS population with incomes below the poverty level is twice the level of the official rate.

Piketty and Saez provided an explanation of their method in a footnote on the forty-ninth spreadsheet of their data, revealing several problems: they did not account for transfer income like Social Security, they did not account for changes in household sizes over the last quarter-century, and they did not use the best gauge of inflation. They reported that adjusting their data for all of those factors would result in incomes among the bottom 90 percent of Americans actually rising by 50 percent over the period of analysis. Consequently, IRS data as reported by Piketty and Saez is not comparable with other data sets and should not be used in the debate about changes in living standards for middle-class Americans.

MIT economists Frank Levy and Peter Temin showed that the Piketty and Saez data implied that 82 percent of income gains from 1980 to 2005 went solely to the richest 1 percent of tax filers. By revising the raw IRS data (using the more common measure of accounting for inflation and adjusting for family size), I found that 39 percent of income growth went to the top 1 percent. After sharing my results, Piketty decided to change the price deflator that they used and changed the data that he provides online; Levy and Temin also modified their online paper to make a similar adjustment and found that less than half of income gains went to the top 1 percent.

Christian Weller and the "Typical" Couple

The Center for American Progress was formed in 2005 by John Podesta, the former White House Chief of Staff to President Clinton. The center now employs several hundred people at its Washington, D.C., office, and is among the chief resources for Democrats in Congress. Christian Weller, the center's chief economist, wrote in late 2005 that the "typical" two-earner family had an income that year of $49,600. The Census Bureau's Current Population Survey (CPS), which economists generally consider the best measure of income, said the "median" income of two-earner families in 2005 was $82,600—a full $33,000 or 60 percent higher than Weller's couple.[135] Weller concludes that the

---

[135] That figure of "median" income means that half the two-earner families in America earn more than $82,600 and the other half earns less. Economists often use median income to describe a "typical" family. Median income, by the way, is distinct from "average" income, which you would derive by adding up all the incomes in America and dividing by the number of families. Economists generally consider that this does not provide a useful measure of typical income because a few rich folk, like Bill Gates, skew "average" income significantly upward.

"combination of stagnant incomes and staggering cost increases for important middle-class items—housing, health care, education, and transportation—have left families with less money to save and spend than just a few years ago, while working longer to achieve the same results as in 1980."[136]

Weller constructs his "hypothetical" family from data on the weekly earnings of nonsupervisory production workers.[137] These data, however, only apply to 80 percent of workers; they don't include managerial and professional high earners—that is, the top 20 percent of earners. Weller's typical couple is really the midpoint of the bottom 80 percent, or the 40th percentile, rather than the 50th percentile. Still, the income of the 40th percentile of the population in 2005 was $71,836, which is still $22,000 higher than Weller's hypothetical couple.

Weller estimates a husband's income on the basis of average weekly earnings of nonsupervisory workers, but this average includes men *and* women *and* full and part-time workers. Husbands in two-earner couples, however, are among the most stable workers, and virtually all of them work full-time, full-year. As Table A-1 shows, Weller's hypothetical husbands worked 1,751 hours and were paid $16 an hour; by contrast, real husbands in two-earner couples at the 40th income percentile in 2005 worked 2,154 hours, with an hourly wage rate of $18.73 an hour. That means that the real husbands earned over $12,000 more than Weller's husbands.

The situation for wives is slightly different. Weller claims to look at couples in which the husband and wife both worked full-time, full-year. Consequently, he gives the wives the same number of hours as the husbands. This figure is very close to the hours of working wives in families at the 40th percentile. To determine the wives' hourly wage, Weller reduces the husbands' wages by the level of the gender gap—the gap between men's to women's earnings. But, as shown above, Weller artificially reduced the husband's wage by including the wages of the

---

[136] "Middle Class Progress? Families Work Longer to Pay for Middle-Class Living than a Quarter-Century Ago," Washington, DC: Center for American Progress, 2005.
[137] The methodology is only briefly described in the report and was obtained through private communication with the author.

TABLE A.1
COMPARISON OF CPS DATA VERSUS WELLER'S
HYPOTHETICAL COUPLE

	Actual 40th percentile 2005	Weller 2005 simulation	Difference Actual − Weller
Husband's Hours	2,154	1,751	403
Wife's Hours	1,767	1,751	16
Husband's Wage Rate	$18.73	$16.00	$2.73
Wife's Wage Rate	$14.50	$12.32	$2.18
Husband's Earnings	$40,355	$28,021	$12,334
Wife's Earnings	$25,618	$21,576	$4,042
Total Earnings	$65,973	$49,596	$16,377
Nonlabor Income	$5,863	$0	$5,863
Total Income	$71,836	$49,596	$22,240

wives'. Now, in applying the gender gap, he also artificially reduces the wife's hourly wage: his hypothetical wife had a wage of $12.32 an hour, while real wives at the 40th percentile had an average wage of $14.50 an hour.

Finally, in calculating family income, Weller does not include the $5,863 in average nonlabor income of two-earner couples at the 40th percentile (e.g., interests, dividends, rents, unemployment insurance, and business income). When you add this to Weller's calculations, you find a total gap of more than $22,000 between the incomes of real two-earner couples at the 40th percentile and that of Weller's "typical" two-earner couples.

Weller next compares his hypothetical couple to a similar one in 1980, arguing that the 2005 income does not provide sufficient spending power because the prices of necessities have risen faster than the overall rate of inflation. Consequently, he argues that the 2005 couple has less money in real terms available for discretionary expenses than its 1980 counterpart. In essence, Weller says that the official consumer price index (CPI) does not adequately reflect the real conditions of moderate-income people. To be sure, the index is based on consumption patterns throughout the entire economy. Because wealthy people enjoy a disproportionate share of the income, their consumption patterns have a bigger effect on spending.

Forbes developed a separate price index for the rich and found that these prices rise faster than the overall rate of inflation. Other researchers claim that prices for the poor rise faster than the overall price index. Weller maintains the price for those in the middle rise faster for the average household.

However, prices for everyone in a group can't be rising faster than prices for the group as a whole or else we would have the classic case of everything being "above average." The federal Bureau of Labor Statistics (BLS) computes the CPI based on the work of hundreds of representatives, who go to stores around the country and note specific prices of hundreds of commodities and services. BLS analyzes the data to make sure the commodities stay the same over time. While that's easy for something like a bottle of milk, businesses constantly change some commodities and services, offering new features and technologies. Government researchers evaluate each commodity and service separately, making the necessary adjustments to separate pure price changes from quality improvements. With these individual estimates, BLS then creates a combined index by weighting the effect of each good/service by its share in the.overall consumption expenditures in the economy as a whole.

Weller does not dispute the inflation estimate of each good or service. Rather, he questions whether the weighting factors that are derived from the economy as a whole are the right ones for estimating the changes in prices of the goods that middle-class people consume. BLS researchers, also concerned about this issue, used the Survey of Consumer Expenditures to determine the consumption basket of poor households. They then reweighted the price changes of individual goods and services on the basis of what poor people consumed. They found negligible differences over time between the official CPI and the newly constructed one for poor people.[138] These researchers later expanded this approach to households all along the income ladder. At

[138] Garner, Johnson, and Kokoski, "An Experimental Consumer Price Index for the Poor," *Monthly Labor Review,* September 1996, pp. 32–42. Available at http://www.bls.gov/opub/mlr/1996/09/art5full.pdf.

each level, they reweighted individual price changes by the shares of goods consumed by different households on the income ladder.[139] Again, they found no significant changes between their new CPI and the standard one, concluding that the CPI is a good measure for all households.

Weller found large price changes for selected commodities, such as medical care, college tuition, and housing. With those price changes in mind, he argued that prices vary more for middle-income people than for others, leaving less available for the income of his hypothetical family to purchase necessities: "$19,542 [is] left to pay for basics—such as clothing, food, and utilities—to save for retirement, to improve their economic well-being, and to spend on any leisure and recreation. That is . . . $1,702 less than in 1980."

But, it is these "basics" that had lower rates of price changes. If Weller used the individual price adjustments, then the $19,542 would have bought more in 2005 than the same sum of money bought in 1980.

Elizabeth Warren and the Two-Income Trap

Elizabeth Warren, a lawyer who teaches at Harvard Law School, and Amelia Tyagi, her daughter and a sociologist, write in *The Two-Income Trap* that two-earner couples in the early 2000s had less disposable income than one-earner couples in the early 1970s, a finding that is cited as a troubling sign of the times. Warren and Tyagi focus on married couples with two children, aged four and seven. In 2002, both the husband and wife worked full-time and spent $10,000 a year on child care; in 1972, only the husband worked while the wife stayed home and took care of the children. They then show how the 1972 couple with one earner was actually better off.

While many people pass through this stage of working life, it's hardly typical. Of all couples in which the husband was less than sixty years old in 2008, only 15 percent had two or more children under the age of eight (the age of the children is important because older children do not require as much child-care expense). In 42 percent of these couples, one parent

---

[139] Personal communication with Thesia Garner, and see http://stats.bls.gov/ore/pdf/ec020030.pdf and http://stats.bls.gov/ore/pdf/ec020060.pdf.

was not working. In another 25 percent, the wives worked part-time. In 43 percent, the wives worked full-time, full-year—thus, only *6 percent* of couples were like Warren and Tyagi's "typical" couple, with two full-time earners and two children under the age of eight.

Census data show that couples use a variety of strategies to provide child care.[140] Two-thirds of families with working mothers use husbands, grandparents, older siblings, or other relatives to care for their children at least some of the time. Thus, almost a third of families with working mothers of preschoolers had no, or minimal, out-of-pocket child-care expenditures. About a third of all families with preschoolers used organized large care facilities (day-care centers, preschool, and Head Start) as their primary source of day care, while another 25 percent relied on non-relative care in the child's own home or the home of the provider. "[O]n average, mothers with one child paid $75 per week, while those with two or more children paid about $114 per week" for regular child care expenses, and just 10 percent of two-earner couples with two children seven or younger spent the $10,000 that Warren and Tyagi claim.[141] To be sure, some families pay $10,000 or more for child care. But they tend to be dual professional couples with high incomes. The median income of two-earner couples with two young children who spent at least $10,000 on child care was $96,000, and, there were virtually no families in the income range of the Warren and Tyagi study that spent that much.

So, *less than 1 percent* of couples fit the profile of the two-income trap—two full-time working parents with two children seven or younger, and spending more than $10,000 a year on child care.

After choosing an unrepresentative family, the authors turn to the rest of their typical family's budget and divide goods into fixed expenditures and discretionary items. Once again, this division is arbitrary, as Warren and Tyagi label food and clothing as discretionary, and label all items as necessary the price of which rose faster than the overall rate of inflation. They conclude, even though two-earner families had incomes in 2002 that were $35,000 higher than one-earner families in 1973, that two-earner families had less discretionary income than a one-earner family had thirty years earlier.

---

[140] Johnson, Julia, "Who's Minding the Kids?" Child Care Arrangements: Winter, 2002. Available at http://www.bls.census.gov/sipp/p70s/p70-101.pdf.
[141] "Who's Minding the Kids?" p. 16.

In the end, their argument that two-earner couples in the early 2000s had a lower standard of living (lower discretionary income) than one-earner couples in the early 1970s is built on inventing a fictitious two-earner family that is atypical, and then incorrectly computing their living standards.

The History of the Panel Study
on Income Dynamics

STARTING IN 1968 (and asking questions about incomes from the previous year), the Panel Study on Income Dynamics (PSID) began collecting information on people's experiences in 1967 and continues to follow up by contacting the original members, plus their children and their children's children. This is a very rich source of information providing a multiyear perspective, which permits researchers to compare periods decades apart. There is no other longitudinal data set with as much information for as long a time period as we find in this study. There have been many studies showing that the results from the PSID align with the results from other data sets (in particular the yearly CPS). Many ask what happens when participants can no longer be contacted and drop out of the study. The largest number of leavers occurred at the beginning of the study but there has been a small trickle of additional people dropping out each year. The leaders of the study account for these changes by adjusting the weighting of each case to try to keep the study representative of the entire population. The one major weakness of the study is the underrepresentation of people of Hispanic descent. Because the study started in 1967 when the Hispanic population was relatively small and only adds the descendants of the original members as they form their own households, Hispanics are now underrepresented in the PSID. This makes it very difficult to study the experiences of Hispanics using the PSID, but the general estimate of the share of the population who are low income using the PSID is comparable to that derived from the CPS and other data sets. Therefore, most researchers have concluded that the PSID is not overly biased toward higher-income households.

Growth Rates 1993–2005

	Income per capita	Employment
United States	21.4	22.9
Alabama	25.3	15.6
Alaska	8.5	21.2
Arizona	23.9	59.7
Arkansas	20.5	19.0
California	22.5	24.7
Colorado	27.6	36.5
Connecticut	23.2	12.1
Delaware	21.3	24.6
District of Columbia	41.1	3.6
Florida	21.7	43.5
Georgia	18.9	33.6
Hawaii	5.5	11.5
Idaho	17.9	41.0
Illinois	18.7	14.5
Indiana	18.4	14.4
Iowa	27.6	15.6
Kansas	22.4	17.4
Kentucky	21.4	18.7
Louisiana	6.1	17.3

	Income per capita	Employment
Maine	24.2	17.9
Maryland	27.7	24.3
Massachusetts	30.4	15.0
Michigan	16.4	13.9
Minnesota	29.6	23.4
Mississippi	22.5	16.3
Missouri	18.4	16.7
Montana	22.2	29.6
Nebraska	25.5	18.6
Nevada	18.0	84.3
New Hampshire	27.1	29.3
New Jersey	22.8	18.2
New Mexico	23.7	28.0
New York	19.8	13.1
North Carolina	19.1	24.3
North Dakota	32.6	18.2
Ohio	16.0	13.2
Oklahoma	26.2	20.0
Oregon	20.6	30.2
Pennsylvania	20.5	13.2
Rhode Island	22.6	13.1
South Carolina	20.9	21.6
South Dakota	34.1	20.9
Tennessee	20.6	22.5
Texas	25.6	33.0
Utah	23.3	46.2
Vermont	26.2	20.4
Virginia	25.6	25.8
Washington	19.2	25.6
West Virginia	18.2	12.9
Wisconsin	22.9	19.0
Wyoming	40.2	25.8

BIBLIOGRAPHY

Akerlof, George and Robert Shiller. *Animal Spirits: How Human Psychology Drives the Economy, and Why It Matters for Global Capitalism.* Princeton, NJ: Princeton University Press, 2009.

Alterman, Eric. *Why We're Liberals: A Political Handbook for Post-Bush America.* New York: Viking, 2008.

Ariely, Dan. *Predictably Irrational: The Hidden Forces That Shape Our Decisions.* New York: HarperCollins, 2008.

Atwood, Margaret. *Payback: Debt and the Shadow Side of Wealth.* Toronto: House of Anansi, 2008.

Baker, Dean. *Plunder and Blunder: The Rise and Fall of the Bubble Economy.* Sausalito, CA: PoliPoint Press, 2009.

Berenson, Alex. *The Number: How the Drive for Quarterly Earnings Corrupted Wall Street and Corporate America.* New York: Random House, 2004.

Bernstein, Jared. *Crunch: Why Do I Feel So Squeezed? (And Other Unsolved Economic Mysteries).* San Francisco: Berrett-Koehler Pubishers, Inc., 2008.

Bernstein, Peter L. *Against the Gods: The Remarkable Story of Risk.* Hoboken, NJ: John Wiley and Sons, 1996.

Bhagwati, Jagdish. *In Defense of Globalization.* New York: Oxford University Press, 2004.

Bitner, Richard. *Confessions of a Subprime Lender: An Insider's Tale of Greed, Fraud, and Ignorance.* Hoboken, NJ: John Wiley and Sons, 2008.

Brownlee, Shannon. *Overtreated: Why Too Much Medicine Is Making Us Sicker and Poorer.* New York: Bloomsbury USA, 2008.

Caballero, Ricardo, and Krishnamurthy Arvind, "Financial System Risk and the Flight to Qualify" http://econ-www.mit.edu/files/165, Nov 2005.

Carnevale, Anthony, and Stephen J. Rose. "Education for What? The New Office Economy." Princeton, N.J.: Educational Testing Service, 1998.

————. "Inequality in the New High-Skilled Service Economy." In *Unconventional Wisdom: New Perspectives in Economics,* Jeff Madrick, ed., New York: The Century Foundation Press, 2000.

————. "Low Earners: Who Are They? Do They Have a Way Out?" *Low Wage Workers in the New Economy,* Richard Kazis and Mark Miller, eds. Washington, DC: Urban Institute Press, 2002.

————. "Socioeconomic Status, Race/Ethnicity, and Selective College Admissions." In *America's Untapped Resource: Low Income Students in Higher Education.* Richard Kallenberg, ed. New York: The Century Foundation Press, 2004.

Choate, Pat. *Dangerous Business: The Risks of Globalization for America.* New York: Alfred A. Knopf, 2008.

————. *Saving Capitalism: Keeping America Strong.* New York: Vintage Books, 2009.

Cohan, William D. *House of Cards: A Tale of Hubris and Wretched Excess on Wall Street.* New York: Doubleday, 2009.

Cox, W. Michael, and Richard Alm. *Myths of Rich and Poor: Why We're Better Off Than We Think.* New York: Basic Books, 1999.

Das, Satyajit. *Traders, Guns & Money: Knowns and Unknowns in the Dazzling World of Derivatives.* London: Prentice Hall Financial Times, 2008.

Davidson, Steven M. *Gods at War: Shotgun Takeovers, Government by Deal, and the Private Equity Implosion.* Hoboken, N.J.: John Wiley and Sons, 2009.

Davis, Bob, and David Wessel. *Prosperity: The Coming 20-Year Boom and What It Means to You.* New York: Random House, 1998.

Dickens, Williams, and Stephen J. Rose. "Blinder Baloney: Today's scare talk of job outsourcing is grossly exaggerated," *The International Economy,* October 2007.

Dobbs, Lou. *War on the Middle Class: How the Government, Big Business, and Special Interest Groups Are Waging War on the American Dream and How to Fight Back.* New York: Viking, 2006.

Easterbrook, Gregg. *The Progress Paradox: How Life Gets Better While People Feel Worse.* New York: Random House, 2004.

Einhorn, David. *Fooling Some of the People All of the Time.* Hoboken, NJ: John Wiley and Sons, 2008.

Emanuel, Rahm, and Bruce Reed. *The Plan: Big Ideas for America.* New York: Public Affairs, 2006.

Epstein, Gene. *Econospinning: How to Read Between the Lines When the Media Manipulate the Numbers.* Hoboken, NJ: John Wiley and Sons, 2006.

Faux, Jeff. *The Global Class War: How America's Bipartisan Elite Lost Our Future— and What It Will Take to Win It Back.* Hoboken, N.J.: John Wiley and Sons, 2006.

Ferguson, Niall. *The Ascent of Money: A Financial History of the World.* New York: The Penguin Press, 2008.

Fishman, Ted. *China, Inc.: How the Rise of the Next Superpower Challenges America and the World.* New York: Scribner, 2005.

Fleckenstein, William. *Greenspan's Bubbles: The Age of Ignorance at the Federal Reserve.* New York: McGraw Hill, 2008.

Frank, Robert H. *Falling Behind: How Rising Inequality Harms the Middle Class.* Berkeley, CA: University of California Press, 2007.

———. *The Economic Naturalist: In Search of Explanations for Everyday Enigmas.* New York: Basic Books, 2007.

Friedman, Thomas L. *The World is Flat: A Brief History of the Twenty-First Century.* New York: Farrar, Straus and Giroux, 2005.

Galbraith, James K. *The Predator State: How Conservatives Abandoned the Free Market and Why Liberals Should Too.* New York: Free Press, 2008.

Goldin, Claudia, and Lawrence F. Katz. *The Race Between Education and Technology.* Cambridge, MA: Bleknap Press of Harvard University, 2008.

Goodman, Peter S. *Past Due: The End of Easy Money and the Renewal of the American Economy.* New York: Times Books, 2009.

Gosselin, Peter. *High Wire: The Precarious Financial Lives of American Families.* New York: Basic Books, 2008.

Grant, James. *Mr. Market Miscalculates: The Bubble Years and Beyond.* Mount Jackson, VA: Axios Press, 2008.

Greenhouse, Steven. *The Big Squeeze: Tough Times for the American Worker.* New York: Knopf, 2008.

Hacker, Jacob S. *The Great Risk Shift: The Assault on American Jobs, Families, Health Care, and Retirement and How You Can Fight Back.* New York: Oxford University Press, 2006.

Hellwig, Martin. "Systemic Risk in the Financial Sector: An Analysis of the Subprime-Mortgage Financial Crisis." Max Planck Institute, Bonn, Germany, 2008.

International Monetary Fund. *Global Financial Stability Report.* Washington, DC, April, 2009.

Johnston, David Cay. *Free Lunch: How the Wealthiest Americans Enrich Themselves at Government Expense (and Stick You with the Bill).* New York: Portfolio, 2008.

Kim, Anne, Stephen J. Rose, and David B. Kendall. "Checking Up on Harry and Louise: The Health Care Coverage of the Middle Class." Washington, D.C.: Third Way, May 2009.

Kindleberger, Charles P., and Robert Z. Aliber. *Manias, Panics, and Crashes: A History of Financial Crises,* 5th edition, Hoboken, NJ: John Wiley and Sons, 2005.

Krugman, Paul. *The Conscience of a Liberal.* New York: W. W. Norton and Company, 2007.

Kuttner, Robert. *Obama's Challenge: America's Economic Crisis and the Power of a Transformative Presidency.* White River Junction, VT: Chelsea Green, 2008.

Kuttner, Robert. *The Squandering of America: How the Failure of Our Politics Undermines Our Prosperity.* New York: Knopf, 2007.

Landsburg, Steven. *More Sex is Safer Sex: The Unconventional Wisdom of Economics.* New York: Free Press, 2007.

Lardner, James, and David Smith, eds. *Inequality Matters: The Growing Economic Divide in America and Its Poisonous Consequences.* New York: The New Press, 2005.

Lewis, Michael. *Liar's Poker: Rising Through the Wreckage on Wall Street*. New York: W. W. Norton, 1989.

———, ed. *Panic: The Story of Modern Financial Insanity*. New York: W. W. Norton, 2008.

Lindsey, Brink. *Age of Abundance: How Prosperity Transformed America's Politics and Culture*. New York: HarperCollins, 2007.

Madrick, Jeff. *The Case for Big Government*. Princeton, NJ: Princeton University Press, 2008.

McDonald, Lawrence G. and Patrick Robinson. *A Colossal Failure of Common Sense: The Inside Story of the Collapse of Lehman Brothers*. New York: Crown Business, 2009.

Minsky, Hyman. *Stabilizing an Unstable Economy*. New York: McGraw Hill, 1986.

Morris, Charles R. *The Sages: Warren Buffett, George Soros, Paul Volcker, and the Maelstrom of Markets*. New York: Public Affairs, 2009.

Muolo, Paul. *$7000 Billion Bailout: What It Means to You, Your Money, Your Mortgage, and Your Taxes*. Hoboken, NJ: John Wiley and Sons, 2008.

Muolo, Paul, and Mathew Padilla. *Chain of Blame: How Wall Street Caused the Mortgage and Credit Crisis*. Hoboken, NJ: John Wiley and Sons, 2008.

Murray, Charles. *The Trillion Dollar Meltdown: Easy Money, High Rollers, and the Great Credit Crash*. New York: Public Affairs, 2008.

Phillips, Kevin. *Bad Money: Reckless Finance, Failed Politics, and the Global Crisis of American Capitalism*. New York: Penguin, 2008.

Posner, Richard A. *A Failure of Capitalism: The Crisis of '08 and the Descent into Depression*. Cambridge, MA: Harvard University Press, 2009.

Prins, Nomi. *Other People's Money: The Corporate Mugging of America*. New York: The New Press, 2004.

Reich, Robert. *Supercapitalism: The Transformation of Business, Democracy, and Everyday Life*. New York: Knopf, 2007.

Reinhart, Carmen M., and Kenneth S. Rogoff, "This Time Is Different: A Panoramic View of Eight Centuries of Financial Crises." National Bureau for Economic Research, Working Paper 13882 (2008). Available at http://www.nber.org/papers/w13882.

———. *This Time is Different: Eight Centuries of Financial Folly*. Princeton, NJ: Princeton University Press, 2009.

Rose, Stephen J. "Does Productivity Growth Still Benefit Working Americans? Unraveling the Income Growth Mystery to Determine How Much Median Incomes Trail Productivity Growth," The Information Technology & Innovation Foundation, June, 2007.

———. *Social Stratification in United States*. New York: The New Press, 2007, 2000, and 1992; formerly published as *The American Profile Poster: Who Owns What, Who Makes How Much, Who Works Where, and Who Lives with Whom*. New York: Pantheon Books, 1986.

———. "The Challenge of Measuring Earnings Mobility and Career Paths in the United States." *Indicators: the Journal of Social Health Vol 1, No. 4,* 2002.

Rose, Stephen J. and Heidi Hartmann. "*Still a Man's Labor Market: The Long-Term Earnings Gap.*" Washington, D.C.: Institute for Women's Policy Research, 2004. Reprinted in a condensed version as "The Long-Term Gender Gap." *Challenge,* Vol 47, No. 5, 2004.

Rose, Stephen J. and Scott Winship. "Ups and Downs: Does the American Economy Still Promote Upward Mobility?" Pew Economic Mobility Project. June 2009.

Schwaub, Klaus, and Michael Porter. *The Global Competitiveness Report, 2008–2009.* Geneva, Switzerland: World Economic Forum, 2008.

Shelp, Ron, with Al Ehrbar. *Fallen Giant: The Amazing Story of Hank Greenberg and the History of AIG.* Second Edition: Hoboken, NJ: John Wiley and Sons, 2009.

Shiller, Robert J. *The Subprime Solution: How Today's Global Financial Crisis Happened, and What to Do About It.* Princeton, NJ: Princeton University Press, 2008.

Silverstein, Michael J. *Treasure Hunt: Inside the Mind of the New Consumer.* New York: Penguin, 2006.

Smick, David. *The World Is Curved: Hidden Dangers to the Global Economy.* New York: Portfolio, 2008.

Sorkin, Andrew Ross. *Too Big to Fail: The Inside Story of How Wall Street and Washington Fought to Save the Financial System from Crisis—and Themselves.* New York: Viking, 2009.

Soros, George. "The Crisis and What to Do About It." *New York Review of Books,* December 4, 2008.

———. *The New Paradigm for Financial Markets: The Credit Crisis of 2008 and What It Means.* New York: Perseus Books Group, 2008.

Sperling, Gene B. *The Pro-Growth Progressive: An Economic Strategy for Shared Prosperity.* New York: Simon and Schuster, 2005.

Taleb, Nassim Nicholas. *The Black Swan: The Impact of the Highly Improbable.* New York: Random House, 2007.

Tett, Gillian. *Fool's Gold: How the Bold Dream of a Small Tribe at J.P. Morgan Was Corrupted by Wall Street Greed and Unleashed a Catastrophe.* New York: Free Press, 2009.

Vyse, Stuart. *Going Broke: Why Americans Can't Hold On to Their Money.* New York: Oxford University Press, 2008.

Wessel, David. *In Fed We Trust: Ben Bernanke's War on the Great Panic.* New York: Crown, 2009.

Whitman, David. *The Optimism Gap: The I'm OK—They're Not Syndrome and the Myth of American Decline.* New York: Walker and Company, 1998.

Wilmarth, Art. "The Dark Side of Universal Banking: Financial Conglomerates and the Origins of Subprime Crisis," *Connecticut Law Review,* May 2009.

Wolf, Martin. *Fixing Global Finance.* Baltimore: Johns Hopkins University Press, 2008.

Yago, Glenn. *Junk Bonds: How High Yield Securities Restructured Corporate America.* New York: Oxford University Press, 1990.

Zandi, Mark. *Financial Shock: A 360 Degree Look at the Subprime Mortgage Implosion and How to Avoid the Next Financial Crisis.* Upper Saddle River, NJ: FT Press, 2008.

INDEX